Africa's Global Engagement: Perspectives from Emerging Countries

Series Editor
Ajay Dubey
ASA India Centre of African Studies
African Studies Association of India
New Delhi, India

The 21st century has been characterized by a global rush to engage African countries. Unlike in the past, globalization has given African countries options to select and diversify their engagements. Though traditional powers are still trying to reinforce their links, African countries have generally found it more empowering to reduce their traditional dependence and develop more equitable relations with counties of the South, especially with emerging economies. Different regions and countries of the world find different opportunities and challenges in their attempts to engage the African region. Similarly, African countries, along with the African Union and other regional organizations, find different advantages in diversifying their traditional dependence. However, the new engagements have neither replaced the traditional engagement of Africa, nor are they wholly unproblematic from African perspectives. In this context, it is essential to understand and analyse emerging Africa's global engagements.

To that end, this series will cover important countries and regions, including traditional powers, that engage African countries, the African Union and African regional organisations. The book series will also address global and regional issues that exclusively affect African countries. Books in the series can be either monographs or edited works.

Expected Content:

The series will focus on the following aspects, among others:

- In its current global engagement, is Africa still a "helpless" player? Who dictates the terms of Africa's new engagement, and how it impacts various African countries?
- In the current competition between traditional powers and emerging economies to engage Africa, is Africa's global engagement merely undergoing a geographical shift, or is it moving toward increasingly equitable international relations? How traditional powers have re-strategised themselves to retain their influence on Africa and how Africa is responding to them?

How is Africa involved in the issues of global governance and how it negotiates and navigates its positions on issues of global concerns?

More information about this series at
http://www.palgrave.com/gp/series/15417

Nikola Pijović

Australia and Africa

A New Friend from the South?

Nikola Pijović
Africa Research and Engagement Centre
University of Western Australia
Perth, WA, Australia

Africa's Global Engagement: Perspectives from Emerging Countries
ISBN 978-981-13-3422-1   ISBN 978-981-13-3423-8   (eBook)
https://doi.org/10.1007/978-981-13-3423-8

Library of Congress Control Number: 2018966693

© The Editor(s) (if applicable) and The Author(s), under exclusive license to Springer
Nature Singapore Pte Ltd., part of Springer Nature 2019
This work is subject to copyright. All rights are solely and exclusively licensed by the
Publisher, whether the whole or part of the material is concerned, specifically the rights
of translation, reprinting, reuse of illustrations, recitation, broadcasting, reproduction
on microfilms or in any other physical way, and transmission or information storage and
retrieval, electronic adaptation, computer software, or by similar or dissimilar methodology
now known or hereafter developed.
The use of general descriptive names, registered names, trademarks, service marks, etc. in this
publication does not imply, even in the absence of a specific statement, that such names are
exempt from the relevant protective laws and regulations and therefore free for general use.
The publisher, the authors and the editors are safe to assume that the advice and
information in this book are believed to be true and accurate at the date of publication.
Neither the publisher nor the authors or the editors give a warranty, express or implied,
with respect to the material contained herein or for any errors or omissions that may have
been made. The publisher remains neutral with regard to jurisdictional claims in published
maps and institutional affiliations.

Cover image: boommaval, shutterstock.com
Cover design by eStudio Calamar

This Palgrave Macmillan imprint is published by the registered company Springer Nature
Singapore Pte Ltd.
The registered company address is: 152 Beach Road, #21-01/04 Gateway East, Singapore
189721, Singapore

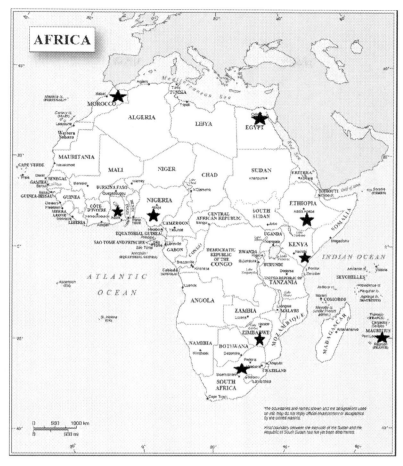

Map of Australian Embassies and High Commissions in Africa, 2018. *Source* Based on United Nations Geospatial Information Section and customized by the author. *Note* Australia's High Commission in South Africa was opened in 1946; the Embassy in Egypt was opened in 1950; the High Commission in Ghana was opened in 1958, closed in 1985, and re-opened in 2004; the High Commission in Nigeria was opened in 1960; the High Commission in Tanzania was opened in 1962 and closed in 1987; the High Commission in Kenya was opened in 1965; the Embassy in Algeria was opened in 1976 and closed in 1991; the High Commission in Zambia was opened in 1980 and closed in 1991; the High Commission in Zimbabwe were opened in 1980; the High Commission in Mauritius was opened in 1984; the Embassy in Ethiopia was opened in 1984, closed in 1987, and re-opened in 2010; the Embassy in Morocco was opened in 2017.

PREFACE

This book began its life in mid-2012 when I first started looking into Australia's engagement with Africa. As I was putting together a research proposal and other documents necessary to apply for Ph.D. study in Australia, I began seriously reading about Australia and Africa. Realizing that there was very little written on the topic at the time, I began daydreaming about one day writing a book capturing the entirety of Australia's engagement with Africa. Six and something years later, here I am. As corny and clichéd as it sounds, I think dreaming about it was essential for actually completing the book. Off course, there were many hurdles to pass between those initial daydreams in 2012 and this end product—being accepted into a Ph.D. program, researching the topic and contributing something original to it, actually passing the Ph.D., finding a publisher who wants to publish it as a book, and then substantially redrafting the research into a book manuscript. But once you get there—to the book publication stage—you realize that it was the dream of writing and publishing the book that was most important; the thing that kept pushing you to do such silly things like—after feeding your screaming infant and putting her back to sleep at 3 a.m.—staying up to work on a book proposal that has already been turned down by 6 different publishers.

Australia and Africa—A new friend from the South? is the product of three and a half years of Ph.D. research conducted between 2013 and 2017. It was a fun book to write mostly because it tells a largely unknown story, and I have been very fortunate to ask people questions

viii PREFACE

no one had ever asked them before, which meant they were overwhelmingly happy to take time out of their—usually very busy—schedules and talk about the topic. One of my fondest memories from this time was meeting up in April 2015 in a small café in Canberra's suburb of Kingston with a very senior Australian diplomat who had just come back from serving at the United Nations. This was at a time when every university and foreign policy think-tank in Australia was trying to get a hold of him because he was key in spearheading the country's successful 2012 Security Council campaign, and was intimately involved in pretty much every meeting Australia attended at the United Nations. Even some of my senior academic colleagues had contacted him repeatedly for interviews, but he didn't have the time. Figuring that he was a pretty busy man, I asked him to squeeze me in for a 30-min chat, and he said ok; two hours later, we exited the café, made a time for a follow-up meeting, and I spent the rest of the day marvelling at what a great interview I just did. And why did he give me two hours of his life? Because a good friend of his asked him to, and because I was asking him about Australia and Africa, and he wanted to talk about it.

When I began daydreaming about this book, it was with one motivation in mind—to leave something original and of substance to future generations. Yes, academics write books to satisfy their egos, secure promotions, gain prominence etc., but the main reason I wrote this book is because no one had thus far told the story of Australia's engagement with Africa, and it is a story worth telling. Australians and especially the almost 400,000 African-born ones do not have many outlets for informing themselves about their country's engagement with African states, and this book should help alleviate that situation. My hope is that one day, as Australia's engagement with Africa becomes more robust and extensive, many more people will write and talk about this topic, and this book will become an outdated reminder of how peripheral the study of Australia's engagement with Africa once was. Until then, I hope this book will serve as an easily digestible source for anyone interested in the topic of Australia and Africa.

I am indebted to many people for their time and thoughts in making this research viable. The primary thanks go to all the participants in my research, and specifically ex Australian Foreign Ministers Gareth Evans, Alexander Downer, and Stephen Smith. I am also particularly grateful to the Australian Department of Foreign Affairs and Trade, and Australian Aid Agency officials for their insights into Australia's engagement with

Africa. At the Australian National University, I must thank Prof. Michael Wesley for supporting my Ph.D. research with great ideas, patience, and just being a kind human being; and Associate Professor Bjorn Dressel for helping me to hone my thinking and tighten up key arguments. Also, many thanks to Professor Ajay Dubey and the team at Palgrave Macmillan for helping this book to come about.

My final thanks are reserved for the person closest to me, and the one who suffered the most from my overwhelming focus on writing this book. Thank you Soma Tata. You have been my most persistent and understanding critic, supporter, discussant, and promoter. With your usual grace and understanding, you have endured everything. I cannot thank you enough for your support. Hvala ti ljubavi.

Za Amandlu i novu generaciju.

Pretoria, South Africa   Nikola Pijović

PRAISE FOR *AUSTRALIA AND AFRICA*

"Australia may not know what it wants in Africa, but Nikola Pijović knows that Africa needs to be on the Australian political map, even if it is not a central pillar to its foreign policy engagement. Pijović's thorough, insightful and in-depth research has captured, in one volume, the complete history of Australia's engagement with Africa. This book is a brilliantly crafted and unique contribution to understanding the political significance of Australian-African relations."

—Dr. Tanya Lyons, *Editor of the* Australasian Review of African Studies *and former President of the African Studies Association of Australasia and the Pacific*

"Australia is an important 'emerging engager' in Africa, with a distinctive history and profile. This well-written, empirically-based book shows the importance of both domestic politics and ideas in Australia's African engagements. As such it makes a very valuable addition to the literature on foreign power interest in Africa."

—Dr. Pádraig Carmody, *Trinity College Dublin and the University of Johannesburg, and author of* The New Scramble for Africa

"A comprehensive examination of Australia's ambivalent and inconsistent engagement with sub-Saharan Africa, this book makes an important contribution to the scholarship on Australia's foreign relations. Provocative and carefully argued, it looks at Australia-Africa relations from the inside and outside. It examines the drivers, inhibitors and prejudices that have shaped Australia's approach to the continent; as well as comparing the results of Australia's record with those of other new engagers with Africa."

—Professor Michael Wesley, *Dean, College of Asia and the Pacific, Australian National University*

Contents

1	Introduction: A New Friend from the South?	1
2	From the Boer War to the End of Apartheid	19
3	Australia Tries to Forget Africa	51
4	Australia Re-discovers Africa...and Then Tries to Forget It Again	73
5	Political Partisanship and Australia's Volatile Aid to Africa	123
6	Conclusion	159
	Appendix: Australia's Merchandise Trade with Africa	177
	Index	183

About the Author

Dr. Nikola Pijović is a Research Fellow at the Africa Research and Engagement Centre (AfREC), University of Western Australia. He specializes in Australian foreign policy, and is a leading authority on Australia's engagement with Africa, having published academic and media articles on Australia and Africa, as well as provided submissions to the Australian Parliament on the country's relations with African states. Dr. Pijović's research also focuses on comparative foreign policy-making in two-party political systems, and especially the distinctions between 'core' and 'peripheral' foreign policy. He has published on statehood, insurgency, and terrorism in Somalia and Somaliland.

LIST OF FIGURES

Fig. 4.1	IMF Fuel Price Index 1996–2017 (*Source* IMF [n.d.]; based on May 2018. *Note* Index 2005 = 100)	80
Fig. 4.2	IMF Metals Price Index 1996–2017 (*Source* IMF [n.d.]; based on May 2018. *Note* Index 2005 = 100)	80
Fig. 4.3	Total Africa oil production 1990–2016, '000 barrels per day (*Source* BP 2017)	81
Fig. 4.4	Total Africa gas production 1990–2016, billion cubic metres (*Source* BP 2017)	81
Fig. 5.1	Total Australian ODA to SSA, current prices, 1989/1990–2015/2016, AUD '000	143
Fig. 5.2	Total Australian ODA to SSA as a percentage of total Australian ODA, 1989/1990–2015/2016	143
Fig. 6.1	A snapshot of G20 member states' Embassies and High Commissions in Africa in 2018. *Note* South Africa is excluded	174
Fig. A.1	Australia's total two-way merchandise trade with Africa, 1988–2017, AUD million (*Source* Author calculations based on Australian Bureau of Statistics 5368.0 Tables 14a and b, May 2018)	178

LIST OF TABLES

Table 5.1	Total Australian ODA to SSA, and as a percentage of total ODA, 1989/1990–2015/2016	142
Table 5.2	Budget estimates for total Australian ODA to Africa between 2007 and 2013, AUD Million	146
Table 5.3	Year-on-year cuts to Australia's total ODA to SSA 2011/2012–2017/2018, current prices, AUD Million	150
Table A.1	Australia's top merchandise export markets in Africa, 1996–2017, AUD million	179
Table A.2	Australia's top merchandise import source countries in Africa, 1996–2017, AUD million	180
Table A.3	Composition of major Australian exports to African states	181
Table A.4	Composition of major Australian imports from African states	181

CHAPTER 1

Introduction: A New Friend from the South?

In January 2011, Australia's foreign minister, Kevin Rudd, made a trip to Ethiopia, delivering his first-ever address to the Executive Council of the African Union (AU). In elaborating on his country's approach to dealing with Africa, Rudd told the gathering that Australia's perspective was that of 'a developed country', but one from the global 'south', and not the 'north'; after all, Rudd had travelled to Ethiopia from the southern hemisphere (Rudd 2011). By pitching his country as one from the 'south' and without colonial baggage in Africa, and interested in mutually beneficial partnerships rather than traditional 'donor–recipient' relationships, the Australian foreign minister was highlighting Australia's uniqueness when compared to other Western developed nations in North America and Europe. And, in summing up his remarks, Kevin Rudd made it clear that after years of neglect by previous Australian governments, his country was interested in a 'new' engagement with Africa. By the time Kevin Rudd's term in office was up in February 2012, he had become the Australian foreign minister with by far the most visits to Africa. Between October 2010 and February 2012, Rudd visited Africa seven times. By contrast, Australia's longest-serving foreign minister, Alexander Downer, made only four visits to Africa in his 11 years in office between 1996 and 2007, and Australia's current foreign minister, Julie Bishop, has only made one visit to mainland Africa since 2013. But why this explosion of interest in Africa in such a short time span? And, more importantly, why so little engagement with Africa before and after Kevin Rudd's time in

© The Author(s) 2019
N. Pijović, *Australia and Africa*, Africa's Global
Engagement: Perspectives from Emerging Countries,
https://doi.org/10.1007/978-981-13-3423-8_1

1

office? This book will answer these and many more questions, and for the first time relate the largely unknown story of Australia's engagement with Africa.

* * *

When one thinks of 'new' actors and emerging countries engaging with Africa, Australia does not normally spring to mind. Usually, such terms are reserved for a number of countries that have ramped up their engagement with Africa since the turn of the millennium, and do not fit into the category of traditional donors and 'old' colonial powers in Africa. But, as this book will show, Australia's engagement with Africa is unique because the country straddles both the categories of traditional donor and emerging country engaging with Africa. However, it is also unique because it does not happily sit in any of those categories. The question mark in the title of this book—*A New Friend from the South?*—is there to highlight several contradictions inherent in Australia's engagement with Africa. Is Australia a *'new'* friend to Africa; that is, can it be called an emerging engager or 'new' actor in Africa? Yes and no. Yes, because like many other countries, Australia has since the turn of the millennium—and really in the past decade—tried to enhance, broaden, and generally re-invigorate its engagement with Africa. No, because Australia is an Organisation for Economic Co-operation and Development (OECD) member and 'traditional' donor, and actually has a long history of engagement with Africa, albeit a history that is largely—and one might add conveniently—forgotten because it involves a long period of supporting British colonialism, and sympathy for racism and apartheid.

Moreover, is Australia a friend from the '*South*'; that is, regardless of its geography in the southern hemisphere, can it be considered a country whose engagement with Africa is bereft of colonial baggage, and consistent with the shared experience of colonialism, shared respect for sovereignty and non-interference, and shared emphasis on 'mutual development' that at least rhetorically marks 'south–south cooperation', rather than the traditional 'donor–recipient' relationships characterizing OECD countries' engagement with Africa? Again, yes and no. Yes, because Australia was never a foreign power directly administering an African colony, but was itself a colony of Britain. No, because Australia played its part in supporting Britain's colonization of Africa, and the country's domestic political tradition, and the values and objectives its foreign policy seeks to spread share many more commonalities with wealthy

1 INTRODUCTION: A NEW FRIEND FROM THE SOUTH? 3

Western and previously imperial countries than they do with developing or 'Southern' countries—and its development assistance is very much characterized by traditional 'donor–recipient' relationships.

These contradictions highlight the richness of the topic of Australia's engagement with Africa. In trying to untangle and explain such contradictions, this book offers a twofold purpose and contribution. On the one hand, this is a book about Australia's engagement with Africa, and as such, its primary purpose is to tell the story of around 130 years of that engagement. In making such a long time period more easily understandable, Australia's engagement with Africa is broken down into two periods: historical and contemporary. The former refers to Australia's engagement with Africa from its earliest days to the end of the Cold War, while the latter examines the time period since then. On the other hand, the book also has comparative value, and its secondary purpose is to add further empirical detail to the literature on emerging countries' engagement with Africa. However, it does this by highlighting Australia's uniqueness as compared to other emerging countries and the commonalities marking their engagement with Africa.

With these two contributions in mind, the book tries to answer two central questions, making several key arguments along the way. As the emphasis of the book is on investigating Australia's contemporary engagement with Africa, the first central question this book seeks to answer is: *What does Australia want in Africa?* Answering this question involves examining the 'why' and 'how' Australia engages with Africa. The key arguments made here are that Australian decision-makers are unable to offer a politically bipartisan justification for why Australia should engage with Africa, and are therefore also unable to assess their country's strategic and long-term interests in Africa—as such *Australia does not know what it wants in Africa.* For almost one century, from roughly the 1880s up until the early 1970s, Australia's engagement with Africa was defined by support for colonialism and sympathy with racism and apartheid. This has left the country with a 'flawed' history that has for the most part been conveniently forgotten, but every now and then spring up in the attitudes and pronouncements of Australian politicians. While both of Australia's two main political forces—the conservative Liberal-National Party coalition, and the centre-left Labor Party—have a history of displaying colonialist and racist attitudes towards engagement with Africa, since the 1970s, it has been mainly the conservative side that has displayed a (neo)colonialist and racist sentiment regarding engagement with African states and issues. On the other hand, while between the 1970s and 1990s there was a period of politically bipartisan focus on the fight against apartheid, that ended with apartheid's ultimate demise in 1994. Since then, Australia's contemporary engagement with Africa has become highly politically partisan, resulting in an episodic engagement, revolving around the country's need to secure African support for its multilateral goals—such as United Nations Security Council (UNSC) membership—and exhibiting a parochial, superficial and cyclical short-term outlook.

The second central question the book seeks to answer is *What kind of an emerging engager with Africa is Australia?* Answering this question is only possible after answering the first question, and taking into account the commonalities shared by other emerging countries' engagement with Africa. The key arguments made here are that because Australia does not know what it wants in Africa, its engagement with the continent is not driven by the same motives and enacted in the same way as that of many other emerging countries—as such *Australia is a unique emerging engager with Africa.* Much of the literature on 'new' or emerging countries' engagement with Africa focuses on countries like China, India, Japan, Russia, Brazil, Turkey, or the Republic of Korea, and at its core, suggests three main features common to most emerging countries' engagement with Africa: an engagement motivated by (a) the desire to secure resources for domestic economies and (b) geopolitical strategies (such as offsetting and countering the influence of strategic rivals); and an engagement conducted through a significant degree of collusion between national governments and businesses (or in many cases, through state-owned companies) (Cheru and Obi 2010; Carmody 2013, 2016; Allan et al. 2013; Van der Merwe et al. 2016; Stolte 2015). All of that highlights the very strategic—if at times incoherent—nature of emerging countries' engagement with Africa. Australia, on the other hand, is unique because its engagement with Africa features none of those commonalities: it is rarely, if ever, strategic, and is certainly not guided by the government's desire to secure resources for the Australian economy, and even less by geopolitical strategies or offsetting and countering the influence of a strategic rival. And its engagement with Africa is not coordinated between the national government and Australian business companies—the latter operate completely independently of the government and generally only seek diplomatic support with host African government contacts in the hope of positively influencing the ease of doing business. Although Australian businesses operating in Africa are predominantly in the resources sector, their activities are not guided by the desires of the government of the day, or geostrategic and geopolitical considerations. Hence, Australia appears *sui generis* when compared to other emerging countries engaging with Africa, and highlights that not all emerging countries engage with Africa with the same motivations and in the same ways.

Australia and Africa: A Snapshot

The African continent is home to a very diverse set of 54 states. Although there are similarities between the historical experiences of (de)colonization and independence of many of them, there are also very vast socio-economic, cultural, linguistic, and religious differences across these states as well as within them. Australia, however, has a history of engaging with only a minority of African states, so that even talking about engagement with 'Africa' is something of a misnomer: one has to look very hard and will find very little to write about regarding Australia's engagement with, for example, Senegal, Mauritania, Togo, Chad, or Angola. Australia's contacts with the African continent have always been strongest at the extremes (Egypt and South Africa), and traditionally more focused on Commonwealth member states, and eastern African countries (given that they share Australia's Indian Ocean geography).

However, this should not suggest that Australia's contacts with African states do not have a long history. The country's earliest official contacts with Africa served the interests of colonialism and British empire-building, and were bloody affairs. From the 1880s and the British war against Mahdist forces in the Sudan, up until the end of World War II, the experience of expeditionary war-making was central to Australia's engagement with Africa. When the newly formed Commonwealth of Australia came into existence in 1901, one of the first items on its agenda was sending troops to fight alongside the British in the Boer War. Much pomp and heroism have been accorded to these earliest Australian imperial expeditions to Africa, even though the behaviour and service of some Australian soldiers in the Boer War were far from exemplary (Reynolds 2016, 191–195). Although Australia's imperial expeditions in Africa are today presented as noble fights for freedom, these military engagements were not tasked with 'liberating' anyone; their purpose was upholding the status quo of colonization, and subjugating the indigenous populations.

But Australia's troubled engagement with Africa is not only confined to the days before the 'winds of change' and decolonization. For reasons of colonial links, a common British cultural heritage, and sympathies for racially discriminatory immigration, Australia had for almost a century (from the 1880s and well into the 1970s) maintained a strong interest in, and affinity for Africa's white settler societies. These were predominantly situated on the southern end of the continent: South Africa and Zimbabwe (or Rhodesia, as it was called until 1980). Australia's ties of 'kith and kin' with whites there, and sympathies for apartheid South Africa and white-minority-led Rhodesia are not well known, and rather unfashionable to acknowledge as they highlight an ever-present dormant streak of racism in Australia's own white settler society, and amongst its conservative politicians. But such sympathies were real, and there were many at the highest echelons of Australia's political class who sympathized with the 'plight' of 'outnumbered' whites in southern Africa. And so it was that up until the early 1970s Australia officially treated apartheid governance as an internal South African issue and one it would not criticize internationally. Furthermore, although Rhodesia's 1965 Unilateral Declaration of Independence from Britain was not recognized by the Australian government—at that time led by the conservative Liberal-Country Party coalition—many of its top political brass, including then Prime Minister Robert Menzies, remained openly sympathetic to Rhodesia's white-minority government, and racial segregation in general. All of this was to a great degree motivated by the colonialist and racist mindset exhibited by Prime Minister Menzies and his key ministers, and remained spiritually consistent with the country's own racially discriminatory 'White Australia' immigration policy.

During these years, there were not many prominent Australian politicians willing to openly criticize apartheid and racism in Africa. However, two individuals, Gough Whitlam and Malcolm Fraser, both as leaders of their political parties, and Australian prime ministers between 1972 and 1983, exhibited an unambiguously anti-racist and anti-apartheid rhetoric. Whitlam was leader of the Australian Labor Party and his election to the prime ministership in late 1972 (after some 22 years of conservative rule) ushered symbolic changes to Australia's engagement with Africa. Whitlam changed Australia's stance on abstaining from United Nations (UN) votes condemning apartheid, and in 1974, Australia even voted in favour of a UNSC resolution seeking to expel South Africa from the organization. However, while rhetorically condemning racism in South

Africa, Australia during this time still maintained strong trade links with the apartheid government, leading many to charge the Labor government with hypocrisy.

The conservatives, on the other hand, were back in power between 1975 and 1983, and many of their politicians was still very much sympathetic to apartheid and Rhodesia's white-minority government. Luckily for Australia, they were led by a man wholeheartedly committed to the fight against racism and apartheid, Prime Minister Malcolm Fraser. Although Malcolm Fraser and Gough Whitlam were great political rivals, in their condemnation of racism, they represented a united front, and Fraser often cut a lonely figure standing in opposition to many in his conservative government by making the fight against apartheid a bipartisan plank of Australia's engagement with Africa. Fraser played a prominent role in trying to broker Zimbabwe's independence at the 1979 Commonwealth Heads of Government Meeting in Zambia, but his outspoken anti-racism almost turned his own Cabinet against him. Fraser had to dismiss his own Minister-elect for Veterans' Affairs, Senator Glenister Sheil, a day before he was to be sworn into office, because the latter had made favourable statements about apartheid; and Fraser's government—to its great embarrassment—could not close down the Rhodesian Information Centre in Sydney because of a backbench revolt against the move.

The struggle against apartheid between the early 1970s and 1990s was the only period where Australia's engagement with Africa displayed a long-term focus. It was also the only time it received bipartisan political support. The downside to all of this was that the anti-apartheid struggle removed the focus from any other possible interests the country might have in Africa. As the Cold War came to an end, and with it the final dismantling of apartheid in South Africa, Australia's engagement with Africa experienced a recalibration of intensity. Between roughly the mid-1990s and mid-2000s Australia, under the conservative government of Prime Minister John Howard, did not appear to pay much attention to African issues, and this attitude only changed with the election of another Labor government in late 2007. Partially motivated by its pursuit of UNSC membership in 2012 and the country's expanding aid budget, the Labor government sought to 'broaden' and 'deepen' ties with the African continent, highlighting its above-mentioned 'new' engagement with Africa. Australian foreign ministers made a flurry of visits to Africa and the country's aid budget to Africa grew significantly, reaching almost 10% of Australia's total Official Development Assistance (ODA) budget in 2011–2012. Then, when it seemed that a closer focus on, and engagement with Africa would become a more durable feature of Australia's foreign policy agenda, another conservative government came to power in 2013 and Australia's engagement with Africa has since fizzled out. The polarizing political partisanship plaguing Australia's contemporary engagement with Africa struck again to rob the country of a unified, strategic, and long-term approach to understanding and pursuing its interests in Africa.

This sketch of Australia's engagement with Africa highlights four key themes that will be re-invoked throughout the book. Firstly, engagement with Africa has on the whole been sporadic and episodic rather than strategic. Aside from the support for the fight against apartheid between the 1970s and 90s and a short interlude between 2008 and 2012, issues were dealt with on an ad hoc basis, without any 'grand plan' considerations or a wider framework justifying why it made sense for Australia to engage with African states. Secondly, while Australia's engagement with Africa has been underpinned by wider structural factors (such as global trends and regional dynamics), the active policy-making of successive Australian governments, and the agency of the country's key foreign policy decision-makers (prime ministers and foreign ministers) bears primary responsibility for determining the course of Australia's engagement with Africa. Thirdly, the Commonwealth (and to a lesser extent the UN) has been Australia's traditional 'window' into Africa, and multilateralism has traditionally been the main conduit for Australia's engagement with Africa. Finally, and particularly since the end of apartheid in South Africa, engagement with Africa has been uniquely politically partisan, and this, coupled with the omnipresent (neo)colonialist, parochial, and racist mindset still readily found mainly on the conservative side of Australian politics, accounts for the ultimate inability of Australia's decision-makers to understand their country's strategic interests in Africa.

The Literature on Australia and Africa

The study of Australia's foreign policy has generally concentrated on accounts of the country's relations with its immediate region (Asia, South Pacific), or its relationships with key strategic allies and trade partners [United States (US), China, United Kingdom (UK), Japan, Indonesia, New Zealand]. The consequences of this study focus have been profound for students interested in African studies, and Australia's relationship with the African continent in particular. African studies in Australia are virtually non-existent, and the study of Australia's foreign policy towards Africa receives only scant and episodic attention. While it may be easy to criticize the paucity of Australian scholarship on the country's engagement with Africa, it must be acknowledged that this is to a large extent influenced by a lack of empirical study material. Africa's marginal status in Australia's overall foreign policy context has influenced its marginal status in Australia's scholarly writing. Academics cannot be criticized for not paying much attention to an area of foreign policy which has traditionally received little attention from policy-makers, and it is hardly surprising that one would find it impossible to sustain an academic career in Australia by focusing only on Australia's engagement with Africa.

Nevertheless, even with these limitations in mind, the dearth of scholarly studies of the topic is concerning. In the period between 1980 and 2012, Australia's most prominent journals of international affairs, political science, and history published just over a dozen scholarly articles dealing with Australian foreign policy towards Africa (Mickler and Lyons 2013, 7–8). Since then, only anther three have been added (Makinda 2015; Mickler and Pijović 2015; Pijović 2016). While there have been a few book chapters over the past 20 years dealing with aspects of Australia's engagement with Africa, most of Australia's prominent foreign policy textbooks pay marginal attention to Africa. For example, Gareth Evans and Bruce Grant (1995) in *Australia's Foreign Relations in the World of the 1990s* have a chapter devoted to the Middle East and Africa, but their discussion of Australia's engagement with Africa spans less than 15 pages—and this is one of the few textbooks that actually tries to explain why Australia engages with Africa. Derek McDougall's *Australian Foreign Relations: Entering the Twenty-first Century* gives chapter-length discussions of Australia's main bilateral and regional relations, with no similar discussion of Africa (McDougall 2009), while Carl Ungerer's *Australian Foreign Policy in the Age of Terror* focuses predominantly on Australia's region and relations with key strategic and trade partners (US and China), with no interest in Africa (Ungerer 2008). Stewart Firth's *Australia in International Politics: An Introduction to Australian Foreign Policy* discusses Africa only a few times and with reference to humanitarian issues and aid, or Australia's role in supporting the struggle against apartheid in Southern Africa (Firth 2011).

More recently, Baldino, Carr, and Langlois' *Australian Foreign Policy: Controversies and Debates* examines important controversial foreign policy questions, devoting several chapters to engagement with Australia's region and key bilateral relationships, with no examination of Australia's engagement with Africa or African issues (Baldino et al. 2014). While this is by no means an exhaustive review of all noteworthy Australian foreign policy textbooks, it is representative of the peripheral status accorded to Africa in discussions of Australia's foreign policy and place in the world.

The country's pre-eminent flagship publication on *Australia in World Affairs*, published by the Australian Institute of International Affairs since the 1950s, includes only two chapters specifically devoted to Australia and Africa, one published in 1983, the other in 2011 (Higgott 1983; Lyons 2011). This is not to suggest that the series did not engage with African issues, rather that most discussions of Africa were usually within the context of a broader discussion of Australia's relations with the Commonwealth, UN, or Indian Ocean, with only a few chapters more directly engaged with particular African affairs, such as the Suez crisis of the late 1950s. These works are indispensable in surveying Australia's engagement with Africa until the 1970s, and to them should be added David Goldsworthy's (2002) *Losing the Blanket: Australia and the End of Britain's Empire* which also covers more substantively Australia's engagement with Africa during the 1950s and 1960s. The main strength of Goldsworthy's book lies in its originality and detail of historical research into those early days of Australia's engagement with Africa. However, the book only examined engagement with Africa in the wider context of Australia's foreign policy subservience to Britain, and was not written as a stand-alone history of Australia's engagement with Africa.

It was only in 2013 that a book centrally focused on examining Australia's engagement with Africa was published. David Mickler and Tanya Lyons' *New Engagement: Contemporary Australian Foreign Policy Towards Africa* focused on the period of the Labor government's revival of foreign policy engagement with Africa (roughly 2008–2012). The book argued that Australia's commercial and political interests were central to the motivations behind the country's reengagement with Africa, with the government keen to support substantial Australian interests, involvements, and investments on the African continent in particularly the resources sector, while at the same time working on garnering

African support for the country's upcoming 2012 UNSC membership bid (Mickler and Lyons 2013, 4). This book is also indispensable for understanding why Australia under the Labor government engaged with Africa, but given its narrow temporal scope, lacks the historical context fundamental to understanding Australia's contemporary engagement with Africa.

METHODOLOGY AND DELIMITATIONS

This book is based on primary and secondary literature, and elite interviews with Australian politicians, diplomats, public servants, and Non-Governmental Organization (NGO) and private sector officials. Primary literature refers to documents produced at the time of the events discussed: online archives of speeches and media releases by Australian ministers, departmental and parliamentary reports and documents, recordings and transcripts of interviews with politicians and public officials, correspondence, official governmental websites, and online and print media. Secondary literature refers mainly to sources published after the events discussed took place, including books and academic articles, unpublished theses, political diaries, memoirs, and biographies.

Elite interviews are generally distinguished from 'normal' interviews by two things: they are in-depth examinations focused on specific topics, lasting between 30 minutes and one hour; and often involve high-level decision-makers and politicians. For the purposes of this research, over 20 such interviews were conducted, most of which lasted around an hour. The majority of the interviews were conducted on a non-attributive basis, but the ones involving politicians were 'on the record'. Those interviewed included three former Australian foreign ministers, with the rest being Australian NGO and private sector officials with past and current operations in Africa, and current or retired Australian Department of Foreign Affairs and Trade (DFAT) and Australian Agency for International Development (AusAID) officials occupying various senior positions including ministerial advisers. Half of the interviewed DFAT and AusAID officials were Australian High Commissioners and Ambassadors in Africa prior to and/or during the interviews.

With regard to terminology, the main point that requires explanation is the use of the term 'Africa'. Unfortunately, the vast majority of international and Australian media writing and commentary, as well as books and articles talk about 'Africa' as if it was one country. For those who are even casually acquainted with the great diversity of the African continent, this terminology is infuriating and smacks of intellectual colonialism. This book refers to Australia's engagement with 'Africa' for two main reasons. The first is to highlight the problematic nature of Australian political and public discourse on the country's engagement with the states of Africa. Yes, Australia has limited diplomatic and political, security, trade, and cultural links with most African states, but there is also a great deal of ignorance about African issues and peoples. Simply put, Africa is still a blank space for many Australians (regardless of their socio-economic standing and educational levels), or better said, it is so unknown that generalizations about the politics, trade, and cultures of the continent are the norm rather than the exception. The second reason is because it is simpler to talk of engagement with 'Africa' as a shorthand for many African states, than to try and mention all of those states individually—that would make for a thoroughly unreadable text. While the book identifies particular African countries Australia has engaged with, often, it unfortunately has to resort to the short-hand of engagement with 'Africa'.

BOOK STRUCTURE

This book is divided into six chapters. After this introduction, Chapter 2 of the book examines Australia's engagement with Africa from its earliest official contacts to the end of the Cold War and the fall of apartheid in the early 1990s. The purpose of the chapter is to relate all important and high-profile episodes of Australia's engagement with Africa in this time period, and highlight how engagement with Africa has traditionally been more multilateral than bilateral—usually taking place through the Commonwealth. The chapter also discusses Australia's largely unacknowledged historical 'baggage' in Africa. Up until the early 1970s, Australian governments—while nominally not supporting apartheid—exhibited imperialist and racist tendencies, sympathizing with 'outnumbered' whites and apartheid in Rhodesia and South Africa. While such sympathies were still present on the conservative side of Australian politics, between the early 1970s and the fall of apartheid in the early 1990s, the country still managed to develop a politically bipartisan dedication to the fight against apartheid.

Chapters 3 and 4 tell the story of Australia's contemporary—post-Cold War and post-apartheid—engagement with Africa. They also highlight issues of structure and agency in Australia's engagement with Africa. Discussions about structure and agency revolve around the relationship between political actors and the extent to which their conduct can shape and is shaped by the political, economic, geostrategic, and cultural environment they find themselves in. Structure refers to the context within which political events, outcomes, and effects occur and is beyond the immediate control of the actors directly involved, while agency refers to the conduct of those actors, implying that their behaviour and choices are responsible for the effects and outcomes we are interested in explaining (Hay 2002, 95–96). Since the end of the Cold War, there have been two key structural factors underpinning Australia's engagement with Africa: throughout the 1990s, this was the 'Decline of Africa', and from the late 2000s, the 'Rise of Africa'.

Chapter 3 examines Australia's engagement with Africa during the reign of the conservative John Howard government between 1996 and 2007, arguing that during this time, Australia largely tried to forget Africa. The chapter firstly discusses the structural factor termed the 'Decline of Africa' which to an extent made it easier for the Howard government to perceive Africa as a place of little interest. Since the anti-apartheid struggle was so central to Australia's engagement with Africa for over two decades beforehand, apartheid's ultimate demise in the early 1990s influenced a diminished intensity in that engagement. Also, changes in Australia's political leadership in the early 1990s signalled a lessening interest in the Commonwealth—Australia's traditional 'window' into Africa—as well as an increasing focus on Australia's engagement with Asia, which also took some of the intensity out of engagement with Africa. More broadly, the end of the Cold War took away much of Africa's overall international strategic value, further exposing some of the long-standing development issues prevalent in many African countries, and contributing to a global narrative of a 'hopeless Africa' running through much of the 1990s.

The rest of Chapter 3 examines the Howard government's engagement with Africa, highlighting how the agency of the Australian government, and Prime Minister John Howard and Foreign Minister Alexander Downer affected and determined the nature of that engagement. While the Howard government's engagement with Africa was not monolithic, it was episodic rather than strategic, and in conservative fashion, fairly reactive. Overall, the Howard government did not conceptualize Africa as a policy space with much relevance past the multilateral Commonwealth connection, and the most high-profile episode of engagement with Africa came through Prime Minister Howard's bruising encounters with African leaders during the 2002/2003 Commonwealth suspension of Zimbabwe. Between 2004 and 2007, the government did react to the growth of Australian commercial and consular interests in Africa by opening an Australian High Commission in Ghana in 2004, and an Australian Consulate General in Libya in 2005. However, notwithstanding these initiatives, the Howard government did not seek proactive engagement with African states and issues during its four terms in office.

Chapter 4 looks at Australia's engagement with Africa during the reigns of two ideologically different Australian governments between 2007 and 2018. It tells the story of how between 2007 and 2013, the Labor government re-discovered Africa, embarking on what it called a 'new engagement' with the continent; and how after 2013, the conservative Liberal-National Party coalition governments led by Prime Ministers Tony Abbott and Malcolm Turnbull tried to again forget about Africa. This chapter also begins with an examination of structural factors underpinning engagement with Africa since the late 2000s termed the 'Rise of Africa'. From roughly the turn of the millennium, the continental trend of Africa's greater political stability and macroeconomic growth, coinciding with the global resources boom emerging in the early-2000s, all contributed to a growing recognition that things in Africa were changing for the better. This in turn fed the 'Rise of Africa' narrative as propagated by some of the world's most prominent media outlets, international financial organizations, banking groups and research institutions, which made it easier and more appealing for Australia to embark on a 'new engagement' with Africa. Although African states still face significant developmental and security challenges, and the global resources boom fizzled out by mid-2014, the 'Rise of Africa' remains a vibrant narrative about the continent's future prospects. However, conservative Australian governments since 2013 have largely ignored it.

The second section of this chapter examines in detail the Labor government's 'new engagement' with Africa, arguing that during this time and for the first time in Australia's history, the country's engagement with Africa was more strategic than episodic. It was strategic because the government was able to justify why engagement with Africa made sense—primarily through its 'middle power' approach to foreign policy—and as a result was able to assess its strategic interests on

1 INTRODUCTION: A NEW FRIEND FROM THE SOUTH? 15

the continent, and pursue specific short-, medium-, and long-term goals. The country's pursuit of UNSC membership in 2012 served as the short-term goal, and increasing its ODA budget to 0.5% of Gross National Income by 2015 was the medium-term goal. These two specific policy goals helped to 'super charge' engagement with Africa and the Labor government worked strategically in utilizing its diplomatic outreach, expanding aid budget, and growing commercial interest across the continent to engage with a host of African countries to achieve its long-term goal of broadening bilateral engagement with the continent. During this time, Australia proactively sought to expand and strengthen diplomatic links with African states beyond traditional connections with South Africa and Commonwealth member states. In this vein, the government in 2010 opened an Australian embassy in Ethiopia (also accredited to the AU), two new Australian Trade Commission offices in Ghana and Kenya, and committed itself to joining the African Development Bank (AfDB), and opening a first-ever Australian Embassy in French-speaking West Africa (Senegal).

The remainder of Chapter 4 examines the conservative Australian governments' engagement with Africa since 2013. It argues that the Tony Abbott and later Malcolm Turnbull-led Australian governments in this period disengaged from Africa, retreating into a Howard-era mindset of episodic and reactive engagement with the continent. This disengagement was not influenced by changes in wider structural factors because while the 'Rise of Africa' was still a factor helping to promote or at least sustain Australia's engagement with Africa, the Abbott government made it clear in 2013 and 2014 that it had little interest in maintaining that engagement. This is further proof in support of the argument that while broader structural factors help underpin foreign policy direction, it is the agency of governments and decision-makers that ultimately determines it. Overall, Prime Ministers Tony Abbott and Malcolm Turnbull exhibited no interest in engagement with Africa, but their Foreign Minister Julie Bishop was at least more rhetorically inclined to support that engagement. This was largely because of her Western Australian-based constituents—which included NGOs and businesses operating across Africa—but her rhetorical support for Australia's engagement with Africa extended only to commercial engagement. The conservative government's disengagement from Africa was made clear when it abandoned the previous government's planned opening of the Australian Embassy in Senegal, and decided against pursuing AfDB membership.

Although Chapters 3 and 4 provide ample empirical detail of the political partisanship driving Australia's fickle contemporary engagement with Africa, Chapter 5 explicitly addresses the question of why this is so. This chapter highlights the agency of Australian governments and key decision-makers such as the country's prime ministers and foreign ministers by examining the roles of Australian political party foreign policy outlooks in driving a politically partisan engagement with Africa. Australia's two main political forces—the centre-left Labor Party and the conservative Liberal-National Party coalition—both subscribe to a set of assumptions and propositions about the country's place and role in the world and how they should go about achieving it. These partisan foreign policy outlooks, as adhered to and interpreted by Australian politicians, are expressed in relevant foreign policy documents and speeches, which in turn support and perpetuate those party foreign policy outlooks. Hence, the two are mutually reinforcing: Australian politicians use their party's foreign policy outlooks to frame and justify their foreign policy direction and priorities, thereby also creating traditions of foreign policy outlooks which are in turn invoked by future decision-makers in justifying their own foreign policy direction.

The conservatives subscribe to a foreign policy outlook conceptualizing Australia as a significant regional power, highly pragmatic and realistic in the pursuit of foreign policy, overwhelmingly interested in regional engagement and maintaining links with key strategic and economic allies, and preferring bilateral management of foreign affairs—the 'bilateralist regionalism' approach. Coalition governments are more comfortable following the dictates of great powers than striking a more independent foreign policy path, and in conservative fashion strive to maintain the status quo. Due to this foreign policy outlook, conservative Australian governments led by Prime Ministers John Howard, Tony Abbott, and Malcolm Turnbull have been less compelled to proactively seek out foreign policy engagement with African states, and find it easier to justify their lack of interest in engagement with Africa.

On the other hand, the Labor Party subscribes to a foreign policy outlook conceptualizing Australia as an active 'middle power' which is equally as interested in regional engagement, but still more open-minded to actively seeking engagement with issues and countries outside of the Australia's immediate region, favouring a multilateral management of foreign affairs, and labelling itself a 'good international citizen'—the 'middle power' approach. Labor governments seek to transcend the dictates of great powers by actively fostering coalitions of like-minded states to try and influence global affairs and build a stable and rules-based international order. Due to this foreign policy outlook, Labor governments led by Prime Ministers Kevin Rudd and Julia Gillard found it easier to seek greater engagement with African states, and justify that engagement both on its own merits, as well as within the context of Australia's pursuit of UNSC membership and an expanding ODA budget. After outlining these foreign policy outlooks and how they influence Australian politicians' thinking on engagement with Africa, Chapter 5 highlights how political partisanship has resulted in great volatility in Australia's development assistance to Africa since the early 1990s.

Chapter 5 is followed by the Conclusion which brings together the main arguments made in the preceding chapters. The Conclusion also tackles in more detail Australia's rather unique place in the literature on 'new' actors and emerging countries' engagement with Africa, and finishes with some observations about the future of Australia's engagement with Africa.

REFERENCES

Allan, Tony, Martin Keulertz, Suvi Sojamo, and Jeroen Warner (eds.). 2013. *Handbook of Land and Water Grabs in Africa: Foreign Direct Investment and Food and Water Security.* London: Routledge.

Baldino, Daniel, Andrew Carr, and Anthony J. Langlois. 2014. *Australian Foreign Policy: Controversies and Debates.* Melbourne: Oxford University Press.

Carmody, Padraig. 2013. *The Rise of the BRICS in Africa: The Geopolitics of South-South Relations.* London: Zed Books.

Carmody, Padraig. 2016. *The New Scramble for Africa.* 2nd Edition. Cambridge: Polity Press.

Cheru, Fantu and Cyril Obi (eds.). 2010. *The Rise of China and India in Africa: Challenges, Opportunities and Critical Interventions.* London: Zed Books.

Evans, Gareth and Brice Grant. 1995. *Australia's Foreign Relations in the World of the 1990s.* 2nd Edition. Melbourne: Melbourne University Press.

Firth, Stewart. 2011. *Australia in International Politics: An Introduction to Australian Foreign Policy.* 3rd Edition. Crows Nest: Allen & Unwin.

Goldsworthy, David. 2002. *Losing the Blanket: Australia and the End of Britain's Empire.* Melbourne: Melbourne University Press.

Hay, Colin. 2002. *Political Analysis: A Critical Introduction.* Houndmills, New York: Palgrave Macmillan.

18 N. PIJOVIĆ

Higgott, Richard. 1983. Australia and Africa. In P. J. Boyce and J. R. Angel (eds.), *Independence and Alliance: Australia in World Affairs 1976–80*. Sydney: Australian Institute of International Affairs, 245–261.

Lyons, Tanya. 2011. Australian Foreign Policy Towards Africa. In James Cotton and John Ravenhill (eds.), *Middle Power Dreaming: Australia in World Affair 2006–2010*. Melbourne: Australian Institute of International Affairs, 185–208.

Makinda, Samuel. 2015. Between Jakarta and Geneva: Why Abbott Needs to View Africa as a Great Opportunity. *Australian Journal of International Affairs*. 69:1, 53–68.

McDougall, Derek. 2009. *Australian Foreign Relations: Entering the 21st Century*. Frenchs Forest: Pearson Education Australia.

Mickler, David and Tanya Lyons (eds.). 2013. *New Engagement: Contemporary Australian Foreign Policy Towards Africa*. Melbourne: Melbourne University Press.

Mickler, David and Nikola Pijović. 2015. Engaging an Elephant in the Room? Locating Africa in Australian Foreign Policy. *Australian Journal of Politics and History*. 61:1, 100–120.

Pijović, Nikola. 2016. The Liberal National Coalition, Australian Labor Party and Africa: Two Decades of Partisanship in Australia's Foreign Policy. *The Australian Journal of International Affairs*. 70:5, 541–562.

Reynolds, Henry. 2016. *Unnecessary Wars*. Sydney: NewSouth Publishing.

Rudd, Kevin. 2011. *Executive Council Speech, African Union*. Minister for Foreign Affairs. Speech. 27 January, Addis Ababa.

Stolte, Christina. 2015. *Brazil's Africa Strategy: Role Conception and the Drive for International Status*. London: Palgrave Macmillan.

Ungerer, Carl (ed.). 2008. *Australian Foreign Policy in the Age of Terror*. Sydney: University of New South Wales Press.

Van der Merwe, Justin, Ian Taylor, and Alexandra Arkhangelskaya (eds.). 2016. *Emerging Powers in Africa: A New Wave in the Relationship?* London: Palgrave Macmillan.

CHAPTER 2

From the Boer War to the End of Apartheid

This chapter outlines how Australia's foreign policy engagement with Africa unfolded from its earliest contacts to the end of the Cold War. The purpose of conducting this historical review is to highlight several important themes which help explain Africa's place in Australia's contemporary foreign policy. The chapter will discuss how colonialism and racism influenced the nature of Australia's engagement with Africa, and how because of its overall marginal status on Australia's foreign policy agenda, engagement with Africa took place largely through multilateral settings such as the Commonwealth and the United Nations (UN). Finally, through outlining key issues and episodes dominating Australia's engagement with Africa, the chapter describes how Australia's foreign policy towards Africa since decolonization became overwhelmingly dominated by the issue of apartheid, and how that helped set the scene for a significant recalibration and downgrading of engagement with Africa once apartheid fell in the early 1990s.

Liberators or Colonizers?

Take a walk down Canberra's Anzac Parade—the street built with the sole purpose of displaying monuments commemorating the Australian martial spirit—and you will notice many monuments to Australia's participation in overseas military expeditions. There is the monument to the Australian participation in World Wars I and II, the Korean War, the

© The Author(s) 2019
N. Pijović, *Australia and Africa*, Africa's Global
Engagement: Perspectives from Emerging Countries,
https://doi.org/10.1007/978-981-13-3423-8_2

Vietnam War, and overlooking the whole parade, the Australian War Memorial. As if this was not enough, on 31 May 2017, the Australian government unveiled its latest monument—this time to the Australian participation in the Boer War. Although it was not the first colonial expedition British subjects from Australia would participate in on the African continent—some 770 of them from New South Wales took part in the subjugation of Mahdist forces in the Sudan in the 1880s—the Boer War was the first conflict the newly formed Commonwealth of Australia would play a role in. Having inherited participation in the Boer War from the colonies who had sent troops to South Africa from 1899 onwards, upon the formation of the Federation of Australia on 1 January 1901, the Australian government moved enthusiastically to promote participation in the Boer War. Troops were mobilized, huge crowds gathered to cheerfully farewell the soldiers, and by the end of the war in 1902, just over 16,000 Australian soldiers had participated in the campaign (Coulthard Clark 2001, 57–96; Odgers 2000, 15–32). Since then, and in the general spirt of glorifying its participation in (expeditionary) warfare, the Australian contribution to the Boer War has been promoted by official narratives as loyal, courageous, and valiant service to a just cause fought by the British empire, even earning an official annual Boer War Day.

For example, in his message to the Annual National Boer War Association's Commemoration service in 2014, the then Australian Prime Minister Tony Abbott stated that Australians in the Boer War 'responded to the call to battle and served valiantly alongside British forces', concluding that

> Australians have always served to uphold the rights of the weak against the strong, the rights of the poor against the rich and the rights of all to strive for the very best they can. We don't fight to conquer; we fight to help, to build and to serve. (Abbott 2014)

A year later, in his message to the same commemoration, Australia's Governor General, and previous Chief of the Defence Force, Peter Cosgrove (2015), stated that Australians participating in the Boer War 'did us proud' especially because their knowledge of the bush, riding ability, shooting skills, and loyalty earned them 'universal respect' while showing the rest of the country 'what it was to be an Australian'.

The problem with these official narratives is that they mask the reality of Australia's participation in the Boer War. Firstly, the British, and by extension the Australians supporting them, were not in South Africa to liberate anyone; they were there to incorporate Boer republics into the British empire, while at the same time maintaining the subjugation of the indigenous African population. They were fighting for British imperial expansion at the expense of native Africans. Secondly, in line with British colonialism in general, Australian participation in the Boer War was to a large extent motivated by racism; the pride that many Australians felt in being part of the 'British race' which had by 1900 colonized much of the known world, and in their eyes spread civilization to the four corners of the empire. As one prominent Australian historian observed back in the 1930 when discussing his parents' generation which had lived through the Boer War, 'pride of race counted for more than pride of country' (quoted in Reynolds 2016, 141). Thirdly, Australia was also partially responsible for what would today amount to significant war crimes meted out on the indigenous African, and civilian Boer populations, courtesy of the British concentration camps and 'scorched earth tactics'. These led to the incarceration of 160,000 Boers and more than 100,000 Africans, leaving 28,000 Boers and at least 14,000 Africans dead, the majority of whom were children (Reynolds 2016, 187–188). Moreover, some Australian solders also committed many atrocities against both Boers and Africans. Diaries, letters, and testimonies from Australians fighting in the Boer War reveal how some Australian soldiers engaged in plunder, theft, burning Boer property, shooting war prisoners, and indiscriminately killing Africans who even served alongside them against the Boers. In the words of the prominent Australian historian Henry Reynolds, Australians in general had a 'bad reputation for ill-treating Africans' (Reynolds 2016, 186).

The reality of Australia's participation in the Boer War does not fit neatly into the official narrative of 'Australians as liberators' and has for the most part been conveniently forgotten in Australia. It does, however, fit into the larger theme of Australia's problematic 'baggage' in its historical engagement with Africa. Simply put, Australians fought in the Boer War in the service of conquest and colonialism, with all the underlying attitudes of racism that entailed. And the country's next two major official foreign policy contacts with the African continent were again mainly in the service of the British empire: in both World Wars Australian troops were deployed as part of British imperial forces to serve in North Africa (mostly Libya and Egypt) (Coulthard Clark 2001, x, 174–176). Notwithstanding the fact that Australia was a self-governing dominion nominally independent form Britain since 1901, and that it had its own separate Federal Department of External Affairs, it was only after the conclusion of World War II that Australia began developing a more autonomous and independent foreign policy. Hence, Australia's 'independent' foreign policy prior to the end of World War II was closely aligned and guided by British (imperial) foreign policy, in which colonialism (and its underlying racism) played a central feature. While a colonial mentality would define Australia's engagement with Africa well into the 1970s—and remain a regular feature of some conservative politicians' thinking on Africa to this day—at least with the end of World War II, the country was able to widen its foreign policy engagement with Africa beyond just participating in wars fought on African soil.

White Australia Meets a Decolonizing Africa[1]

In 1956, the Australian Prime Minster Robert Menzies led a delegation to Cairo to try and persuade Egypt's President Gamal Abdel Nasser to reverse his nationalization of the Suez Canal. On a hot day, and in rather jovial mood, Robert Meznies told one of his fellow commissioners, the Ethiopian foreign minister Akiliou Habte-Wold, that no doubt, as an Ethiopian, he did not mind the heat. The latter replied that Menzies was quite wrong, because Akiliou came from Addiss Ababa, which was '7000 feet above sea level' and blessed with a remarkably temperate climate. To this, Menzies joking replied, how come that Habte-Wold was 'easily the most sunburnt man on this committee?' (Menzies 1967, 160–161). Although retold by Menzies himself in a light-hearted manner, this anecdote captures well the attitudes, ignorance, and racial stereotyping that a predominantly white Australia brought to its early encounters with a decolonizing Africa.

* * *

In 1949, Robert Menzies was elected prime minister of Australia, and ushered in a conservative government that was to last until 1972. This was a formative time for Australia's engagement with the world,

---

[1] The rest of this chapter draws on work previously published in Pijović, Nikola. 2014. The Commonwealth: Australia's Traditional 'Window' into Africa. *The Round Table: The Commonwealth Journal of International Affairs*, 103:4, 383–397, parts of which are reprinted here by permission of Taylor & Francis Ltd, on behalf of The Round Table: The Commonwealth Journal of International Affairs.

and given the continuity in the government's approach towards post-colonial matters, it was a time of monolithic uniformity. This period is referred to as the 'Menzies Era' specifically because there was such great continuity between Menzies' approach to engagement with Africa and those of his successors who governed the country between 1966 and 1972. Prime Minister Menzies, Australia's longest-serving prime minister (1949–1966), like many who grew up in the British Dominion of 'white' Australia, did not truly believe that all races and cultures were equal. Politically yes—that everyone was created equal was the mantra of the post-World War II UN system, and Menzies was at least officially in support of that position. But personally—when you strip away the political correctness of public office—Menzies was a strong proponent of the colonial mindset: some races and cultures were better than others and it was their job to govern more backward peoples, eventually preparing them for self-government. Although he was too suave and politically savvy to say so explicitly while in office, these sentiments were often revealed in his memoirs and musings on Africa and apartheid.

The reason why the longest-serving Australian prime minister's personal views on Africa and colonial issues are so important is twofold. Firstly, as noted in the introduction, it has been the agency (proclivities, interests, motivations, and personalities) of the country's key foreign policy decision-makers—particularly prime ministers—that has played a key role in affecting the development and nature of Australia's engagement with Africa. Secondly, Menzies was a towering and key figure in the development of Australian foreign policy for over 15 years, and during his prime ministership, he presided over a time period of great change in Africa. Decolonization swept most of the African continent in the late 1950s and early 1960s, and Africa became home to dozens of the world's youngest states, some of whom had fought long and hard to rid themselves of their European colonizers. Menzies' Australia was now in a position where it had to interact and develop relations with a part of the world it had hitherto only visited in support of colonial military expeditions under the banner of those very same European colonizers the Africans had just rid themselves off. Although this presented an opportunity for Australia to advance its international reputation, unfortunately, the country's engagement with Africa still followed the British line, and where it did not, it was even more colonialist and conservative.

Australia and the Suez Canal Crisis

Australia's first major non-military foreign policy engagement with an African state came with the aforementioned 1956 Suez Canal crisis. The history of this episode is already well covered, and needs only sketching out details as they are relevant to Australia. The breakdown of negotiations between Britain, the United States (US), and Egypt over the financing of the latter's Aswan Dam was followed by President Nasser's nationalization of the Suez Canal Company on 26 July 1956. A month later, an international conference in London was convened to address the matter, and Prime Minister Menzies represented Australia. At the time, the Suez Canal was of vital importance to Australia, but the situation did not represent much of a crisis for Australia since the change in management of the Canal did not adversely affect international shipping (except for Israeli ships). In any case, during his speech to the conference, the Australian prime minister left no doubt about his country's position in the dispute: 'We in Australia applaud the statement made by France, the United Kingdom, and the United States...We cannot accept either the legality or the morality of what Nasser has done' (Menzies 1958, 86).

The Australian government supported the British position in the Canal dispute, which bordered between the use of force to regain control of the Canal, or use of economic sanctions to force Egypt's surrender of it. As the Australian prime minister argued in a September 1956 debate in the Australian parliament, 'an open Canal' was 'essential to British prosperity', and a closed Canal could mean mass unemployment and a financial collapse in Britain, resulting in 'a grievous blow at the central power of our Commonwealth, and the crippling of our greatest market and our greatest supplier' (Menzies 1958, 142). Hence, Australia supported Britain's subsequent armed invasion of the Canal, and Egypt severed diplomatic relations with Canberra. However, support for the British escapade was not unanimous within the Australian government. The Cabinet was itself split between those who supported Britain's use of force (centred on Prime Minister Menzies), and those who opposed it (centred on External Affairs Minister Richard Casey). Menzies ignored Casey's advice who rightly judged that Australia's support for Britain's 'neo-colonial' excursion would jeopardize its friendly relations with many Asian countries. In a rapidly decolonizing world, Australia's support for Britain's 'disastrous policy' was perceived by some in the late 1960 as 'the most serious mis-judgement of Australian post-war foreign policy', which was 'not only ineffective, but damaging to vital Australian international relations with other countries' (Watt 1968, 303–304).

The Commonwealth, UN, and Racism in Southern Africa

From the early 1960s until the early 1990s, Australia's foreign policy engagement with Africa was dominated by issues of apartheid and racism in Southern Africa. During the Menzies Era, this produced many challenges to Australia's international reputation because the conservative government's instincts on apartheid, racism, and relations with newly decolonized countries in Africa were outdated. One thing that clearly illustrated this was Menzies' attitude towards the 'new' Commonwealth. The 'old' or 'crown' Commonwealth was a body made up of the United Kingdom (UK) and white settler dominions banded together by allegiance to the British Crown. In the early 1930s, its membership included the UK, Australia, Canada, New Zealand, and South Africa. This is the Commonwealth Menzies was most comfortable with: enjoying leisurely meetings with (old) white men such as himself—representatives of white settler colonialists who had subjugated the indigenous populations of their countries. By 1960, the Commonwealth had grown by six more member states (India, Pakistan, Sri Lanka, Ghana, Malaysia, and Nigeria), all of which were led by indigenous leaders, who were, to use Menzies' phrase, of a much more 'sunburnt' complexion.

Prime Minister Menzies was an unashamed Anglophile, and a loyal proponent of the British Empire and the 'white' make-up of the old 'crown' Commonwealth before decolonization. He therefore had a problem accepting the rapid changes and growth of the organization. As the Australian historian David Goldsworthy (2002, 18) has argued, 'It was never a secret that Menzies felt little or no sense of familial attachment to the leaders and peoples of the British dependent territories in Asia, Africa, the Caribbean and elsewhere'. The Australian prime minister made his opposition to the changing face of the Commonwealth clear as early as 1950 (discussing India's admission to the organization), arguing that 'we remain in the old dominions, the King's subjects and the King's men' while India, with its presidential republican system had been 'severed from allegiance to the Crown' (Menzies 1950, 2).

In a 1962 letter to Britain's Prime Minister Harold Macmillan, Menzies—who was 'too deeply royalist at heart to live comfortably in a nest of republics'—stated that 'When I ask myself what benefit we of the Crown Commonwealth derive from having a somewhat tenuous association with a cluster of Republics some of which like Ghana are more spiritually akin to Moscow than to London, I begin to despair' (Goldsworthy 2002, 111). In addition to the 'republican' flavour of the 'new' Commonwealth, Menzies was also critical of Commonwealth colleagues such as Ghana's President Kwame Nkrumah. As Menzies (1967, 188) complained, 'modern applications by former British colonies to be members of the Commonwealth "as Republics"' were becoming a matter of routine, and no one emphasized how much of a routine this was than Nkrumah who 'went to London', was sworn in as Privy Councillor—the Privy Councillor's oath being 'just about the most royalist expression in the world'—and then returned to Ghana declaring 'for a Republic, of which he would be the first President!' For Menzies, that was a 'cynical performance' after which it was impossible for him to 'have any personal respect' for Nkrumah, who had at least made it clear that the 'organic' and 'internal' relationship of the Commonwealth which the 'older members'—the 'crown' Commonwealth—still felt, was gone for good. Such attitudes and displeasures at the changing face of the Commonwealth were shared by many of Menzies's fellow conservative politicians in the late 1950s (Watt 1968, 287; Goldsworthy 2002, 166).

At the 1961 Commonwealth Prime Ministers' Meeting in London, South Africa first tabled its application to join the Commonwealth as a Republic, but due to vocal opposition from leaders such as Kwame Nkrumah and India's Prime Minister Jawaharlal Nehru, then withdrew the application fearing it would be rejected (the country did not rejoin the Commonwealth until 1994). Menzies was unhappy with the 'decolonized' Commonwealth members' criticisms of South Africa's apartheid system of governance, and had warned South Africa's Prime Minister Hendrik Verwoerd a year earlier in a private letter that he did not 'regard it as quite certain that an application by a Republic of South Africa will be accepted by all Prime Ministers…I am afraid in particular of what attitude may be of Nehru and Nkrumah' (Menzies 1967, 201).

In his attempts to keep South Africa in the Commonwealth, Prime Minister Menzies adopted a legalistic approach to apartheid, arguing that it was 'a domestic matter and that we in other countries should not interfere' (Menzies 1967, 192). However, Menzies' legalism was not consistent or coherent, but rather selectively applied when it suited his argument or Australia's interests. A testament to this can be found in his memoirs and his reflections on the Suez Canal affair. The Australian prime minister was very disappointed with the American position in the Suez Canal fiasco, and recounted an episode of confronting John Foster Dulles over it. Dulles was the US Secretary of State at the time of the affair and highly critical of the British-led invasion of the Suez Canal. Meeting him some years later in Australia, Menzies asked Dulles if US vital interests were threatened by China in Taiwan, would his country take the issue to the UN or send US troops to defend those interests. Dulles said that he would send in the troops, 'of course'. Then Menzies asked Dulles why he took the UK and France to the UN over their invasion of the Suez, given that their vital interests were challenged by Egypt. To this, Dulles replied that the US had a treaty with Taiwan, implying that there would be legal basis for US military action, something the British and French were missing in the Suez affair. Menzies was unhappy with this answer, reiterating that he always thought that Nasser's nationalization of the Suez Canal was 'a gross breach of international law' (Menzies 1967, 184–185). But it was not: as the Australian prime minister knew very well given that he was a lawyer, Egypt's President Nasser was operating within international conventions of the time, in which every country was within its sovereign rights to nationalize any company operating on its territory.

Menzies' application of legal arguments was selective: Dulles' legalism was problematic because it was against Britain's (and by extension Australia's) interest, while Menzies' legalism on apartheid was fine, because it shielded Australia from international condemnation and allowed his government to mask its sympathies for racism and apartheid. As the Australian prime minister argued in a 1961 speech to the Australian parliament, he did not favour apartheid, but thought that if the door was open to discussing domestic politics within the Commonwealth, no member state would be beyond reproach (Menzies 1961). As Menzies stated immediately after the Commonwealth meeting in 1961, the issue of apartheid was 'a matter of domestic policy in South Africa which South Africa does not seek to apply to any other country' and was 'as much a matter of domestic policy to South Africa as Australia's migration policy is a matter for us' (quoted in Watt 1968, 282–283). Obviously, in supporting South Africa in the Commonwealth, Menzies had Australia's own racially discriminatory 'White Australia' immigration policy in mind. He even wrote to British Prime Minister Macmillan that 'the South African precedent meant it would henceforth be "quite legitimate" for the Commonwealth to discuss, for example, the Australian immigration policy which is aimed at avoiding internal racial problems by the expedient of keeping coloured immigrants out. I hope my fears are not justified' (Goldsworthy 2002, 26–27). The Australian government's legalistic position on apartheid presented a challenge to the country's international reputation, and by maintaining such an attitude during the hey-day of decolonization, Prime Minister Menzies was a 'living embodiment of attitudes which the new African members of the Commonwealth regarded as out of date' (Miller 1968, 428).

Australia's sympathetic attitude toward South Africa did not win her many friends within the Commonwealth, and this was the situation within the UN as well. UN members had for years debated the legitimacy of South Africa's administration of South-West Africa (present-day Namibia), its treatment of people of Indian origin in South Africa, and its racial discrimination of native Africans. On the issue of South West Africa, Australia had, under both Labor and conservative governments throughout the 1940s and 1950s, defended South Africa (Miller 1968, 442). However, given that the UN finally terminated South Africa's mandate to administer South West Africa in 1966—making South Africa's occupation illegal—Australia did become slightly more critical of South Africa's role in South West Africa. Unfortunately, this criticism did not extend to the issue of apartheid within South Africa itself, and here, the Australian government maintained its rigid legalistic position arguing that apartheid issues brought for consideration before the UN were a matter of domestic concern for South Africa. Therefore, between 1956 and the early 1960s, Australia found itself either in a small group of countries opposing UN resolutions against South Africa and apartheid, or an equally small group abstaining from voting on such resolutions.

South Africa's neighbour, Rhodesia (present day Zimbabwe) was also a thorny issue for Australia's engagement with Africa. Racism and white-minority governance in Rhodesia had since the early 1960s regularly made their way to the agendas of the Commonwealth and UN, but things really came to a head when Prime Minister Ian Smith's white-minority government unilaterally declared independence from Britain in November 1965. There was a Commonwealth conference called to debate the issue, but Australia decided not to attend. The Menzies government justified its absence by arguing that Australia had already refused to recognize Rhodesia, and that it also disagreed with proposals to use armed force against Rhodesia, which were at the time advanced by some Commonwealth members. The Australian government further argued that Britain was ultimately responsible for Rhodesia's status, and reiterated its by now well-known legalistic position that it was not the Commonwealth's business to intervene in the internal affairs of its members—in this case, those of Britain since Rhodesia was still formally a dominion (Menzies 1967, 221–222).

Officially, Australia considered Rhodesia's declaration of independence illegal, but there is little doubt that the highest echelons of the Australian government were sympathetic to white-minority governance and Rhodesia's international plight. Firstly, Menzies himself (1967, 218), in his memoirs written only a few years after the event, displayed a classically colonialist attitude towards empowering the black majority in Rhodesia: universal suffrage would eventually come, but only 'after a reasonable period of years' in which the natives were educated and reasonably trained to competently 'accept the responsibilities of full citizenship'. Secondly, as one of Menzies' colleagues, the Liberal politician Peter Howson (1984, 175–176), revealed in his diaries, Menzies, Howson, and their Cabinet colleagues exhibited a considerable degree of sympathy toward their 'white brethren' in Rhodesia. In a diary entry for 28 September 1965, Howson noted that he had a 'nightcap' in the ante-room with Menzies, who at times exhibited 'a series of violent prejudices' which on that night included his dislike of the UN and hopes it would 'fold up', a desire for his country to 'never alter the White Australia Policy', and his hopes that Rhodesia would 'delay self-government in any form, especially to Africans'. Two months later, the day after Rhodesia declared independence, Menzies called a special Cabinet meeting. Howson (1984, 185) noted in his diary that 'although we have to nominally support the UK there was a general feeling that for too long we have been "swimming with the tide of majority opinion" on the winds of change', and that the time had come for Australia to 'support our white brethren in Southern Rhodesia even if it means that we are going to suffer at the UN'. Howson recalled that Cabinet agreed that Ian Smith was 'ill advised to move so soon' on the declaration of independence, but now that he had, the government would not 'move very rapidly to impose sanctions as requested by Britain'. Howson was not alone in such thinking and as he noted, Minister for Housing Les Bury and Minister for Territories Ceb Barnes agreed 'whole-heartedly' with his 'views on supporting Rhodesia'.

Finally, on 18 November 1965, Prime Minister Menzies addressed the Australian parliament on Rhodesia, outlining his government's reservations about, but adherence to, economic sanctions against the country, with Howson (1984, 186) noting in his diary: 'We talked about PM's speech. Some of us (Gorton, Fairhall, and me) felt he had leant too far forwards supporting UK. But in general we agreed that he couldn't have done much less. It is obvious our sympathies are with the Rhodesians'. Even the British Foreign Office was 'not entirely satisfied with the Australian attitude towards sanctions', arguing that the Australian collaboration with the UK on this issue was 'less close than we would have expected' (Goldsworthy 2002, 91). A few months after that speech, Prime Minister Menzies retired, and his successor as Australian prime minister, Harold Holt, maintained Menzies' attitude towards Rhodesia. On a visit to London in mid-1966, Holt expressed his view that white Rhodesians would be committing racial suicide by conceding to majority rule, leaving the British Foreign Office to conclude that there 'was no doubting Mr. Holt's sympathy for the Smith regime' (Goldsworthy 2002, 92).

The conservative prime ministers who came after Menzies—Harold Holt, John McEwen, John Gorton, and Billy McMahon—all maintained Menzies' positions on apartheid and Rhodesia. In June 1968, the UN passed a resolution proclaiming that South West Africa be known as Namibia, and urgently requesting the Security Council to take measures for the removal of South Africa from the territory. Australia, alongside Britain, Canada, and the US abstained from voting (Harper and Greenwood 1974, 17). In the late 1960s and early 1970s, Australia voted in very small company against widely supported UN resolutions demanding the use of force against Rhodesia; aid for rebels fighting the white Rhodesian government; and sanctions against Portugal and South Africa for having allegedly supported the Rhodesian government. While not officially condoning apartheid and racism in Southern Africa, the Australian government between 1949 and 1972 did very little to actively challenge it.

Summing Up the Menzies Era

There were two dominant influences on Australia's engagement with Africa during the Menzies Era. The first was the perception of Africa as a place of important interest to British foreign policy and well-being, and only because of that relevant to Australia. This much was clearly highlighted by Prime Minister Menzies' speech to the Australian parliament in the wake of the Suez Canal crisis where he firstly noted the adverse effects the closure of the Canal could have on the British economy, and only by extension the Australian one. The second influence was the deeply seated colonialist mindset and sympathy for white settler societies in Southern Africa prevalent within the Australian government, coupled with its own racially discriminatory 'White Australia' immigration policy. Prime Minister Robert Menzies and his successors continued to endorse the virtues of empire which paradoxically brought them out of step with Britain's own commitment for accelerated decolonization in Africa. Although politically astute enough to not explicitly endorse apartheid, Prime Minister Menzies was too much a product of his colonial 'white man's burden' mindset to fully reject apartheid's appeal. After all, under his watch, Australia was not interested in accepting black Africans into the country. After retiring from politics, Menzies would ridicule those who thought apartheid to be 'a rude word', as it merely meant 'separate development', an idea for which he had great sympathy. When the Labor opposition called on his government to cut all trade ties with South Africa in the wake of the 1960 Sharpeville massacre in which South Africa's predominantly white police force killed over 60 unarmed black protesters, Menzies was unmoved. As he recalled later in his memoirs, such arguments were 'a sort of racism in reverse': while coloured people were killing coloured people for religious and political reasons all over India and Africa, people were only protesting against government-led violence when white people were involved (Menzies 1970, 282). This charge of 'reverse discrimination' would remain a regular feature in Australian conservative politician's pronouncements on apartheid and Southern African issues, invoked in various forms to this day. In the late 1980s, one of Menzies' keenest political worshippers, the conservative leader John Howard, would invoke it to argue that Australia's immigration policy was discriminating against white South Africans looking to immigrate to Australia. And, in 2018, Australia's Home Affairs Minister Peter Dutton would invoke the violence against, and prosecution of, white South African farmers as a reason why his department would pay 'special attention' to how they could be helped to migrate to Australia (Karp 2018).

The Menzies era set the foundations for perceiving Africa as marginal to Australia's overall foreign policy interests and agenda. In light of the very limited commercial, immigration, cultural, and defence and strategic links between Australia and African states, this may seem as self-evident, but it was not necessarily destined to be so. Australia's cultural and colonial links were strong with Southern Africa, and the limited immigration links were a direct product of the government's own racially discriminatory immigration policy. It was the active decision-making of the Menzies Era conservative Australian governments that failed to foster any substantive links with African states past the already established connections with the Commonwealth, and Southern African white settler societies. Although this will remain a historical hypothetical, perhaps if Australia had been governed by a more progressive party in the 1950s and 1960s, its foreign policy-makers would have perceived Africa somewhat differently, and would have made concerted efforts at engaging African states to help build more durable connections.

CHANGE IS COMING

After more than two decades of post-World War II conservative governments, Australia, in late 1972, elected a Labor government headed by Prime Minister Gough Whitlam. As noted in the introduction, Gough Whitlam was one of the few prominent political leaders in Australia during the long reign of conservative governments to openly criticize apartheid, and challenge his country's government on issues of racism and discriminatory immigration. Although Australia had been very slowly loosening discriminatory restrictions on its immigration intake of non-white peoples since the late 1960s, it was Prime Minister Whitlam who finally ended the country's 'White Australia' immigration policy. With regard to engagement with Africa, Whitlam's election would set the foundations for what would later become an era of bipartisan focus on the fight against apartheid, and one which would for the first time instil at least some long-term vision to Australia's interests in Africa, and garner the country some friendship amongst African states.

The Commonwealth, UN, South Africa, and Rhodesia

As was the case in the 1950s and 1960s, Australia's engagement with African states during the 1970s was primarily conducted through the Commonwealth and to a lesser extent the UN. However, the great novelty in the country's changing engagement with Africa was not a change from a largely multilateral to a bilateral engagement, but rather a markedly changed attitude towards engaging with African states and issues through multilateral fora. During the Menzies era, Australian prime ministers viewed African Commonwealth members with a degree of suspicion, and given that African states made the majority of the Commonwealth, the forum itself was neglected as a tool of Australian foreign policy. Prime Minister Whitlam understood and recognized that the Commonwealth, United Nations, and other multilateral fora presented an opportunity for Australia to enhance and change its reputation, and utilized them to that effect, especially in Australia's relations with developing countries in Asia and Africa.

Back in 1961, during the parliamentary debate on South Africa's exit from the Commonwealth, Gough Whitlam was one of few Australian politicians to vocally criticize Prime Minister Menzies' approach to South Africa and apartheid, as well as his expressed dislike of the changing composition of the Commonwealth. When debating South Africa's exit from the Commonwealth, Whitlam (1961) reminded Menzies of the Commonwealth's importance for Australia, arguing that the organization was 'the best bridge' between developed 'European type countries' on the one hand, and the countries of Asia and Africa, on the other hand. Menzies had 'gone out of his way' to suggest that the Commonwealth had been weakened by the defection of South Africa, and Whitlam wanted to make it clear that the Commonwealth was in fact stronger by not having South Africa, 'under its present outlaw government' as a member. Upon becoming Australia's prime minister, Gough Whitlam's engagement with multilateral settings such as the Commonwealth and UN was aimed at shedding Australia's racist image in the world—an image influenced by his predecessors' sympathy for, and lack of criticism of apartheid, and Australia's own restrictive immigration policies. In an address to the UN General Assembly in 1974, Prime Minister Whitlam (1974) stated that the international community needed to be 'unremitting' in its efforts to 'break the illegal regime in Rhodesia, to end South Africa's unlawful control over Namibia and to end apartheid'. His government, conscious that Australia's own record on racial discrimination was 'seriously flawed', was determined 'to remove all forms of racial discrimination' within Australia, 'notably now, as notoriously in the past, against our own Aboriginals'.

In late 1973, Australia began its term as a non-permanent member of the UN Security Council (UNSC), and used the forum, in addition to the UN in general, to establish itself as a vocal critic of apartheid South Africa. A few days after Labor formed government in December 1972, Australia banned South Africa's racially selected sports teams from traveling to or passing through the country, and from 1973 onwards, Australia supported and co-sponsored a number of anti-South Africa resolutions in the UN, going as far as supporting a 1974 UNSC resolution calling for South Africa's expulsion from the UN (Clark 1980, 149, 153; Albinski 1977, 116). Prime Minister Whitlam was an outspoken critic of apartheid and racism, and in a late 1973 television interview went as far as comparing the leaders of South Africa and Rhodesia to Adolf Hitler (Albinski 1977, 102). By that time, the leader of South Africa, Prime Minister J. B. Vorster had already expressed his dislike of Whitlam by stating 'I say to Mr Whitlam: When you are just an unpleasant memory in Australia, we'll still be governing South Africa' (quoted in Loshak 1973).

On the issue of Rhodesia, the Australian government quickly moved towards the side of Afro-Asian nations in the Commonwealth and UN, and while it did not favour an armed intervention against the white-minority government, it did support sanctions against the country, arguably with more vigour than the Menzies Era governments. Whitlam's government also unsuccessfully attempted to close down the Rhodesian Information Centre in Sydney, but it was successful in banning any further sales of wheat to the country and clamping down on issuing visas to Rhodesians (Albinski 1977, 113, 114). Considering that Australia had actually issued Rhodesian officials and diplomats with valid passports from the late 1960s, the government's tough policy on Rhodesian travel documents arguably saved the country from international embarrassment. As Whitlam would later state (1985, 68), taking aim at his Menzies Era conservative predecessors, since no other government recognized Rhodesian 'passports' and the British were not issuing passports to Rhodesians, the Rhodesian government's 'contacts with the outside world had been conducted by courtesy of the Australian Government'.

Although the Australia government had at this time at least rhetorically done much to change Australia's reputation and image in the world regarding apartheid and racism, it was still criticized for its continued trade with the apartheid regime. This highlighted the discrepancy between Australia's anti-apartheid rhetoric, on the one hand, and its beneficial trade relationship with South Africa, on the other. Australia's trade with South Africa had flourished since the late 1960s, and the government's position on possibly suspending that trade was quite clear. By the end of 1972, South Africa was the fourth largest market for Australian manufactures, and the Australian government was not interested in bilaterally imposing sanctions or a trade embargo. Australia's Minister for Overseas Trade, Dr. Jim Cairns, explicitly shunned the idea of disrupting trade with other countries, regardless of how unsavoury their governance seemed, stating that 'You can't stop trade with countries just because you don't like their policies. If we did that, we would stop trading with just about every country except Sweden and Switzerland' (quoted in *The Australian* 1973). In the end, Australia's dilemma regarding trade with South Africa, while noticeably controversial, was not an overly difficult one. Without UN sanctioned embargos against South Africa, Australia was under no obligation to stop trading with a very beneficial trading partner, and regardless of its anti-apartheid rhetoric, the government continued to promote trade with South Africa (Witton 1973).

A Lonely Figure Ushers a Politically Bipartisan Dedication to the Anti-apartheid Struggle

In December 1975, the conservative Liberal-National Party coalition was back in power, and many of its members were still holding a deep sympathy for apartheid and minority-white governance in Rhodesia. Luckily for Australia, the prime minister, Malcolm Fraser, was not one of them. A man whose foreign policy exhibited a relatively unique mixture of 'hard lined conservatism on East-West issues with quite radical liberalism on North-South issues' (Renouf 1986, 132), Prime Minister Fraser's dedication to the anti-apartheid struggle made Australia's engagement with Africa politically bipartisan for the first time since the continent's decolonization. While previous—Menzies Era—conservative Australian governments also nominally did not support apartheid, they were too colonialist and racist in mindset, and ultimately too sympathetic with white Southern Africans and their racial governance to seriously fight apartheid and racism. Although the conservative side of Australian politics was still predominantly populated by such politicians, what was different this time was that at least the conservative leader, and Australia's prime minister, was outspokenly and genuinely anti-racist and interested

36   N. PIJOVIĆ

in ending apartheid. Malcolm Fraser's personal dislike of racism and his outspoken anti-apartheid stance often saw him in conflict with members of his own government, and Australia's strong and proactive preference for engaging with Commonwealth issues (particularly African ones) during his prime ministership was deeply at odds with the foreign policies of his conservative predecessors. But Fraser persevered, and Australia's engagement with Africa was now, under both Labor and conservative coalition governments, explicitly and unambiguously guided by the anti-apartheid struggle.

The Commonwealth, South Africa, and Rhodesia

The conservative government's continuation of Labor's anti-apartheid stance and policies, and the ensuing emerging political bipartisanship in Australia's engagement with Africa is interesting because Malcolm Fraser was highly critical of the Labor government's foreign policy while he was in opposition. Fraser did not support the government's strong anti-racist changes to the country's immigration and naturalization, and in 1975 was vocally critical of Australia's tough stance on apartheid, and its provision of humanitarian aid to African national liberation movements (Renouf 1986, 133). As misplaced and wrong as those criticisms now seem, given Fraser's anti-racist record when in office, they can be seen as reflecting his domestic political calculations. Malcolm Fraser was first a foremost a politician trying to win an upcoming election, and he would have been well aware of the strong and vocal constituency in Australia exhibiting a significant degree of sympathy for white Southern Africans—the same constituency that would end up making it difficult for him to push his own anti-racist and anti-Rhodesian policies when in office. Racism, during this time, 'was an issue which sat lightly with many Australians' (Bolton 1990, 197), and even the government's own 1979 report on relations with the Third World noted that 'developments in southern Africa and our official response towards them are issues of considerable public interest and controversy within Australia. Many Australians feel ties of kith and kin with white populations of southern Africa and sympathize with their predicament...' (Harries 1979, 164). Malcolm Fraser (Fraser and Simons 2010, 505) himself noted that some of his own party room members questioned his support for the 'communists' and 'terrorists' in the ANC against 'our blood brothers, the Afrikaners'. During parliamentary debates on Rhodesia in the late

1970s, members of parliament from Fraser's own coalition government would routinely question their government's line on Rhodesia, exhibiting strong sympathies for white-minority rule there. They would openly disagree with the prime minister that minority rule was a valid enough reason to isolate and sanction the Rhodesian government, and even local state governments within Australia disagreed with the Australian federal government's policy. Hence, the Premier of Western Australia, Charles Court, stated in 1976 that he was interested in resettling 100,000 white Rhodesians in his state (Lee 2017, 13–15, 32).

Two incidents which best highlight the considerable opposition Fraser's government faced from within its own ranks on the issue of Rhodesia came early in his tenure as prime minister, in 1977. One of the conservative coalition's most outspoken critics of the government's stance on Rhodesia was the Queensland-based member of parliament, Glenister Sheil. Sheil was nominated by Prime Minister Fraser to be Australia's minister for veterans affairs, but the night before his swearing into office made remarks to a reporter that Australia 'had a lot to learn from policies in South Africa and Rhodesia', and that if the Australian indigenous population wanted it, he was in favour of introducing apartheid in Australia (*Sydney Morning Herald* 2008). Sheil's 'ministerial' reign lasted 43 hours—although he was never officially sworn in as minister—before Prime Minister Fraser dismissed him for such utterances which were clearly contradicting government policy. The second incident involved the unsuccessful attempt by Fraser's government to close down the Rhodesian Information Centre in Sydney. Such information centre was Rhodesia's quasi-embassies and after the UNSC passed a resolution making sanctions against Rhodesia mandatory for all UN members, they were closed down around the world. This meant that leaving the one in Sydney open would have remained an international embarrassment to Australia. However, although the Australian government made genuine attempts to close the centre down, it suffered a backbench 'revolt' with as many as 40 of the 91 conservative coalition members of parliament disagreeing with the move (Lee 2017, 24; *Daily Graphic* 1977, 2). Overall, because of such sympathies towards white Rhodesians and apartheid, while Prime Minister Fraser was in 1979 and 1980 internationally lauded as a statesman due to his role in helping broker Zimbabwe's independence, at home, he was 'greeted with considerable hostility' with his personal approval ratings plummeting below 30% (Higgott 1983, 239).

However, the domestic public and political support and sympathy for white-minority rule in Rhodesia and apartheid in South Africa did not constrain Prime Minister Fraser's foreign policy agenda of fighting racism and apartheid, and he utilized the Commonwealth for his most prominent and best-known episode of diplomatic engagement with Africa (see below). Back in the 1961 parliamentary debate following South Africa's withdrawal from the Commonwealth, Malcolm Fraser was one of few conservative members of parliament who defended the importance of the Commonwealth for Australia—contradicting what his own party leader, and the Australian prime minister was saying at the time. Malcolm Fraser (1961) was out of step with many in his own party at the time by openly attacking apartheid and racism, and concluding that he regarded the Commonwealth 'as a bridge between the people of different races and colours', and that Australia should 'try to maintain this bridge'. However, Prime Minister Fraser's support for the Commonwealth stemmed from various reasons not necessarily directly related to the issue of racism. The Commonwealth was the forum through which Australia could have access to Third World leaders it normally had little bilateral contacts with; it was a forum where Australia genuinely could be influential and seen as a 'big player'; it was also a forum through which Fraser's government could try and counter the Soviet Union's growing influence—particularly in southern Africa, which was a foreign policy concern for Fraser; and 'the Commonwealth offered an arena for those kinds of gestures that cement relationships at a political level without costing a great deal in practical or financial terms' (Higgott 1983, 248).

Since Australia's connections with Africa were primarily developed through the Commonwealth—all of the country's diplomatic missions in Sub Saharan Africa were in Commonwealth countries—policy towards South Africa 'tended to be developed in a Commonwealth context' (Neuhaus 1989, 162). The Commonwealth was also the forum thought which Prime Minister Fraser established himself as a vociferous and internationally prominent critic of racism and apartheid, and it was through the Commonwealth that his diplomacy most directly engaged with the fight against racism. At the June 1977 Commonwealth Heads of Government meeting (CHOGM) held in London, Malcolm Fraser delivered his most famous anti-apartheid speech, in which he also for the first time publicly referred to Rhodesia as Zimbabwe. As the Australian prime minister argued at the time 'Policies based on the false and pernicious premise of one race's superiority over another, one race's right to subjugate another, are the most flagrant violation of fundamental human decency', further stating that 'Apartheid cannot succeed even in terms of its own logic. A policy that pretends to foster equal social development but which involves permanent separation of the races and imposes permanent political inferiority on one race will not, and cannot, succeed'. It was because of all of this that Fraser argued for 'a rapid move towards majority rule in Zimbabwe' (Fraser 1977).

The Fraser government's bipartisan continuity of the previous government's proactive attitude towards the Commonwealth, coupled with Malcolm Fraser's own vocal criticism of apartheid and white-minority rule in Rhodesia, generated much goodwill towards Australia. It was also thanks to that goodwill and Fraser's international prominence in criticizing apartheid that he was able to act as a mediator between African leaders and the British Prime Minister Margaret Thatcher on the issue of Rhodesia/Zimbabwe's ultimate decolonization. The Rhodesian government began implementing limited governance reforms in the late 1970s, even electing its first black prime minister—Bishop Abel Muzorewa. But, these changes did not appear fully democratic or representative of the wishes of the black majority, and as a result, rebel leaders like Robert Mugabe continued their insurgency against the government. What many Commonwealth members feared was the international recognition of Muzorewa's government, especially as the newly elected prime minister of the UK, Margaret Thatcher, favoured an internal solution to Rhodesia's status. Australia's most prominent engagement with African issues during Prime Minister Fraser's tenure in office came with him helping to broker the 1979 CHOGM Lusaka Agreement. The country's diplomacy was mobilized on an unprecedented scale for the Lusaka meeting—some 'two dozen Australian diplomats and officials' accompanied the prime minister to Zambia—and the Australian prime minister's role mostly revolved around helping to mediate between Afro-Asian Commonwealth leaders and Margaret Thatcher (Fraser and Simons 2010, 503–512; Simson and McDonald 1979). Fraser's effort in brokering the deal which paved the way for the signing of the December 1979 Lancaster House Agreement—in turn bringing about Zimbabwe's independence and black majority rule—was highly publicized by Australian media, and he was widely presented as a 'peacemaker' central to the negotiations (*The Australian* 1979; Colless 1979). Although the Australian prime minister's importance in negotiating the Lusaka Agreement and by extension Zimbabwe's independence has been

40   N. PIJOVIĆ

questioned, with some downplaying his, and even the Commonwealth's significance in the affair (Higgott 1983, 250; Renouf 1986, 141), it is overall not that important how decisive Fraser's role actually was. As far as Australia's engagement with Africa is concerned, the country was—through its prime minister—prominently involved in brokering Zimbabwe's ultimate independence and black majority rule, and a focus on Rhodesia/Zimbabwe dominated that foreign policy engagement for much of Prime Minister Fraser's time in office.

THE END OF AN ERA

In 1983, the Australian Labor Party came into power, with Bob Hawke serving as prime minister of Australia between 1983 and 1991. Hawke would eventually be replaced by Paul Keating, who served as prime minister until 1996. Australia's engagement with Africa remained overwhelmingly focused on the anti-apartheid struggle well into the early 1990s, when the independence of Namibia, and then the 1994 end of white-minority rule in South Africa removed apartheid from the forefront of that engagement. This represented the end of an era because the fight against apartheid had been so central to Australia's overall engagement with Africa, and its final demise set the scene for a decrease in the interest in, and intensity of Australia's engagement with Africa. Although Australia would, in the early 1990s, see its largest military involvement in Africa since the end of World War II (as part of UN deployments to Western Sahara, Somalia, and Rwanda), that involvement generated much less political and foreign policy interest than the fight against apartheid. The fall of apartheid underpinned Australia's disengagement from Africa, which became especially visible in the second half of the 1990s.

The Commonwealth and South Africa

From the early 1970s and his union leadership days, Prime Minister Bob Hawke was a well-known and vocal critic of apartheid, and his Labor governments maintained Australia's opposition to apartheid in South Africa. The Australian government banned South African sporting teams from Australia in 1983, and in 1985 banned certain exports to, and imports from South Africa (things such as agricultural produce, oil, uranium, coal, iron, and military hardware) (Osei-Amo 2004, 221–228).

However, it is questionable how much such decisions were really effective at anything more than highlighting Australia's anti-apartheid credentials. The decision to ban South African athletes from traveling to Australia reportedly only affected South African amateur athletes while leaving the professionals to travel to the country freely (Grattan and Davis 1983). Nevertheless, aside from such symbolic decisions against the apartheid regime, Australia utilized the Commonwealth for one of its most advertised anti-apartheid initiatives, still regularly re-invoked by Australian diplomats and ministers to this day.

In his memoirs, Bob Hawke (1994, 317) claimed that his 'faith in the Commonwealth was repaid' throughout his prime ministership, especially as CHOGMs 'became the powerful, leading force in mobilizing world opinion against apartheid', and 'bringing to an end that evil system'. Indeed, it was through the Commonwealth that, according to Hawke, Australia would initiate the idea of financial sanctions against South Africa, which in the end broke the back of apartheid. As Hawke tells it, he realized that economic sanctions were ineffective against South Africa, and what was needed was investment (financial) sanctions which would make it almost impossible for the apartheid regime to finance its borrowing and debts. Hawke noted South Africa's Finance Minister Barend du Plessis publicly stating that sanctions were hurting his country, and this he thought was a blow to arguments (advanced by the likes of the British Prime Minister Margaret Thatcher) that sanctions would not have an effect on South Africa (Pijović 2014, 391). 'Against this background I conceived an initiative which, when accepted and implemented, finally broke apartheid' (Hawke 1994, 331).

The initiative that Australia came up with was presented at the 1987 CHOGM in Vancouver. Prime Minister Hawke invited a New York-based Australian banker, Jim Wolfensohn, to meet with Commonwealth leaders and further argue Hawke's financial sanctions ideas. According to Hawke (2014, 2) and his Foreign Minister Gareth Evans (2014, 1, 3–4), it was Australia's Commonwealth initiative that paved the way for other important international players such as the US and European Economic Community to adopt financial sanctions against South Africa, and ultimately bring an end to apartheid. The official narrative is that Australia played an important role in developing financial sanctions against South Africa because it: firstly, initiated a study on the potential impact of such sanctions, and that study became 'widely influential in international financial circles'; and secondly, funded a centre at the London School of

Economics which assessed the role of international capital flows in and out of South Africa (Evans and Grant 1995, 294). Australia's Foreign Minister Gareth Evans would later state that it was conceded to him in discussions he had 'with a number of ministers and officials during his visit to South Africa in June 1991...that it was the financial sanctions more than any other form of external pressure that had ultimately forced' the apartheid government to the negotiating table (Evans and Grant 1995, 294). Evans (2014, 3) maintains this view, reiterating that when he visited South Africa in 1991, he spoke to 'the Governor of the Reserve Bank and others' about the impact of financial sanctions, and that they left him in 'absolutely no doubt that it was the financial sanctions' that were 'the crucial tipping-point factor' in bringing the apartheid regime to the negotiating table.

It would appear that even South Africa's first black president, Nelson Mandela, accepted the view that Australia played a globally prominent role in helping to bring about financial sanctions against the apartheid regime. According to Bob Hawke, Mandela, during his 1990 visit to Australia, told the then Australian prime minister 'I want you to know, Bob, that I am here today, at this time, because of you' (Hawke 1994, 335; 2014, 10). However, it is important to adopt a dose of healthy scepticism towards politicians' self-proclaimed achievements while in office. Certainly Nelson Mandela may have been grateful for Australian support for the liberation struggle, and the country's sanctions against the apartheid regime. But whether Mandela's comment implies direct responsibility for bringing down apartheid—as Bob Hawke implies—as opposed to astute diplomatic niceties, remains difficult to tell. In any case, there have been criticisms of Prime Minister Hawke and his Foreign Minister Evans' 'myth-making' interpretation of the globally important role Australia played in ending apartheid. As some have argued, Australia could have applied bilateral sanctions against South Africa, but did not because they would have hurt its beneficial trade with the country, and in any event, Australia lagged behind states such as the US in applying sanctions against the apartheid regime. Therefore, Australia was hardly a leader in helping to bring down apartheid (Cox 1997, 139–140). Moreover, Australian newspapers at the time of the 1987 CHOGM only reported Hawke's proposal for a study of the impact international financial sanctions could have on South Africa as one of several proposals in the debate on South Africa (Steketee 1987a, b). And even the Australian banker James Wolfensohn, who by Hawke's interpretation played a key

2 FROM THE BOER WAR TO THE END OF APARTHEID   43

role in pitching financial sanctions to Commonwealth leaders in 1987, in his own autobiography in which he is anything but shy about highlighting his own professional and personal achievements, does not mention Bob Hawke, the 1987 CHOGM, or South Africa (Wolfensohn 2010). One would expect that if Wolfensohn had played such a significant role alongside Bob Hawke in helping to broker the ultimate demise of apartheid, he would have at least mentioned it in the story of his life.

A Slow Disengagement Begins

Since Australia's foreign policy engagement with Africa was wholly dominated by the apartheid issue since the early 1960s, its high political profile would help mask the country's slow on-the-ground diplomatic disengagement from Africa during the 1980s. The mid-1980s saw the publication of two important government reports which in many ways set the course for Australia's foreign policy towards Africa in the future. In 1984, the *Report of the Committee to Review The Australian Overseas Aid Program* was published (known as the Jackson Report after the committee's chairman, Gordon Jackson), and in 1986, the *Review of Australia's Overseas Representation* was also published (known as the Harris Report, after the report's author Stuart Harris). Many of the findings and recommendations of both of these reports would have important implications for Australia's engagement with Africa, lasting to this day.

The overall argument of the Jackson Report was that Australia should focus its aid on its neighbourhood, implying that this was where Australian aid could make the most difference and satisfy the country's foreign policy interests. It recommended that development aid should not be directed towards African countries, and that emergency aid, technical assistance, and training should 'continue to be the principal forms of assistance for Africa' (1984, 7). Although the report was careful to point out that this should not imply a complete withdrawal of Australian aid to Africa, it nevertheless disadvantaged the region. Most importantly, the report's recommendations were accepted by the Australian government, and the Jackson Report influenced successive Australian governments' attitudes towards aid engagement with Africa.

The *Review of Australia's Overseas Representation* was published a year before its author, the secretary of Australia's Department of Foreign Affairs Stuart Harris, would oversee the merger of the Departments of

Foreign Affairs and Trade. That merger was itself a good indication of the Australian government's changing understanding of foreign policy priorities, and the higher primacy given to economic relations in the pursuit of foreign policy advancement (Harris 2002). At the time of the writing of the Harris Report, Australia had 10 diplomatic missions in Africa (Algeria, Egypt, Ethiopia, Tanzania, Zambia, Zimbabwe, South Africa, Nigeria, Kenya, and Mauritius). What makes the Harris Report so important for Australia's engagement with Africa is that it predicted—and probably influenced—the closure of several diplomatic posts in Africa. While Australia's representation in Egypt was deemed 'appropriate to prosecute Australia's political and commercial interests', Harris (1986, 205) noted that it would be difficult to maintain and justify the mission to Algeria due to limited economic prospects in the country. Australia's mission in Algeria was eventually closed in 1991 'owing to budgetary pressures', the declining significance of commercial interests, and 'civil conflict' (DFAT 2010, 24). Harris further noted that essential Australian interests in Africa were limited, and outlined which posts were of little significance to the country's foreign policy interests (Lusaka, Harare, Dar Es Salaam, Lagos). As the report noted (Harris 1986, 208), 'The Commonwealth connection, Australia's opposition to apartheid and involvement in the Rhodesian settlement have led to a pattern of representation in black Africa beyond that essential to Australia's immediate interests'.

The Harris Report highlighted how economic interests and not necessarily political ones served the best basis for opening and closing Australian diplomatic posts. This is clearly seen in Australia's engagement with Africa. A year before Harris' report came out, Australia closed its post in Ghana after operating in the country since 1958, partially because of political instability and partially due to lacking economic interests in West Africa and Ghana. Australia also closed its posts in Ethiopia in 1987 (due to budget cuts, and probably the loss of interest in the East African famine, the post was initially opened in 1984 to coordinate the humanitarian relief effort there); in Tanzania in 1987 (again due to budget cuts and low economic interests); and in Zambia in 1991 (due to lacking economic and political interests, the latter influenced by the fall of apartheid in South Africa). On the other hand, the Australian government did open a new diplomatic post in Mauritius in 1984, but that mission effectively replaced Tanzania as the centre for diplomatic representation for the Indian Ocean, and was part of the reason for the closure of the post in Tanzania three years later (DFAT 2010, 24–25). As one senior Australian diplomat noted, from the 1980s onwards, there was always a 'zero-sum' game with regard to diplomatic posts in Africa, exhibited in a pattern of opening a post in one place but having to close in another. All of this was 'a real problem' for Australia's development of an 'Africa policy', because one of the consequences of this 'zero-sum' attitude was that 'no one wanted to make their career in Africa because it was quite clear that this was not going to be an area of expansion' within Australian foreign policy and the country's Department of Foreign Affairs and Trade.[2]

CONCLUSION

The historical review of Australia's engagement with Africa conducted in this chapter has highlighted several key themes and recurring issues which have helped to establish Africa's 'place' in Australia's wider foreign policy agenda. Ironically, although this wider foreign policy agenda has experienced significant changes in the time period under review—such as Australia's move from a UK-dominated foreign and strategic policy, to a US-dominated one, and the country's growing enmeshment in Asia—Africa's place in it has remained relatively constant. It began its life in Australia's autonomous and independent foreign policy as a space of rather marginal interest, and more than sixty years later, notwithstanding limited efforts to the contrary, it largely remains in that same policy space. With this in mind, a few conclusions can be made about the foundations of Australia's engagement with Africa.

Firstly, Australia's engagement with Africa has traditionally been more multilateral than bilateral. While the UN has been an important forum, it was really the Commonwealth that proved to be Australia's traditional 'window' into Africa. What all of the various episodes of Australia's engagement with Africa through the Commonwealth demonstrate is that the organization has been an almost invaluable forum for the development of Australian diplomatic expertise on African issues, and the advancement of the country's reputation internationally. The Commonwealth is the one multilateral forum that regularly brings Australia close to African states, and it is the only such forum

[2] Phone interview with senior DFAT official, 9 April 2014.

where Australia can objectively be considered an influential player. It is therefore 'very difficult to imagine Australia not only substantially engaging, but also exercising a significant amount of influence over issues such as anti-racism and the fight against apartheid, or the settlement of Rhodesia/Zimbabwe's international status, outside of the Commonwealth forum' (Pijović 2014, 394).

Secondly, Australia's historical engagement with Africa has by and large been focused on apartheid and racism in Southern Africa. From at least the days of South Africa's exit from the Commonwealth in 1961, to the election of South Africa's first black president in 1994, the prism through which successive Australian governments saw the African continent was either with sympathy for, or objection to, apartheid. The anti-apartheid struggle was for good and for bad the principal driver of Australia' attention to Africa, and the long-term negative effect of this preoccupation was that it excluded any discussion about other possible interests Australia might have in Africa. This in turn resulted in a diminishing Australian engagement with Africa in the 1990s, and was one of the reasons why it was quite easy for the incoming conservative John Howard-led Australian government in 1996 to perceive Africa as a place with almost no observable foreign policy interests or objectives for Australia.

Lastly, one of the central pillars of Australia's engagement with Africa has been the perception of Africa as marginal to Australia's overall foreign policy interests and agenda. In light of the very limited commercial, immigration, cultural, and strategic links between Australia and African states, this may seem self-evident, but it was not necessarily destined to be so. Africa was a space of potential commercial, strategic, and foreign policy opportunity during the late 1950s and especially in the wake of the mass decolonization movement which by the early 1960s gave birth to so many African states. However, it was the active decision-making of successive conservative Australian government between 1949 and 1972 that failed to foster any substantive links with African states past the already established interests in, and sympathy for Southern African white settler societies.

References

Abbott, Tony. 2014. *National Boer War Memorial Association Annual Commemoration and Reconciliation Service 2014.* Message from the Prime Minister. 30 May. http://www.bwm.org.au/boer_war_day/Boer_War_Day2014.php. Accessed on 6 May 2018.

Albinski, Henry Stephen. 1977. *Australian External Policy Under Labor: Content, Process and the National Debate.* St. Lucia: University of Queensland Press.

The Australian. 1973. Cairns Defends Trade Visit. 27 July.

The Australian. 1979. It's Fraser the Statesman. 8 August.

Bolton, Geoffrey Curgenven. 1990. *The Oxford History of Australia: Vol. 5, 1942–1988 the Middle Way.* Melbourne: Oxford University Press.

Clark, Claire. 1980. The United Nations. In W. J. Hudson (ed.), *Australia in World Affairs 1971–75.* Sydney: Allen & Unwin, 126–162.

Colless, Malcolm. 1979. Fraser Hails Zimbabwe Peace Formula. *The Australian.* 7 August.

Cosgrove, Peter. 2015. *Message for Boer War Day 2015.* http://www.bwm.org.au/boer_war_day/Boer_War_Day2015.php. Accessed on 6 May 2018.

Coulthard Clark, Chris. 2001. *The Encyclopaedia of Australia's Battles.* St. Leonards: Allen & Unwin.

Cox, Dave. 1997. Boosterism and Myth-Making: Testing the Veracity of the Hawke Government's South Africa Foreign Policy. In Richard Leaver and Dave Cox (eds.), *Middling, Meddling, Muddling: Issues in Australian Foreign Policy.* Sydney: Allen & Unwin, 120–142.

Daily Graphic. 1977. Fraser Faces Revolt. Issue 8346, 19 August, 2. https://books.google.co.za/books?id=GIj0qoFmb8kC&pg=PA2&lpg=PA2&dq=daily+graphic+19+August+1977+rhodesia&source=bl&ots=n5nbs5VjV1&sig=gFQFwURbxzK-5L2FlB9qZJEFDjM&hl=en&sa=X&ved=0ahUKEwidq-7xhe_aAhXMIMAKHUuHDLgQ6AEILTAB#v=onepage&q=daily%20graphic%2019%20August%201977%20rhodesia&f=false. Accessed on 6 May 2018.

DFAT. 2010. *Supplementary Submission Responding to Additional Questions.* Joint Standing Committee on Foreign Affairs, Defence and Trade, Inquiry into Australia's Relationship with the Countries of Africa. Submission No. 94. 15 November.

Evans, Gareth. 2014. Interview with Gareth Evans. *Commonwealth Oral History Project.* http://www.commonwealthoralhistories.org/2015/interview-with-the-hon-gareth-evans/. Accessed on 15 February 2016.

Evans, Gareth and Brice Grant. 1995. *Australia's Foreign Relations in the World of the 1990s.* 2nd Edition. Melbourne: Melbourne University Press.

Fraser, Malcolm. 1961. Question: International Affairs Speech. *House of Representatives.* 12 April.

Fraser, Malcolm. 1977. *Prime Minister's Address to the Royal Commonwealth Society.* 3 June. London. https://pmtranscripts.dpmc.gov.au/release/transcript-4414. Accessed on 15 February 2016.

Fraser, Malcolm and Margaret Simons. 2010. *Malcolm Fraser: The Political Memoirs.* Melbourne: The Miegunyah Press.

Goldsworthy, David. 2002. *Losing the Blanket: Australia and the End of Britain's Empire.* Melbourne: Melbourne University Press.

48 N. PIJOVIĆ

Grattan, Michelle and Ian Davis. 1983. Policy Change to Bar Most South African Amateurs. *The Age*. 26 October.

Harper, Norman and Gordon Greenwood. 1974. *Australia in World Affairs, 1966–1970*. Melbourne: Cheshire for the Australian Institute of International Affairs.

Harries, Owen. 1979. *Australia and the Third World: Report of the Committee on Australia's Relations with the Third World*. Canberra: Australian Government Publishing Service.

Harris, Stuart. 1986. *Review of Australia's Overseas Representation 1986*. Canberra: Australian Government Publishing Service.

Harris, Stuart. 2002. The Merger of the Foreign Affairs and Trade Departments Revisited. *Australian Journal of International Affairs*. 56:2, 223–235.

Hawke, Bob. 1994. *The Hawke Memoirs*. Port Melbourne: William Heinemann Australia.

Hawke, Bob. 2014. Interview with Bob Hawke. *Commonwealth Oral History Project*. http://www.commonwealthoralhistories.org/2015/interview-with-the-hon-bob-hawke/. Accessed on 15 February 2016.

Higgott, Richard. 1983. Australia and Africa. In P. J. Boyce and J. R. Angel (eds.), *Independence and Alliance: Australia in World Affairs 1976–80*. Sydney: Australian Institute of International Affairs, 245–261.

Howson, Peter. 1984. *The Howson Diaries: The Life of Politics*. Ringwood: Viking Press.

Jackson, R. Gordon. 1984. *Report of the Committee to Review the Australian Overseas Aid Program*. Canberra: Australian Government Publishing Service.

Karp, Paul. 2018. Australia Considers Fast-Track Visas for White South African Farmers. *The Guardian*. 14 March. https://www.theguardian.com/australia-news/2018/mar/14/dutton-considers-fast-track-visas-for-white-south-african-farmers. Accessed on 22 May 2018.

Lee, Alexander. 2017. *Conservatives Divided: Defending Rhodesia Against Malcolm Fraser 1976–1979*. Unpublished Master's Thesis, Australian National University.

Loshak, David. 1973. Toe Line or Else, Vorster Tells Papers. *The Australian*. 21 September.

Menzies, Robert Gordon. 1950. The British Commonwealth of Nations in International Affairs. *Roy Milne Memorial Lecture*. Adelaide: The Australian Institute of International Affairs. 26 June.

Menzies, Robert Gordon. 1958. *Speech Is of Time: Selected Speeches and Writings*. London: Cassell.

Menzies, Robert Gordon. 1961. Question: International Affairs Speech. *House of Representatives*. 11 April.

Menzies, Robert Gordon. 1967. *Afternoon Light: Some Memories of Men and Events*. London: Cassell.

Menzies, Robert Gordon. 1970. *The Measure of the Years*. Melbourne: Cassell.
Miller, J. D. B. 1968. Australia and the Indian Ocean Area, 1961–1965. In Norman Harper and Gordon Greenwood (eds.), *Australia in World Affairs 1961–1965*. Melbourne: Cheshire for the Australian Institute of International Affairs, 416–444.
Neuhaus, Matthew. 1989. A Useful CHOGM: Lusaka 1979. *Australian Journal of International Affairs*. 42, 161–166.
Odgers, George. 2000. *100 Years of Australians at War*. Melbourne: Ken Fin Books.
Osei-Amo, Yaw. 2004. *Australia's Foreign Policy Towards Sub-Saharan Africa 1972–96*. PhD Thesis, The University of Queensland.
Pijović, Nikola. 2014. The Commonwealth: Australia's Traditional 'Window' into Africa. *The Round Table: The Commonwealth Journal of International Affairs*. 103:4, August, 383–398.
Renouf, Alan. 1986. *Malcolm Fraser and Australian Foreign Policy*. Sydney: Australian Professional Publications.
Reynolds, Henry. 2016. *Unnecessary Wars*. Sydney: NewSouth Publishing.
Simson, Stuart and Hamish McDonald. 1979. The Ambitious Safari of Statesman Fraser. *The National Times*. 23 June.
Steketee, Mike. 1987a. Commonwealth to Shift Away from Sanctions. *Sydney Morning Herald*. 14 October.
Steketee, Mike. 1987b. Plan to Curb S African Finance. *Sydney Morning Herald*. 16 October.
Sydney Morning Herald. 2008. Former Senator Sheil Dies Aged 79. 6 October. https://www.smh.com.au/news/obituaries/no-chance-to-grow-old-as-veter-ans-affairsminister/2008/10/14/1223750030243.html. Accessed on 6 May 2018.
Watt, Alan. 1968. *The Evolution of Australian Foreign Policy 1938–1965*. London and New York: Cambridge University Press.
Whitlam, Gough. 1961. Question: International Affairs Speech. *House of Representatives*. 11 April.
Whitlam, Gough. 1974. *Address by the Prime Minister of Australia, Mr E.G. Whitlam, at the United Nations General Assembly*. New York, 30 September. https://pmtranscripts.dpmc.gov.au/release/transcript-3410. Accessed on 15 February 2016.
Whitlam, Gough. 1985. *The Whitlam Government 1972–1975*. Ringwood: Viking.
Witton, Ron. 1973. Australia and Apartheid—Ties That Bind. *Australian Quarterly*. 45:2, 18–31.
Wolfensohn, James D. 2010. *A Global Life: My Journey Among the Rich and Poor, from Sydney to Wall Street to the World Bank*. Sydney: Pan Macmillan.

CHAPTER 3

Australia Tries to Forget Africa

As outlined in the previous chapter, Australia's engagement with Africa in the first half of the 1990s started experiencing a slow change in intensity. However, that change in intensity, leading to Australia's disengagement from Africa in the 1990s was not destined to happen. Australia's slow disengagement from Africa was to an extent underpinned by wider structural factors such as the end of the Cold War and especially end of apartheid in South Africa, but that disengagement was considerably accelerated after the election of the John Howard conservative government in 1996. As this chapter will show, the Howard government largely tried to forget Africa in the 1990s, and only recognized the need to invest resources in that engagement in the mid-2000s. Although Australia under the Howard conservative government lacked substantial interest to engage with Africa, events in Africa forced it to maintain at least an episodic engagement with the continent. The first section of this chapter will examine the structural context in which the Howard government found itself upon entering office, and explain how that underpinned a diminishing Australian engagement with Africa. The second section of the chapter examines the agency of the Australian government, and particularly the roles of Prime Minister Howard and his Foreign Minister Alexander Downer in ultimately determining and affecting the shape and course of Australia's engagement with Africa.

© The Author(s) 2019
N. Pijović, *Australia and Africa*, Africa's Global
Engagement: Perspectives from Emerging Countries,
https://doi.org/10.1007/978-981-13-3423-8_3

The Decline of Africa

The end of the Cold War changed the half-century-old structure of the international political system from a bipolar to a largely unipolar one. The final disintegration of the Soviet Union in the early 1990s had significant repercussions for countries around the world and African ones in particular. From the early days of decolonization, most African countries were in some way affected by the strategic Cold War rivalry between the Americans and Soviets, and this made Africa arguably more relevant to international politics than would have been the case otherwise. Another issue that kept Africa globally relevant during the Cold War was the struggle against racism, apartheid, and institutionalized white-minority governance in Southern Africa.

Some of the most infamous cases of proxy wars between the United States (US) and Soviet Union took place in Africa, such as the conflict in Angola throughout the 1980s; and some of the most infamous cases of great power support for dictatorial regimes also took place in Africa, whether it was US support for Samuel Doe in Liberia and Mobutu Sese Seko in Zaire (today's Democratic Republic of Congo), or Soviet support for Mengistu Haile Mariam in Ethiopia.[1] During the four decades of the US–Soviet competition, 'anticolonial nationalists, prodemocracy activists, and issues of good governance and development were ignored or opposed' if they interfered with American strategic interests, and 'no regime was deemed too corrupt or repressive for American support so long as it allied with the United States in the Cold War' (Schmidt 2013, 127). US foreign policy towards Africa 'was shackled by the Cold War' and from the end of World War II until at least the mid-1980s, American 'interest in the continent fluctuated with changing estimates of the threat posed by real or imagined Soviet gains' (Clough 1992, 2). The same can, off course, be said of the Soviets and their calculations vis-a-vis the US (Schmidt 2013, 228). Overall, with the end of the Cold War, such calculations were no longer necessary and having lost its strategic value 'Africa was even more marginal internationally' (Somerville 2015, 179).

The end of the Cold War was relevant to Australia's engagement with Africa primarily, in that it helped to bring about (or speed up) the

---

[1]On the Americans in Zaire, see Clough (1992, Chapter 10) and Meredith (2006, Chapter 17). On the Soviet Union in the Horn of Africa, see Patman (1990). In general on foreign intervention in Africa, see Schmidt (2013).

end of apartheid in South Africa. As the US and Soviet Union relaxed their strategic rivalry in Africa in the second half of the 1980s, Western governments moved more forcefully to condemn and sanction South Africa's apartheid regime (previously a partner in the Cold War battle against communism). Although the Reagan administration was stuck in the Cold War mentality and averse to open and high-profile criticisms of the apartheid regime, the relaxing of the Cold War rivalry forced the US government to change tack. For example, as late as July 1986, Ronald Reagan attacked the African National Congress' (ANC) anti-apartheid struggle in South Africa, labelling their activities as 'calculated terror' and arguing that 'the South African government has a right and responsibility to maintain order in the face of terrorists', further re-invoking the country's strategic value vis-à-vis the fight against communism (Clough 1992, 106). However, such scaremongering was no longer enough to maintain support for the apartheid government because by 1985–1986, most US senators and congressmen 'were at least as worried about being labelled "soft on racism" as they were about being declared "soft on communism"' (Clough 1992, 106).

By this time, Australia had already been (at least rhetorically) active in global criticisms of apartheid, and the country's development assistance to Africa was mainly concentrated on supporting frontline states in the fight against apartheid in South Africa. Given the centrality of the fight against apartheid for Australia's engagement with Africa, the dismantling of white-minority rule in South Africa was highly salient in underpinning a changing foreign policy engagement with Africa. This much was confirmed by Gareth Evans, Australia's foreign minister between 1988 and 1996, who argued that although the prospect of the end of the Cold War in general 'created a more relaxed, fluid, and open environment' in Africa, all of Australia's 'eggs were in the South Africa basket' and the fight against apartheid was 'the driving dynamic' of Australia's engagement with Africa.[2] Since the early 1960s, and South Africa's departure from the Commonwealth, racism and apartheid were the main (and often only) issues Australia had to consistently deal with in its engagement with Africa, and were particularly prominent for that engagement since the early 1970s and Australia's open and prominent criticism of apartheid. This is why the demise of apartheid resulted in a recalibration

[2] Interview with Gareth Evans, Canberra, 17 September 2015.

of the nature and intensity of Australia's engagement with Africa. As Gareth Evans further argued

> There was certainly, as foreign minister, nothing like the same intensity of engagement once the South Africa [apartheid] issue had been resolved... We still had an interest, and [Bob] Hawke had a particular interest in the Commonwealth... but it was not centre-front as a policy preoccupation in the way it had been during the apartheid years...So just in the nature of things the intensity of that engagement did fall away. It was not a deliberate choice, just that there were so many other preoccupations elsewhere, and that when a problem is basically solved, and things are looking better, you move on.[3]

With no more apartheid to fight, Australia's engagement with Africa entered a new phase of lower intensity and less direct policy preoccupation. As the dismantling of apartheid started to gain traction in the early 1990s, Australia's development assistance to Southern Africa experienced a decrease, and the Australian High Commission in the frontline state of Zambia was closed. Paradoxically, Australia's defence deployments to Africa were at their highest levels during the early 1990s, but only through UN missions (Western Sahara, Somalia, and Rwanda) which did not really necessitate the government's high-profile political and diplomatic preoccupation (in the way that the anti-apartheid struggle did).

There were two other factors which also jointly helped to diminish the intensity of Australia's engagement with Africa. One was the change in Australian prime ministers from Bob Hawke to Paul Keating in the early 1990s. Bob Hawke maintained a strong interest in Commonwealth affairs, and by extension (given its historical centrality for Australia's engagement with Africa) African issues such as apartheid. Even Gareth Evans (2014, 6, 7) noted that Hawke took the Commonwealth connection more seriously than either himself or Paul Keating.[4] As one of Australia's diplomats with several head-of-mission postings to Africa remembered, when leaving the 1995 Commonwealth Heads of Government Meeting (CHOGM) in Auckland for the Asia-Pacific Economic Cooperation (APEC) summit in Japan, Prime Minister Paul Keating reportedly stated that he was now going to 'a real international

---

[3] Interview with Gareth Evans, Canberra, 17 September 2015.

[4] Interview with Gareth Evans, Canberra, 17 September 2015.

conference' (Neuhaus 2013, Part 1, 3; 2014, Part 3, 3). Prime Minister Keating was 'sceptical about the Commonwealth', and Evans (2014, 7) himself as Australia's foreign minister did not ascribe the forum much importance in the 'larger scheme of things', arguing that 'since the South Africa [anti-apartheid struggle] days' the Commonwealth just didn't have the same sort of resonance in Australia. Also at that time, and running through the 1990s, greater engagement with Asia was 'the main game' of Australian foreign policy under both Labor's Prime Minister Paul Keating and his conservative successor John Howard (Evans 2014, 7). In the aftermath of Australia's leading role in the founding of APEC, Paul Keating's time in government coincided with a growing recognition of Asia's tremendous economic rise (World Bank 1993). Keating displayed a very strong focus on regional integration with Asia, and even his government in its last few years was criticized for not proactively increasing engagement with Africa (JSCFADT 1996, 5; Neuhaus 2013, Part 1, 3).[5] In the aftermath of the dismantling of apartheid, Australian interests in Africa during the 1990s were perceived to be minimal, and other foreign policy priorities, such as engagement with Asia, were more pressing.[6] These trends and perceptions were largely maintained by the incoming conservative Howard government in 1996, and as Howard's foreign minister, Alexander Downer, argued

> ... given the priorities of Australian foreign policy it [engagement with Africa] just did not feature as a high priority, because we did not, we had some, but we did not have huge interest in Africa...compared to other parts of the world, our interests there were fairly modest...I mean in those days the priority for Australia was to build its engagement more successfully with Asia. And consolidate its relationships with traditional partners [such as the US].[7]

The second factor contributing to the decline in the intensity of Australia's engagement with Africa was the overall negative and

---

[5] For Paul Keating's focus on Asian integration, see Keating (2000). Keating's general lack of interest in African issues can also be gauged from Don Watson's portrait of Paul Keating, *Recollections of a Bleeding Heart*, which in over 730 pages offers almost no reference to African issues; one reference each to Rwanda and Somalia, and one to the 1991 CHOGM in Zimbabwe; see Watson (2002).

[6] Interview with Gareth Evans, Canberra, 17 September 2015.

[7] Phone interview with Alexander Downer, 28 October 2014.

pessimistic global narrative of Africa as a deeply troubled continent (Easterly and Levine 1997; Collier and Gunning 1999). This was encapsulated by *The Economist* magazine's May 2000 front-page headline 'The Hopeless Continent'. In the post-Cold War decade, many African states witnessed economic decline or at best stagnating growth coupled with a number of high-profile humanitarian and man-made disasters, leading *The Economist* (2000) to lament the despair surrounding the African continent. In the context of the raging civil war in Sierra Leone, the magazine generalized about the continent's 'many dreadful wars', with Sierra Leone epitomizing 'so much of the rest of Africa', and concluding that while no one could 'blame Africans for the weather', most of the continent's shortcomings 'owe less to acts of God than to acts of man'. And while 'brutality, despotism and corruption' were not inherently African traits, 'African societies, for reasons buried in their cultures, seem especially susceptible to them'.

The period between the mid-1970s and mid-2000s has come to be considered as Africa's 'lost quarter century', with the continent's severest economic decline taking place between 1980 and 1995 (Noman and Stiglitz 2015, 3). During this time, average per capita incomes in Africa declined steadily, many countries were subject to Structural Adjustment Programs mandated by international donors and financial institutions which in many cases only exacerbated economic difficulties, and the numerous highly publicized conflicts in Rwanda, Somalia, Sierra Leone, Angola, the Democratic Republic of Congo, and the Sudan, only served to further weaken political and economic governance across the continent (Noman and Stiglitz 2015, 1–29). Throughout the 1990s, the world appeared to be 'giving up' on helping Africa to develop, and there was a 'growing international perception that Africa is beyond help' (JSCFADT 1996, 5). The Organization for Economic Cooperation and Development's (OECD) aid to Africa decreased by around US 10 billion throughout the 1990s, from just over US 25 billion in 1990 to US 15.5 billion in 1999, only increasing to its 1990 levels in 2003 (OECD 2015). With this in mind, and although the situation was far from uniform across this very heterogeneous continent, much of the global perception of Africa in the 1990s was fairly pessimistic. To summarize, the end of the Cold War and apartheid, Australia's increasing emphasis on Asian engagement, and global perceptions of a 'hopeless' Africa all set the context for the 'Decline of Africa' in Australian foreign policy. This is not to suggest that engagement with Africa was a key plank of the country's foreign policy agenda before this time, but that the struggle against apartheid was an important policy preoccupation which regularly mobilized Australian foreign policy attention towards Africa from at least the early 1970s. With the end of apartheid, all of the above-noted issues contributed to a context more biased towards a generally declining and diminishing Australian interest in engagement with Africa in the 1990s.

THE HOWARD GOVERNMENT'S EPISODIC ENGAGEMENT WITH AFRICA

After the longest period of a Labor government Australia had ever seen (1983–1996), in March 1996, the country elected the conservative Liberal-National Party coalition to power. The conservatives were led by Prime Minister John Howard, and Howard's pick for his foreign minister, Alexander Downer, would become the country's longest-serving foreign minister. Both Howard and Downer remained in their respective portfolios for the full four terms of their government (1996–2007), and both men remained two central figures of Australia's foreign policy-making. As one senior Australian Department of Foreign Affairs and Trade (DFAT) official noted, Howard's foreign policy focus was very firmly on Australia's deeper engagement with Asia and strengthening ties with the US; 'Africa simply wasn't on the radar'.[8] John Howard (2011, 234) himself noted in his autobiography that upon entering office, he wanted to change his predecessor's 'seemingly Asia-only foreign policy focus'. While for Howard 'Asia was the first and most important region of political and economic interaction' for Australia, it was not the only one, and he felt that over the years Australia had allowed its 'traditional links with the United States and the United Kingdom to be taken for granted'. Howard also had a 'tainted' history on anti-apartheid issues, being vocal in his criticisms of the Australian Labor government's financial sanctions against the apartheid regime, as well as claiming that Australia's immigration policy in the late 1980s was discriminating against white South Africans.

Foreign Minister Alexander Downer largely followed his prime minister in not espousing much interest in engagement with Africa. As Downer himself stated, during his tenure in office, engagement with

---

[8] Phone interview with senior DFAT official, 13 October 2014.

58 N. PIJOVIĆ

Africa was 'a low priority' and 'more episodic than strategic'.[9] This was an honest and fair assessment of Australia's engagement with Africa not only during his time in office, but also for its entire history. Still, one Australian diplomat who served as High Commissioner to an African country during Downer's time in office stated that the foreign minister 'barely took an interest in Africa', and that 'a key dynamic of Downer's foreign policy years was his desire to get the consular service more into shape' because by providing better consular service, DFAT could gain greater public recognition. 'That was the only bit of Downer's foreign policy that really had a pro-Africa edge'.[10] This much was substantiated by another senior DFAT official who had been involved in the internal departmental debates around the opening of Australia's High Commission in Ghana in 2004, and even Alexander Downer stated that one of the reasons why the Ghana post was opened in 2004 was because Australia did not have enough consular coverage in Africa.[11] In any case, when interviewed for this research, Alexander Downer did not leave the author with the impression of having no affinity for African issues, strongly arguing that personalities have little to do with foreign policy-making and that if the structural factors during his time in office were supportive of Australia's greater engagement with Africa—i.e. if there were more Australian economic, diplomatic, strategic interests in Africa—he would have tried to increase his government's engagement with African states. As Downer noted, Australian interests in Africa during his time were thin, and hence, foreign policy focus on the region followed that trend.[12] However, when quizzed about where Africa fitted in his conceptualization of Australia's place and role in the world—which he often asserted was that of 'a significant country and pivotal power'—the former foreign minister simply stated that 'as a significant country we obviously have global interests, and Africa is included in our global interests'.[13] Without being unfair to Downer, this was a rather generic statement rather than a strategic illumination of Australia's interests in Africa.

[9] Phone interview with Alexander Downer, 28 October 2014.

[10] Both quotes are from a phone interview with a senior DFAT official, 13 October 2014.

[11] Interview with senior DFAT official, Canberra, 9 September 2014. Phone interview with Alexander Downer, 28 October 2014.

[12] Phone interview with Alexander Downer, 28 October 2014.

[13] Phone interview with Alexander Downer, 28 October 2014.

It may be true that Australian interests in Africa during Alexander Downer's tenure were slim, but it is also true that his government didn't make much of a proactive effort to enhance them. While the conservative government tried to forget Africa during the late 1990s and early 2000s, events on the continent coupled with Australia's membership of the Commonwealth would necessitate at least—as Downer stated—an episodic engagement with African issues. The most high-profile episode in that engagement came during the 2002 and 2003 Commonwealth meetings, and the suspension of Zimbabwe from the Commonwealth. This episode simultaneously represented the culmination of Australia's diplomatic mobilization in support of engagement with a prominent African issue, and a low point in its overall relations with its largest African trading partner, South Africa. The paradox here was that while the episode played out through the Commonwealth, by his own admission, Downer's government at the time was 'pretty sceptical' about the organization, and 'did not invest a lot of time and energy' in it.[14] Engagement with Africa picked up some traction in the last few years of the Howard government, coinciding with the strengthening of Australian commercial interests in Africa and the global resources boom. Thus, the conservative government, while largely reactive in fostering engagement with Africa, was not completely blind to changes on the continent, and in 2004 and 2005 moved to support growing Australian commercial and consular interests in Africa.

Africa and Australia's Failed 1996 UNSC Membership Bid

Soon after being elected to government, and in the context of the country's United Nations Security Council (UNSC) campaign launched by the previous Labor government, the Foreign Minister Alexander Downer attended a meeting of the Organization of African Unity in Cameroon in early July 1996 (Downer 1996a). Downer also appointed ex-Prime Minister Malcolm Fraser as Australia's special envoy to Africa in an attempt to lobby African governments in support of the country's UNSC campaign (Downer 1996b). However, although the conservative government made an attempt to support the UNSC bid, the campaign ended terribly for Australia. In the lead up to the October 1996

---

[14] Phone interview with Alexander Downer, 28 October 2014.

60   N. PIJOVIĆ

vote, there was a high degree of confidence in Australia's chances of winning a UNSC seat, and Australia's ambassador to the UN spearheading the campaign, Richard Butler, was highly optimistic (Stewart 1996). However, as the vote got closer, reports started indicating that it would be a very close race and there was even talk of Portugal buying African votes—some African states, such as Chad and Sao Tome and Principe had been in arrears with their UN dues for two or more years, but suddenly paid those dues and were eligible to vote (Littlejohns 1996). When the vote finally took place on 21 October 1996, Australia—who ran against Sweden and Portugal—lost out disastrously. In the first round, Sweden pooled 153 votes, Portugal 112, and Australia 91. But in the second round runoff with Portugal, Australia polled only 57 votes compared to Portugal's 124 (United Nations 1996). Considering that the Portuguese were the last colonizers to leave Africa only twenty years earlier, and that the previous (Labor) Australian government considered itself as a frontrunner in the global fight against apartheid, the country's embarrassment was significant. The loss shocked many, not only the diplomats and DFAT officials involved in managing Australia's bid, but also Prime Minister Howard and Foreign Minister Downer (*Daily Telegraph* 1996a). Downer admitted his surprise by stating that he did not know 'what went wrong with the calculations', while a day after the vote, Prime Minister Howard requested DFAT to explain the gap between the predictions of a successful vote and what had transpired (McPhedran 1996; Murdoch and Baker 1996; *Daily Telegraph* 1996b). In the post-election analysis, a variety of issues were raised as to why Australia was unsuccessful in its UNSC membership bid: Portugal bought African votes; the Australian government's stance on East Timor (recognizing Indonesia's sovereignty in contrast to Portugal's support for East Timor's independence); Ambassador Richard Butler's own arguably abrupt and arrogant personal style of 'diplomacy' which alienated other UN diplomats; strained relations with France over opposition to its nuclear testing in the Pacific; and Australia's unflinching support for the US especially with regard to airstrikes on Iraq (*The Canberra Times* 1996; Attwood 1996a). For his part, the man leading the campaign, Richard Butler, did admit that his own style of 'diplomacy' may have been an issue, but assessed that 'we lost this vote in Africa', implying that Australia simply had not done enough to garner African support (Attwood 1996b). It would appear that Australia's lobbying of African votes was a 'lesson in failure', even though it was recognized by

DFAT during the campaign that Africa was always assessed as a 'potential weakness'. Although Australia had apparently 'invested a lot of time and energy winning the Africans over' those efforts did not pay off, and DFAT officials conceded that Africa was 'the region where the greatest drift in support for Australia probably occurred' (Greenlees 1996).

The shocking failure of the country's UNSC membership campaign, and the overall narrative dominating the post-election analysis which pinpointed a large part of the blame on shifting (or bought) African votes probably affected the Howard government's attitude towards engagement with Africa. Although in the wake of the UNSC election failure some within DFAT were prompted 'to question not only the style of Australia's campaign but also what weight needs to be given to cultivating [relations with] regions outside the obvious foreign policy priorities', at the same time, there were reports that Australia was set to close down four diplomatic posts, one of which was in Nigeria (Greenlees 1996; Miranda and Mckenzie 1996). The closure of the post in Nigeria did not eventuate, but neither did the reconsideration of the importance Australia should give to cultivating relationships with regions outside the government's obvious immediate foreign policy priorities. In any case, Alexander Downer noted that Australia would have received some votes from Africa, but that in the overall terms of Australia's UNSC membership support, Africa 'was not our heartland'.[15] The perceived and substantial lack of support from Africa for Australia's UNSC membership bid probably further entrenched in the minds of conservative political leaders the idea that engagement with Africa offered very few foreign policy rewards.

The Peak of Engagement with Africa: The Commonwealth's 2002/2003 Suspension of Zimbabwe

During the Howard government's time in office, no foreign policy issue related to Africa was more high-profile and demanding of the prime minister's focus than that of Zimbabwe and its suspension from the Commonwealth. In 2002, Prime Minister Howard was chair of the CHOGM taking place in Australia, where he played a prominent role in also chairing the appointed 'Troika of Leaders' (including South Africa's

---

[15] Phone interview with Alexander Downer, 28 October 2014.

President Mbeki, and Nigeria's Obasanjo) whose job was to engage Zimbabwe's President Mugabe and 'respond to the expected report of Commonwealth election observers, in order to help find a solution that would benefit all the people of Zimbabwe' (McKinnon 2004, 406). The Zimbabwean presidential election itself took place a week after the CHOGM in Australia, and the Commonwealth election observers' team 'expressed concern about the high level of politically motivated violence and intimidation which preceded the poll', concluding that 'the conditions in Zimbabwe did not adequately allow for a free expression of will by electors' (McKinnon 2004, 406–407). In March 2002, the Troika announced Zimbabwe's suspension from the councils of the Commonwealth, stopping short of suspending the country's full membership of the organization. The Troika of Commonwealth leaders met again in Nigeria in September 2002 where the Australian prime minister was highly prominent in calling for Zimbabwe's full suspension from the organization. As Howard (2002) stated at the time, 'I was arguing that the Troika…should move immediately to fully suspend Zimbabwe from the Commonwealth because of the failure of Zimbabwe to show any sensitivity at all to Commonwealth opinion arising out of the observer group finding on the election'. Howard's hard lined stance caused a rift within the Troika and he was unable to secure Nigeria and South Africa's support for full suspension, but Australia nevertheless moved to institute 'smart' sanctions against the Zimbabwean government (Ford 2003, 27–28; McDougall 2005, 345). While Australia's sanctions did not have any impact on President Mugabe's ability to hold onto power, Prime Minister Howard was successful in advocating for an extension of Zimbabwe's suspension from the Commonwealth. Hence, at the December 2003 CHOGM in Nigeria, the Australian prime minister's hard line stance caused a further rift between Australia and prominent African members of the Commonwealth, but the Commonwealth did extend Zimbabwe's suspension, upon which President Mugabe withdrew his country from the organization altogether (Neuhaus 2013, Part 1, 14).[16]

[16]This paragraph is based on work previously published in Pijović, Nikola. 2014. The Commonwealth: Australia's Traditional 'Window' into Africa. *The Round Table: The Commonwealth Journal of International Affairs*, 103:4, 383–397, parts of which are reprinted here by permission of Taylor & Francis Ltd, on behalf of The Round Table: The Commonwealth Journal of International Affairs.

During these Commonwealth encounters and discussions of Robert Mugabe's regime in Zimbabwe, Prime Minister Howard experienced a particularly bruising relationship with South Africa's president Thabo Mbeki. As Howard (2011, 525) remembered, given the divergence in opinion between the two on Zimbabwe's status, he even had to resort to threats to induce Mbeki to attend a preparatory CHOGM meeting scheduled for September 2002 in Abuja. Upon receiving a message that Mbeki was not attending the Abuja meeting, Howard instructed Australia's High Commissioner in Pretoria to 'convey in the appropriate terms my displeasure' at Mbeki's planned absence. Howard told his top diplomat in South Africa to tell the South Africans that Mbeki's non-attendance in Abuja would be insulting, risking 'doing real damage to the relationships between Australia and South Africa'. Mbeki, in the end, turned up at the meeting.

Howard and Mbeki's difficult relationship extended beyond just disagreements over Zimbabwe. Firstly, John Howard, like his political idol Robert Menzies—Howard has since written a biography of the 'Menzies Era'—was very much of the 'old Commonwealth' mindset (Neuhaus 2013, Part 1, 14). As Don McKinnon (2013, 11), the Secretary of the Commonwealth at the time of the Zimbabwe episode argued, Howard 'was old Commonwealth', and McKinnon's 'father's generation' when it came to views on the UK, Commonwealth, and British monarchy, all of which were a result of Howard's personal outlook: 'old style...out of the stable of Robert Menzies'. Such an outlook would have from the very beginning made Howard more inclined to have strong views on the values that Commonwealth countries and their leadership should exhibit, and the organization should promote. Since Howard was also 'not a natural negotiator', this would have made it difficult to avoid confrontation over Mugabe's contentious governance in Zimbabwe, and his country's status in the Commonwealth (Neuhaus 2013, Part 1, 14).

Secondly, Thabo Mbeki (and his governing ANC in general) were well aware of John Howard's and his conservative Liberal-National coalition's 'flawed' history with decolonization, and historical sympathy for apartheid and 'outnumbered whites' in Southern Africa. John Howard was one of several high-profile Liberal party officials who disagreed with Prime Minister Malcolm Fraser on his government's policy of sporting sanctions against the apartheid regime, and as leader of the opposition in the late 1980s, Howard was critical of economic sanctions against South Africa, even arguing that the Australian Labor government's immigration policy was 'discriminating against white South Africans' (Walters 1987; Dunn 1987; Ramsey 1999). Although in the lead-up to the 1999 CHOGM in South Africa John Howard admitted that 'he was wrong in opposing sanctions against South Africa in the 1980s' (Wright 1999), he still had a 'tainted' history which President Mbeki would have never forgotten (Neuhaus 2013, Part 1, 14). And as one Australian diplomat who had served as High Commissioner to South Africa in the late 2000s concluded, 'the ANC's perception of the Liberals was never that good'.[17]

In any case, Prime Minister Howard and President Mbeki 'had fallen out very badly' over Zimbabwe's Commonwealth suspension, and the whole episode was 'the low point' in Australia's relations with Africa.[18] As John Howard (2011, 526) himself concluded in his autobiography, the CHOGM 2002/2003 Zimbabwe issue was 'just about the most demoralising foreign affairs issue' he touched in his time as prime minister—and this was a man who took his country to war in Iraq and Afghanistan in the early 2000s! The political relationship between Australia and South Africa deteriorated so much that, as one Australian diplomat who served as High Commissioner to South Africa soon after the events argued, even Foreign Minister Downer used to state that 'our relationship with South Africa was our second worst on earth, the worst being the relationship with Zimbabwe itself'.[19] After 2003, John Howard never visited any African country, and never dealt with any substantive African issue, only throwing out the occasional denunciation of the Mugabe regime. According to one Australian diplomat and Commonwealth official intimately involved in the discussions over Zimbabwe's suspension, Prime Minister Howard came out of the 2003 CHOGM saying 'I'll never meet again', which indicated his overall level of (dis)interest in African issues (Neuhaus 2013, Part 1, 13). When asked if re-elected to the prime ministership in 2007, would John Howard have pursued closer engagement with Africa, a retired Secretary of DFAT and senior Liberal Party official who had a history of working closely with John Howard answered with an unequivocal 'no!'; Howard had a bad experience at the 2002/2003 CHOGMs, was disillusioned with African leaders because of the whole Zimbabwe affair, and had no

[17] Interview with retired senior DFAT official, Canberra, 7 April 2014.

[18] Phone interview with senior DFAT official, 13 October 2014; Phone interview with senior DFAT official, 8 April 2014.

[19] Phone interview with senior DFAT official, 13 October 2014.

interest whatsoever in African engagement.[20] John Howard's involvement in the Commonwealth Troika almost certainly 'hardened his disdain' for African issues (Hawker 2004, 8).

However, Prime Minister John Howard's prominent activity in the Commonwealth's suspension of Zimbabwe represents a paradox: a man who overall exhibited very little interest in African engagement both prior to and after the 2002/2003 CHOGMs, was highly interested and engaged in this one episode of Australia's engagement with Africa.[21] Why? Well, there are two main reasons that help explain the anomaly. The first and simpler one is that engagement with the Zimbabwe issue was mandated by Australia's membership of the Commonwealth, and the Commonwealth is one of few international fora where Australia is a seriously powerful and prominent player. This would not necessarily mandate Prime Minister Howard's personal interest in engagement with the Zimbabwe issue, but what his story of threats to Mbeki in the lead up to the 2002 Abuja meeting reflects is at least the view that Australia's status in the Commonwealth should be taken seriously. Mbeki's non-attendance, as Howard hinted, implied a disregard for Australia's status within the Commonwealth, and Howard's overall activity on the Zimbabwe issue could be seen as playing the role that is expected from one of the organizations major players. The second reason for Prime Minister Howard's interest and activity could be much more personal and tied to his values. Although Howard espoused what he termed a realist and pragmatic approach to foreign policy, his foreign policy thinking was nevertheless very much influenced by his system of values, deeply rooted in his conservatism and Methodist upbringing (Wesley 2007, 31–59). This in itself resulted in a paradox; while on the one hand Howard could back in 1998 proclaim that he was not interested in exporting liberal democratic governance to other countries, and respected 'the right of countries to have the system of governance that they think is best for their society', on the other hand, by 2002, he could exhibit very little of that 'open-mindedness' and tolerance in his engagement with Zimbabwe (Howard 1998). This was because Howard was anything but a cultural relativist: his respect for cultural difference did not mean he was 'a believer in the equal value of all national cultures', and there were

---

[20] Interview with senior DFAT official, Canberra, 12 August 2014.

[21] Although some have argued that Howard's involvement in the CHOGM troika was 'virtually accidental', see Hawker (2004, 8).

66   N. PIJOVIĆ

some 'ways of doing things that are better than others' (Wesley 2007, 56). It was this 'cultural superiority' that helped to drive John Howard's interest in engagement with the Zimbabwe issue, and it must be remembered that this was all taking place at the same time as Australia participated in US-led interventions aimed at changing governance structures and regimes in the Middle East. In short, the Zimbabwe episode not only allowed Australia to exercise its 'big player' status in the one international forum where it could, but it also allowed John Howard to export his own values-driven foreign policy.

The Global Resources Boom, the Growth of Australian Commercial Interests, and Trade with Africa

In addition to the Howard government's recognition that Australia's consular coverage of Africa needed improving, from the early 2000s onwards, many African states began experiencing prolonged periods of political stability and economic growth. The early 2000s saw the beginnings of what would later be recognized as the global resources boom, and an increasing number of Australian-based resources companies became involved in trying to seize the vast opportunities in resource exploration and exploitation in Africa. Hence, from roughly 2002 onwards, the Australian government tried to promote greater trade with North Africa, Egypt, and Libya in particular. This move culminated in the 2005 opening of an Australian Trade Commission (Austrade) post in the Libyan capital of Tripoli, which was opened 'to help' Australian companies 'investing in Libya at the time'.[22] Unfortunately, due to the civil war in Libya, that post would suspend operations in 2011, and formally close down in 2013. It was also in this context of supporting enhanced commercial links with Africa that in May 2005, the Australian Parliament's Joint Standing Committee on Foreign Affairs, Defence and Trade initiated a formal inquiry into expanding Australia's trade and investment relations with North Africa (JSCFADT 2006).

However, aside from its economic engagement with South Africa— which was the one relationship that the conservative government proactively sought to maintain—the Howard government was on the whole reactive to global developments when it came to fostering greater

---

[22] Phone interview with Alexander Downer, 28 October 2014.

economic engagement with Africa. Hence, within the spirit of Africa's growing appeal as an investment destination and the global resources boom driving up prices of primary commodities and minerals, in its last few years, the Howard government moved to react to such forces and support growing Australian commercial interests in Africa. It was in this context that the Australian government reopened its High Commission in Ghana in 2004, thereby increasing the country's diplomatic representation in West Africa to two posts (Nigeria and Ghana). While the reopening of the post was driven by the expansion of Australian mining interests in West Africa, as well as the need to broaden Australia's diplomatic coverage in the region, the reactive nature of it all was the reason why the Australian resources-based business community with operations in Africa perceived that the Howard government generally displayed 'no particular interest' in supporting Australia's economic engagement with Africa.[23]

As can be seen in the Appendix which outlines Australia's historical merchandise trade with Africa, between 1996 and 2007, South Africa remained Australia's most important export market in Africa. The Howard government was proactive in its efforts to formalize regular high-level trade meetings with South African ministers and business delegations and this could have helped foster greater economic cooperation with South Africa. Exports to South Africa rose steadily from AUD 947 million in 1996 to AUD 2.5 billion in 2007, and while due to the nature of Australia's liberal market economy it is impossible to prove causality, the Howard government's focus on promoting and supporting economic links with South Africa may have been beneficial in helping this trade relationship grow. Of Australia's top ten export destinations in Africa during these years, only South Africa, Egypt, Mauritius, and Kenya held permanent Australian diplomatic missions, with the post in Ghana opened in 2004, and the post in Libya opened in late 2005. The opening of these two diplomatic posts did not have a significant effect on boosting exports to those countries, although in the case of Libya, it may have been helpful in boosting Australian exports to neighbouring countries such as Algeria. Exports to Ghana in the few years following the opening of the Australian High Commission rose slightly in line

---

[23] Phone interview with senior DFAT official, 13 October 2014. Phone interview with senior DFAT official, 15 October 2014. Phone interview with senior Paydirt Media official, 31 July 2014.

with the general trend of rising exports there visible before the opening of the diplomatic post, while in Libya, Australian exports to the country were actually much more significant prior to 2002. As has traditionally been the case, Australia's strongest export markets on the African continent were on the extreme north and south. Of the top 10 export destination countries in Africa, two were from Southern Africa (South Africa and Mozambique) and by value of exports most important for Australia; three were from North Africa (Egypt, Algeria, and Libya), with another four from Eastern Africa and the Indian Ocean (Kenya, Sudan, Tanzania, and Mauritius), and one from West Africa (Ghana). As far as Australia's imports of merchandise from Africa are concerned, between 1996 and 2007, South Africa was by far the largest source market for African imports. The largest sources of merchandise imports from Africa during these years were slightly more diversified in terms of geographic location than Australia's largest export markets on the continent. Of the top 10 largest import source countries, two were in Southern Africa (South Africa and Swaziland), three in North Africa (Morocco, Algeria, and Egypt), two in Eastern Africa (Kenya and the Congo), and three in West Africa (Gabon, Nigeria, and Cote D'Ivoire).

Conclusion

This chapter has tried to highlight that although wider structural factors such as the end of apartheid in South Africa, Australia's growing focus on Asian engagement, and a global perception of a 'hopeless' Africa throughout the 1990s underpinned Australia's slow disengagement from Africa, it was the active policy-making of the Howard conservative government that ultimately tried to forget about engagement with Africa. While engagement with Africa through the 11 years of the Howard government was not monolithic, it was, as Howard's foreign minister, Alexander Downer, stated 'episodic rather than strategic'. The first key episode came with Australia's failed 1996 UNSC membership bid, and the second came with the Commonwealth's 2002/2003 suspension of Zimbabwe. It was multilateralism—first the UNSC membership bid and then the Commonwealth—that really forced the Howard government to engage with Africa issues, and on all other fronts, save for economic engagement with South Africa, it would have been more than happy to forget about the continent altogether. This much was certainly evident with regard to Australia's development assistance to Africa which is examined in detail in Chapter 5. However, notwithstanding its efforts to forget Africa, the Howard government—in its last few years in power—began to understand the need for greater diplomatic engagement with the continent, and this recognition was largely driven by the widening of Australian commercial (and to an extent consular) interests across Africa. In the end, the government reacted to such necessities with the opening of an Australian High Commission in Ghana in 2004, and an Austrade run Consulate General in Libya in 2005.

REFERENCES

Attwood, Alan. 1996a. Unseated. *Sydney Morning Herald.* 26 October.

Attwood, Alan. 1996b. Deception and Duplicity: How the Black Prince Was Rolled by the RLBs of the UN (Rotten Lying Bastards). *The Age.* 26 October.

The Canberra Times. 1996. Australia's UN Humiliation. 24 October.

Clough, Michael. 1992. *Free at Last? U.S. Policy Toward Africa and the End of the Cold War.* New York: Council on Foreign Relations Press.

Collier, Paul and Jan Willem Gunning. 1999. Why Has Africa Grown Slowly? *The Journal of Economic Perspectives.* 13:3, Summer, 3–22.

Daily Telegraph. 1996a. Australia's Shock Loss in UN Vote. 22 October.

Daily Telegraph. 1996b. Explain UN Seat Defeat, PM Demands. 23 October.

Downer, Alexander. 1996a. *African Initiatives.* Minister for Foreign Affairs. Media Release. 28 June.

Downer, Alexander. 1996b. *Appointment of Mr Malcolm Fraser as Special Envoy to Africa.* Minister for Foreign Affairs. Media Release. 28 June.

Dunn, Ross. 1987. Lib Welcome Mat for South Africans. *Sydney Morning Herald.* 29 May. 5.

Easterly, William and Ross Levine. 1997. Africa's Growth Tragedy: Policies and Ethnic Divisions. *The Quarterly Journal of Economics.* 112:4, November, 1203–1250.

The Economist. 2000. Hopeless Africa. 11 May.

Evans, Gareth. 2014. Interview with Gareth Evans. *Commonwealth Oral History Project.* http://www.commonwealthoralhistories.org/2015/interview-with-the-hon-gareth-evans/. Accessed on 15 February 2016.

Ford, Jolyon. 2003. Australian-African Relations 2002: Another Look. *Australian Journal of International Affairs.* 57:1, 17–33.

Greenlees, Don. 1996. African Lobbying a Lesion in Failure. *The Australian.* 23 October.

Hawker, Geoffrey. 2004. Australia and Africa: Old Issues, New Connections. *AQ: Australian Quarterly.* 76:1, 6–8, 40.

Howard, John. 1998. *Transcript of the Prime Minister the Hon John Howard MP, Press Conference Regent Hotel.* Department of Prime Minister and Cabinet. Interview. 17 November, Kuala Lumpur.

Howard, John. 2002 *Transcript of the Prime Minister the Hon John Howard MP Radio Interview, BBC4.* Department of Prime Minister and Cabinet. Interview. 25 September.

Howard, John Winston. 2011. *John Howard Lazarus Rising: A Personal and Political Autobiography.* Revised Edition. Sydney: Harper Collins Publishers.

Joint Standing Committee on Foreign Affairs, Defence, and Trade (JSCFADT). 1996. *Inquiry into Australia's Relationship with Southern Africa.* Canberra: Commonwealth of Australia.

Joint Standing Committee on Foreign Affairs, Trade and Defence (JSCFADT). 2006. *Expanding Australia's Trade and Investment Relations with North Africa.* Canberra: Commonwealth of Australia.

Keating, Paul. 2000. *Engagement: Australia Faces the Asia-Pacific.* Sydney: Pan Macmillan.

Littlejohns, Michael. 1996. Close Vote for Security Council Seats. *Financial Times.* 18 October.

McDougall, Derek. 2005. Australia and the Commonwealth. *The Round Table: The Commonwealth Journal of International Affairs.* 94:380, 339–349.

McKinnon, Don. 2004. After Abuja: Africa and the Commonwealth. *The Round Table: The Commonwealth Journal of International Affairs.* 93:375, 403–409.

McKinnon, Don. 2013. Interview with Don McKinnon. *Commonwealth Oral History Project.* Part 1. http://www.commonwealthoralhistories.org/2015/interview-with-sir-don-mckinnon/. Accessed on 18 February 2016.

McPhedran, Ian. 1996. UN Seat Lost in Blow to Aust. *The Canberra Times.* 23 October.

Meredith, Martin. 2006. *The State of Africa: A History of the Continent Since Independence.* London: Simon & Schuster.

Miranda, Charles and Scott Mckenzie. 1996. Envoys Coming Home/Diplomatic Posts to Close After UN Failure. *The Daily Telegraph.* 24 October.

Murdoch, Lindsay and Mark Baker. 1996. Answers Fought for Humiliation at UN. *The Age.* 23 October.

Neuhaus, Matthew. 2013. Interview with Matthew Neuhaus. *Commonwealth Oral History Project.* Part 1, 2. http://www.commonwealthoralhistories.org/2014/interview-with-matthew-neuhaus/. Accessed on 17 February 2016.

Neuhaus, Matthew. 2014. Interview with Matthew Neuhaus. *Commonwealth Oral History Project.* Part 3. http://www.commonwealthoralhistories.org/2014/interview-with-matthew-neuhaus/. Accessed on 16 February 2016.

Noman, Akbar and Joseph E. Stiglitz. 2015. *Industrial Policy and Economic Transformation in Africa.* New York: Columbia University Press.

OECD. 2015. *Distribution of NET ODA.* https://data.oecd.org/oda/distribution-of-net-oda.htm. Accessed on 17 February 2016.

Patman, Robert G. 1990. *The Soviet Union in the Horn of Africa: The Diplomacy of Intervention and Disengagement.* New York: Cambridge University Press.

Ramsey, Alan. 1999. A Sorry Tale of Minute Vision. *Sydney Morning Herald.* 20 November, 49.

Schmidt, Elizabeth. 2013. *Foreign Intervention in Africa: From the Cold War to the War on Terror.* New York: Cambridge University Press.

Somerville, Keith. 2015. *Africa's Long Road Since Independence: The Many Histories of a Continent.* London: Hurst Publishers.

Stewart, Cameron. 1996. Our Man in New York Woos the World in Disarming Style. *The Australian.* 16 September.

United Nations. 1996. *General Assembly Fifty-First Session: 39th Plenary Meeting.* New York. 21 October, A/51/PV.39. http://www.un.org/ga/search/view_doc.asp?symbol=A/51/PV.39. Accessed on 16 February 2016.

Walters, Patrick. 1987. Back White Moderates in South Africa, Howard Urges Govt. *Sydney Morning Herald.* 17 March.

Watson, Don. 2002. *Recollections of a Bleeding Heart: A Portrait of Paul Keating PM.* Milsons Point: Vintage Book.

Wesley, Michael. 2007. *The Howard Paradox: Australian Diplomacy in the Asia 1996–2006.* Sydney: ABC Books.

Wright, Tony. 1999. I Erred on Apartheid: PM. *The Sunday Age.* 14 November, 4.

World Bank. 1993. *The East Asian Miracle: Economic Growth and Public Policy.* A World Bank Policy Research Report. New York: Oxford University Press.

CHAPTER 4

Australia Re-discovers Africa...and Then Tries to Forget It Again

The purpose of this chapter is to tell two stories: one which highlights how the Australian government between 2007 and 2013 tried to re-engage with Africa, and the other which highlights how the Australian government between 2013 and 2018 did its best to try and forget about engagement with Africa. The reason why the Australian government could, in a matter of years, hold such diametrically opposing positions on engagement with Africa is simple: the country was led by two ideologically different governments. The centre-left Australian Labor Party came into government in late 2007 after some 11 years of conservative government, and very quickly established its foreign policy priorities. In line with its traditional 'middle power' foreign policy outlook, the Labor government committed itself to greater activity in its engagement with the world. This included a 'new engagement' with Africa, which, as the government suggested, was necessary because of the previous conservative government's neglect of Africa. That 'new engagement' was 'supercharged' by two specific short- and mid-term policy commitments: the pursuit of United Nations Security Council (UNSC) membership in 2012, and the expansion of Australia's aid budget to the level of 0.5% of Australia's Gross National Income (GNI) by 2015. While these two commitments were aimed at increasing Australia's overall internationalist standing, they helped significantly boost the country's engagement with Africa.

© The Author(s) 2019
N. Pijović, *Australia and Africa*, Africa's Global
Engagement: Perspectives from Emerging Countries,
https://doi.org/10.1007/978-981-13-3423-8_4

73

On the other hand, the conservatives were back in government in September 2013, and under Prime Minister Tony Abbott, and his successor, Prime Minister Malcolm Turnbull did not care much for maintaining Labor's levels of engagement with Africa. As far as the conservatives were concerned, Labor's 'new engagement' with Africa was all about winning the UNSC seat, and once that goal was achieved in 2012, why bother with Africa. Driven by their own traditional 'bilateralist regionalism' foreign policy outlook, the conservatives turned Australia's foreign policy gaze firmly back on its own region, and engagement with Africa simply had no place there.

This chapter proceeds in three main sections. Much like the first section of the previous chapter, the first section of this chapter examines wider structural factors that helped to underpin Australia's changing engagement with Africa in the late 2000s. While in the 1990s it was the 'Decline of Africa' that helped to underpin the Howard conservative government's disengagement from Africa, in the late 2000s, it was the 'Rise of Africa' that helped to underpin the Labor government's re-engagement with the continent. The second section of the chapter examines the Labor government's 'new engagement' with Africa, while the final section of the chapter looks at the Abbott and Turnbull conservative governments' disengagement from Africa. Just like the previous chapter, this chapter also focuses on the agency of Australian governments and especially their prime ministers and foreign ministers in ultimately determining the significant changes Australia's engagement with Africa experienced between 2007 and 2018.

THE RISE OF AFRICA

Since the turn of the millennium, many African economies experienced consistent economic growth, and more durable macroeconomic and political stability. However, it was only towards the end of the 2000s that the explicit and then much-trumpeted recognition of this trend occurred, forming the narrative of the 'Rise of Africa'. This would become a highly influential structural factor helping to shape the Australian government's 're-discovery' of Africa in the mid-2000s. In this context, two interconnected issues were of key relevance for Australia: Africa's general prolonged economic rise, and more specifically, the global resources boom that to an extent drove it. The former set the broader context for a more optimistic perception of Africa, while the latter highlighted specifically the place of Australian business and commercial interests in this context.

The changing narrative of the rise of Africa is best highlighted by a quick examination of headlines from *The Economist*. Between 1997 and 2015, the magazine ran 19 front-page headlines featuring African issues. Its already-discussed May 2000 headline 'The Hopeless Continent', although prominent in its extreme negativity and pessimism, reflected a pattern by which up until the late 2000s, almost all Africa-related headlines were of an Afro-pessimist tone, focusing mainly on the problems with the continent's development, governance, and security. But, fast forward to 2011, and *The Economist* ran a lead story with a markedly different front-page title: 'Africa Rising—The Hopeful Continent'. In a clear example of Afro-optimism that was sweeping through international media and financial organizations and think tanks, the story focused primarily on the beneficial changes taking place on the continent over the past decade. After outlining a 'depressingly familiar backdrop' of corruption, kleptocracy, poverty, drought, and famine, the editorial focused on health, technology and communications improvements, Africa's fast-growing middle class and a steady increase in Foreign Direct Investment (FDI) to the continent. As *The Economist* concluded, 'at a dark time for the world economy, Africa's progress is a reminder of the transformative power of growth' (2011, 13). The narrative of Africa's rise was further confirmed two years later, in March 2013, when *The Economist* ran a special report and front-page story titled 'Aspiring Africa', arguing that celebrations were 'in order on the poorest continent', because never 'in the half-century since it won independence from colonial powers has Africa been in such good shape' (2013, 9).

The Economist was not alone in recognizing that trends in Africa were changing for the better. Perhaps surprisingly for a country that places such marginal importance on African issues, one of the first publications to highlight Africa's rise came from an Australian foreign policy think tank: the Lowy Institute's 2008 *Into Africa: How the Resources Boom Is Making Sub-Saharan Africa More Important to Australia* (Donnely and Ford 2008). The report was not globally significant in shaping the 'Rise of Africa' narrative, but it was significant for Australian foreign policy because it explicitly highlighted Africa's growing appeal for Australian business interests in the resources sector. It also formed the foundation from which the Australian Department of Foreign Affairs and Trade (DFAT) would draw early figures on the estimated value of Australian

76   N. PIJOVIĆ

commercial interests and investments in Africa (Le May 2007; *AAP* 2008). A more globally renowned report was published by the McKinsey Global Institute in June 2010, titled *Lions on the Move: The Progress and Potential of African Economies* (Roxburgh et al. 2010). That report was highly influential in helping shape the wider narrative of Africa's rise both globally and in Australia, and this much was noted by almost all DFAT officials interviewed for this research, who would often cite the McKinsey report as an authority on the 'Rise of Africa' narrative.[1]

What Happened Between 2000 and 2011 in Africa?

As a number of publications have made clear, there were three overarching factors that helped shape Africa's rise: improved political governance and security, improved macroeconomic stability and sustained economic growth, and the global resources boom. The 2008 Lowy Institute report argued that 'improved African fundamentals' such as macroeconomic stabilization and conflict resolution and democratization, coupled with the growth in commodity prices, were some of the main reasons why Africa was becoming an important destination for Australian businesses (Donnely and Ford 2008, 1–13). The McKinsey report stated that while Africa's growth acceleration was helped by the resources boom, it was underpinned by more than just that; 'arguably more important' were government actions to end political conflicts and improve macroeconomic conditions (Roxburgh et al. 2010, 1). *The Economist* (2011, 13) echoed such views, highlighting that Africa was 'at last getting a taste of peace and decent government', while noting that the commodities boom was partially responsible for the fact that 'over the past decade six of the world's ten fastest-growing countries were African'. The consensus was that 'booming commodity prices and mineral discoveries' as well as 'improved macroeconomic management' all made significant contributions to the economic 'Rise of Africa' (Noman and Stiglitz 2015, 1).

As far as improved political governance and security were concerned, from the late 1990s onwards, many African states began experiencing prolonged political stability and relatively higher levels of security. While this in itself does not necessarily imply that there has been a general

---

[1] For other works helping to shape the 'Rise of Africa' narrative, see Radelet (2010), Severino and Ray (2011), and Robertson et al. (2012).

improvement in the quality of political governance across the continent, it has at least allowed for an environment conducive of greater economic activity. The trend towards conflict resolution continent-wide was an important factor in Africa's rise. With the ending of the long-running conflicts in Angola in the early 2000s, Cote d'Ivoire in the mid-2000s, and at least the diminishing intensity of fighting in the Democratic Republic of Congo by the late 2000s, many of Sub Sharan Africa's (SSA) major economies were experiencing increasing political stability which in turn helped to foster economic growth. As the McKinsey report argued, with the average number of serious conflicts in Africa declining from 4.8 each year in the 1990s to 2.6 in the 2000s, economic growth in conflict-free countries rebounded to some 5% a year (Roxburgh et al. 2010, 12).

On the other hand, Africa's macroeconomic stability and economic growth had been, although starting from a low base, relatively resilient and steadfast in the 2000s, especially as compared to the 1990s. As *The Economist* (2011, 76) noted, since 'regrettably' labelling Africa 'the hopeless continent' a decade ago, 'a profound change has taken hold'. In short, much of the continent experienced unimpeded economic growth and changes in a range of economic indicators. Firstly, while SSA's Gross Domestic Product (GDP) largely stagnated through most of the 1990s (between just over US 370 Billion in 1990 and just over US 380 Billion in 2000), from the early 2000s until 2015, it rose steadily and significantly (from just over US 390 Billion in 2002 to just over US 1.5 Trillion in 2015) (IMF 2018). However, Africa's economic rise since the early 2000s did not necessarily mean that African governments were less indebted, but rather that their increasing revenues meant that external debt as a percentage of GDP actually decreased in the 2000s. Although SSA's external debt actually rose significantly from the mid-2000s onwards (from US 186 billion in 2006 to US 358 billion in 2013), as a percentage of GDP, it declined steadily from just above 50% in 2002 to just above 20% in 2013. This is in contrast with the 1990s when external debt was more or less stable at around 50% of GDP (IMF 2018).

Furthermore, over the 2000s and as Africa collectively became a more appealing destination for business investment, FDI flows increased. FDI flows into SSA rose slightly in the 1990s, from around US 1.6 billion in 1990 to around US 8.9 Billion in 1999. But they really exploded after 2001 when their value was around US 16.4 billion, reaching around US 60.2 billion in 2011 (UNCTAD 2017). Another and related significant change was the increase in African countries with FDI levels greater than Official Development Assistance (ODA) levels. Excluding South Africa, in 1990, there were only two countries in SSA where FDI flows were greater than ODA flows (Nigeria and Liberia). By the turn of the millennium, that number had risen to almost 10, and in 2012, some 17 countries experienced greater FDI than ODA inflows (Sy and Rakotondrazaka 2015, 2). This was one indicator that was particularly helpful in feeding the 'Rise of Africa' narrative as it portrayed some African countries as becoming less aid dependent and more appealing to international business investments.

Another thing that also contributed to Africa's economic growth since the early 2000s was a changing pattern of external financial flows—the sum of gross private capital flows, official development assistance, and remittances—to the continent. Since the early 2000s, two significant changes took place. Firstly, the total value of external financial flows to SSA increased from around US 20 billion in 1990, to over US 120 billion in 2012. Just between 2004 and 2012, that increase was threefold. Secondly, the composition of external financial flows to SSA changed dramatically. In 1990, the composition was around 62% development assistance, 31% gross private capital flows, and around 7% remittances, but by 2012, only around 22% made up development assistance, while 54% were gross private capital flows, and around 24% remittances (Sy and Rakotondrazaka 2015, 1). While lower income countries were probably still heavily reliant on development assistance, middle-income countries became increasingly less dependent on aid, and more on private capital flows and remittances. In any case, since the turn of the millennium, the African continent experienced a sustained and relatively robust trend of economic growth. While this growth came from a very low base, it continued even after the Global Financial Crisis struck the world in 2007 and 2008 and left many of its developed economies struggling to maintain economic growth.

The Global Resources Boom

One of the key factors supporting the economic growth of many African countries from the early 2000s onwards was the increasing global demand for primary commodities. Given that the African continent is home to 88% of global platinum reserves, 56% of diamond reserves, 41% of cobalt reserves, 40% of gold reserves, 27% of bauxite reserves, 15%

of iron ore reserves, and 10% of global reserves of oil, it is not difficult to see why the global demand for resources became an important part of the economic growth of many African states. This part of the overall story of Africa's rise, and the growing number of Australian resources companies investing and operating across Africa were key factors underpinning the Australian government's rediscovery of Africa. The number of Australian companies operating and investing across Africa rose significantly from the mid-2000s onwards, as did the reported overall value of their investments on the continent, and this was a story the Australian government in the late 2000s was keen to highlight as further evidence of the country's broadening relationship with Africa.

Data compiled in the figures highlight how much commodity exporting countries would have benefitted from the significant growth in commodity prices during the 2000s. Several reports outlining the 'Rise of Africa' noted the important role the global resources boom played in Africa's economic growth. As the McKinsey report argued back in 2010, 'Oil prices climbed from less than $20 a barrel in 1999 to more than $145 in 2008, enriching Algeria, Libya, and Nigeria and other producers', concluding that 'Not only have African producers benefited from rising global prices, but they also have increased production' (Roxburgh et al. 2010, 10). However, the report also cautioned that the growth of the commodities sector explained 'only part of Africa's broader growth story' (Roxburgh et al. 2010, 10), a caution echoed by *The Economist* (2011, 77) a year later when it noted that 'only about a third of Africa's recent growth is due to commodities'.

Data exhibited in Figs. 4.1 and 4.2 show that global fuel prices rose steadily from 2003 onwards, and quite significantly between 2007 and mid-2014; and global metals prices also rose steadily from 2003, experiencing their highest peaks in 2011. At the same time, between 2000 and 2010, African countries also significantly increased their oil and gas production to cash in on the rising demand for resources (see Figs. 4.3 and 4.4).

The structural changes outlined above—Africa's economic rise coupled with the global resources boom—led to what one senior DFAT official termed a 'new discourse about Africa', not only internationally, but within Australia's foreign policy-making bureaucracy as well.[2] While John Howard's conservative government was generally slow to

---

[2] Phone interview with senior DFAT official, 8 April 2014.

Fig. 4.1 IMF Fuel Price Index 1996–2017 (*Source* IMF [n.d.]; based on May 2018. *Note* Index 2005 = 100)

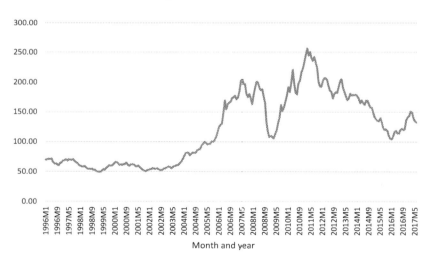

Fig. 4.2 IMF Metals Price Index 1996–2017 (*Source* IMF [n.d.]; based on May 2018. *Note* Index 2005 = 100)

react to such developments, the rise of Africa and Australia's growing economic interests on the continent were not missed by DFAT. As one senior DFAT official with several diplomatic postings in Africa noted,

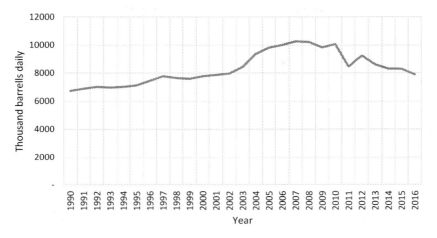

Fig. 4.3 Total Africa oil production 1990–2016, '000 barrels per day (*Source* BP 2017)

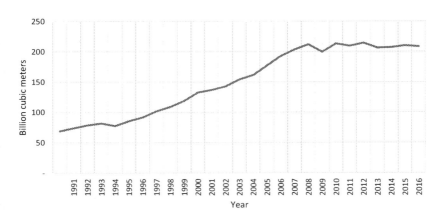

Fig. 4.4 Total Africa gas production 1990–2016, billion cubic metres (*Source* BP 2017)

during the mid-2000s, the department had suggested to then Foreign Minister Alexander Downer that the country's diplomatic footprint in Africa should be expanded even beyond the High Commission in Ghana opened in 2004. However, the idea 'did not get much traction'.[3] But, by the late 2000s, this 'new discourse about Africa'—the recognition that Africa's economic growth was robust and supported by the global resources boom in which many Australian companies were active—made it easier for the Labor government to understand that a greater foreign policy engagement with Africa was beneficial for Australian interests, and push for deepening and widening that engagement. Almost all of the individuals interviewed for this research highlighted that Africa's rise coupled with growing Australian resources investments on the continent had an enabling effect on greater engagement with Africa. The Howard government in its last few years may have started to recognize the importance of these factors, but it was subsequent Kevin Rudd-led Labor government that moved quickly and proactively to utilize them in enacting a closer engagement with African states.

The interconnectedness and relevance of all of these factors for Australia's engagement with Africa was best summarized by a senior DFAT official and one of Kevin Rudd's foreign affairs advisers, who observed that in addition to Australia's UNSC membership bid, two key dynamics driving the country's growing engagement with Africa during the Labor years were the 'phenomenal' growth of Australian mining interests on the continent, and 'the dynamic of reform within Africa itself'.[4] In addition to the real and tangible Australian commercial interests in Africa, what also made it easier for the Labor government to revive Australia's engagement with Africa was the global narrative of the 'Rise of Africa', which, in Afro-optimist fashion, focused more on opportunities and positives, than challenges and negatives. As Rudd's adviser argued, in the past 'anytime we wanted to move forward [on Africa] somebody would write something in the newspaper saying what a terrible human rights record this range of countries had, or how none of them were governed democratically, or how there were all these military people [leaders] there, or how corruption was hopelessly endemic'. But the reforms within Africa, Australian interests there, and the changed global narrative about the continent all 'made it easier to promote Africa' during the Labor government.[5]

---

[3] Phone interview with senior DFAT official, 15 October 2014.

[4] Phone interview with senior DFAT official, 13 November 2014.

[5] Phone interview with senior DFAT official, 13 November 2014.

The Labor Government Re-discovers Africa[6]

In November 2007, after almost 12 years of conservative rule, Australia elected the Labor Party into government, headed by Prime Minister Kevin Rudd. Rudd would in 2010 be replaced by his deputy, Julia Gillard, as the country's Prime Minister, but would soon after become Australia's foreign minister. The two terms of the Labor government were a turbulent time in Australian politics, with the country going through two prime ministers and three foreign ministers. However, regardless of such personnel changes, once the main aspects of Labor's foreign policy agenda were established in 2008, the Australian government exhibited a great deal of foreign policy continuity regardless of who was calling the shots at the top.

In its many contacts with African governments and officials during its time in power, the Labor government made a point to rhetorically highlight its 're-engagement' with Africa. Stephen Smith, Labour's first foreign minister, argued on several occasions in 2008 and 2009 that his government was committed to 'broadening' and 'deepening' engagement with Africa, especially because that engagement had traditionally received less focus and attention than it deserved (Smith 2008b, 2009b, c, f, g). Smith's rhetoric was building on what had already been expressed in the Labor Party's 2004 *Foreign Policy Statement*, and its 2007 *Constitution and National Platform*. As the latter document made clear, the Labor Party was looking to 'rectify the emerging pattern of Australian disengagement from the African continent' because 'Africa lies front and centre in the international community's global development challenge'. Australia, under a Labor government, would 're-engage with Africa' and to that end, Labor would 'establish an Africa-Australia Council' as a vehicle for deepening engagement with Africa. The Labor Party also recognized that Africa presented 'significant opportunities for Australian business—as well as enhancing Australia's multilateral leverage through the UN system' (ALP 2007, 236). Hence, Labor was, at least rhetorically, dedicated to more foreign policy and commercial

---

[6]The rest of this chapter draws on work previously Published in Pijović, Nikola. 2016. The Liberal National Coalition, Australian Labor Party and Africa: Two Decades of Partisanship in Australia's Foreign Policy. *Australian Institute of International Affairs*, 70:5, 541–562, parts of which are reprinted here by permission of Taylor & Francis Ltd, on behalf of the Australian Institute of International Affairs.

engagement with Africa. This dedication was further strengthened by the party's July 2007 pledge to, if elected to government, increase Australia's total Official Development Assistance (ODA) to 0.5% of Gross National Income (GNI) by 2015, and Prime Minister Kevin Rudd's March 2008 announcement that Australia would bid for a temporary seat at the UNSC in 2012 (Rudd 2007, 2008).

In contrast to John Howard's conservative government, Labor's foreign policy engagement with Africa is difficult to break down in distinct episodes because it was more strategic and consistently eventful. Simply put, there was much more happening on the Africa foreign policy front, much of which was of a bilateral nature. This meant that Australia's traditional 'window' into Africa, the Commonwealth, was not the scene of highly prominent episodes in engagement with Africa as it had been during John Howard's tenure in office. Overall, and as hinted above, much of what happened in terms of Australia's engagement with Africa during the Labor government could be seen in the context of two significant policy drivers: the UNSC membership campaign, and the increasing aid budget. However, the overall bilateral as well as continent-wide focus in Africa during the Labor years had a distinct and previously and subsequently unseen rhetorical and policy feel to it. Regardless of what policies helped to drive it, it was a rather uniquely strategic engagement, in that there was a short-, medium-, and long-term vision of why greater engagement with Africa was beneficial for Australia—a vision largely absent during the preceding and succeeding conservative Australian governments.

Foreign Minister Stephen Smith Sets the Foundations for Engagement with Africa

Stephen Smith was the Labor government's minister for foreign affairs between December 2007 and September 2010. Although he played an instrumental role in establishing the government's approach to 'broadening' and 'deepening' engagement with Africa, Smith had no great personal affinity for African issues. During his studies in the late 1970s and early 1980s in London, he followed the Lancaster House 'stuff on Zimbabwe'—the 1979 negotiations over Rhodesia/Zimbabwe's independence—but had done more academic work on India and South East Asia than Africa. In Smith's own words, it was only after he became foreign minister of Australia and started attending the Perth-based Africa Down Under mining conference that he developed an appreciation of what was occurring in Africa and Australia, and how all of Australia's strategic and commercial interests were connected. As Smith stated in an interview for this research, while he did not want to 'over-egg' his affinity for Africa, there were a number of issues that made it easier for him to conclude that enhancing engagement with Africa was 'well worth doing'.[7]

Some of these issues included the already mentioned planned increase in Australia's ODA budget and the country's UNSC membership bid. Smith himself noted that given that he was a Perth and Western Australian-based politician, his approach to foreign policy was more 'west coast' than 'east coast', in that politicians from Western Australia are more familiar with looking West than East, naturally more inclined to be interested in the Indian Ocean region, and can appreciate that 'from a geopolitical strategic point of view Africa is important'.[8] This idea of a 'west coast' outlook on Australia's foreign policy was noted by several DFAT officials interviewed for this research. One noted that being from Western Australia, Stephen Smith would have been very familiar with the growth of Australian commercial interests in Africa, and being a bit closer to Africa would have influenced a 'mental map' which might make that proximity seem more significant from Perth than the east coast of Australia.[9] Another official noted that while 'you would not want to overrate it', there was nevertheless a perception of a 'west coast' foreign policy outlook that was evident in Australia's defence policy in the 1980s 'which had a greater interest in Africa as well'.[10] Being from Western Australia, Stephen Smith also had a large constituency of Australian businesses operating in the resources industry around Africa. As Western Australia's premier, Colin Barnett, noted in a keynote address at the 2014 Africa Down Under mining conference in Perth, of the 220 Australian Stock Exchange-listed companies operating across African nations, more than 70% were Western Australian-based.[11] Given

---

[7] Phone interview with Stephen Smith, 25 September 2014.

[8] Phone interview with Stephen Smith, 25 September 2014.

[9] Phone interview with senior DFAT official, 15 October 2014.

[10] Phone interview with senior DFAT official, 13 October 2014.

[11] Colin Barnett speech at ADU Conference 2014, author personal notes; see also Merrillees (2014).

this constituency, Foreign Minister Smith was also very keen to provide personal support for the Africa Down Under conference, first by setting a precedent of ministerial attendance in 2009, and then even returning as Australia's defence minister in 2011.[12] Smith also kept attending the Africa Down Under conferences after retirement from federal politics in 2013.

Foreign Minister Smith was central in practically implementing the government's approach to greater engagement with Africa. It was his initiative to visit the African Union (AU) in January 2009, and according to one former Secretary of DFAT, such a trip had the department's senior management 'scratching their heads' at the time.[13] As Smith himself argued, it was not surprising that after almost 12 years of 'not much activity' on Africa, there was a bit of reluctance from DFAT towards greater engagement with the continent before 'people got the message'. And what enabled people to 'get the message' was a combination of the demands placed by Smith's office on senior management, Australia's UNSC membership bid, and the efforts of a small group of enthusiastic and committed mid-level and junior officials working on Africa within DFAT.[14] Smith maintained that although the UNSC campaign allowed him to 'knock down barriers' and concentrate efforts in pursuing engagement with Africa, his opinion was that greater engagement with Africa was in Australia's long-term strategic, political, and economic interest, and that it was consistent with the Labor Party's 'middle power' foreign policy outlook and values.[15] This view was supported by Gareth Evans, Australia's foreign minister between 1988 and 1996, who argued that 'certainly' the UNSC membership campaign 'concentrated minds on the need to get our act together in Africa' and that there was 'absolutely no doubt' that the UNSC bid was a 'key motivating factor' for the Labor government's refocus on Africa. However, Evans stated that

---

[12] Interview with retired senior DFAT official, Canberra, 7 April 2014.

[13] Interview with retired senior DFAT official, Canberra, 12 August 2014.

[14] Phone interview with Stephen Smith, 25 September 2014.

[15] Phone interview with Stephen Smith, 25 September 2014. According to a senior DFAT official, 'Stephen Smith was absolutely crucial in developing a policy towards Africa that eventually delivered us victory [in the UNSC membership bid]'. Phone interview with senior DFAT official, 9 April 2014.

he equally had no doubt that there was a perception that Australia had a potential base on which to build greater relations with Africa because of the country's credibility for everything it had done in the anti-apartheid struggle, and that while the UNSC campaign 'was the ideal climate in which to pursue those objectives in a very sharply focused way', it was 'absolutely over-cynical' to write off Australia's renewed engagement with Africa 'as just Security Council-driven'.[16]

Soon after entering office in late 2007, Smith's government made rhetorical moves to enhance its foreign policy engagement with Africa. Taking cue from what was stated in the Labor Party's 2007 *Constitution and National Platform*, DFAT noted in its 2007–2008 annual report outlook that 'Africa will become a more significant focus of the department's attention as we move to enhance Australia's relations with the continent's institutions and nations, through broadening and deepening government and economic linkages' (DFAT 2008, 78). Foreign Minister Smith in 2008 also delivered a major foreign policy speech which outlined his government's 'broadening' and 'deepening' engagement with Africa, exhibiting an Afro-optimist outlook in emphasizing opportunities on the continent which were already being seized by the Australian private sector (Smith 2008a, b).

In January 2009, Stephen Smith became the first Australian foreign minister to attend and address the Executive Council of the AU in Addis Ababa, Ethiopia (Smith 2009a). While Smith was the first Australian foreign minister to attend a meeting of the AU (which has been in existence since 2002), Foreign Minister Alexander Downer had visited a meeting of the Organization of African Unity (the AU's predecessor organization) in 1996. Addressing the AU, Australia's foreign minister pointed out that 'in the past, Australia has not given Africa the priority it requires and deserves', proceeding to outline his government's strategy for supporting greater engagement with Africa (Smith 2009b). While at the AU Smith used the opportunity to do 'a bilateral meeting with any other minister who was there', meeting some 40 African ministers. After such a frenzied schedule, Smith came back to Australia, telling his department that after so many 'bilaterals', they needed to 'hit the ground running and start opening up dialogue with all of the people we had a conversation with' to try and promote Australia's re-invigorated engagement

---

[16] Interview with Gareth Evans, Canberra, 17 September 2015.

with Africa.[17] With the help of the Africa branch and a small Africa Task Force active over the next few months, DFAT came up with an overall strategy for greater engagement with the continent.[18] Part of the strategy involved producing over 40 ministerial letters which provided 'a firm bilateral basis for taking forward these differing African relationships with Australia', with each letter 'produced in targeted fashion, providing information on the impact of Australia's new development assistance programme for Africa as well as economic engagement with the country concerned, and highlighting opportunities for further engagement' (DFAT 2009b).

Australia also at this time formalized diplomatic relations with several African countries such as Liberia, Burkina Faso, Niger, and the Republic of Congo (DFAT 2009a, 73–74), giving further weight to the government's proclaimed strategy of 'broadening' engagement with Africa. Following Foreign Minister Smith's January visit to the AU, Australia's Minister for Defence, Joel Fitzgibbon, also visited the organization a month later in order to open the way 'for increased dialogue with the African Union on peace and security issues' (DFAT 2009a, 74). This, however, did not result in a markedly enhanced level of security cooperation between Australia and the AU. The flurry of official visits to Africa initiated by Smith in early 2009 was followed by the Australian Governor General Quentin Bryce's high-profile visit to nine African countries between mid-March and early April 2009. The Governor General's tour of Africa included mostly areas of traditional Australian interest and links with Africa, namely Eastern and Southern Africa: Mauritius, Namibia, Zambia, Botswana, Mozambique, Ethiopia, Kenya, Tanzania, and the Seychelles (Governor General 2009). The Australian government sought to utilize the Governor General—still the British Queen's nominal administrator of Australia—in a 'head of state' capacity to promote Australia in Africa. Comically, one of the probably more foreseeable issues with this was explaining to African governments—who had fought independence struggles against Britain—what the Governor General actually stood for, and why Australia still had one.[19]

---

[17] Phone interview with Stephen Smith, 25 September 2014.

[18] According to one senior DFAT official, it was in 2009 that DFAT was also given more funds to expand the Africa section into a whole branch—a larger administrative unit with more employees; phone interview with senior DFAT official, 15 October 2014.

[19] Interview with senior DFAT official, Canberra, 10 September 2014.

In any case, Foreign Minister Stephen Smith and the Australian Governor General probably left a positive impression on at least some African ministers during their visits to their countries, which was probably one of the reasons for the unprecedented burst of ministerial visits from African states to Australia, all taking place in the wake of Smith's and the Governor General's trips to Africa. In late May 2009, Bernard Membe became Tanzania's first foreign minister to visit Australia since the late 1980s (Smith 2009d). A few weeks later, Kenya's Minister for Foreign Affairs Moses Wetang'ula led the first official bilateral visit to Australia by a Kenyan foreign minister (Smith 2009e). At roughly the same time, Australia was visited by Rwanda's Minister for Foreign Affairs Rosemary Museminali, and a few days later, Botswana's Foreign Minister Phandu Skelemani also became his country's first-ever foreign minister to visit Australia (Smith 2009g). This flurry of high-level African delegations visiting Australia was rounded off with a September 2009 visit to the country by Mozambique's Foreign Minister Oldemiro Baloi, the first such visit from Mozambique in almost two decades (Smith 2009i). In the space of one month, Australia had been visited by more high-level African ministers than during the whole 11 years of John Howard's conservative government. Foreign Minister Smith's second visit to Africa came in July 2009 when he visited Egypt; and in January 2010, he visited Africa for the third time, this time Botswana and South Africa (Smith 2009h, 2010a, b). Smith became the first Australian foreign minister to visit Botswana bilaterally, and also the first foreign minister to visit the headquarters of the Southern African Development Community. His visit to South Africa was certainly not a first by an Australian foreign minister, but it had been the first visit since Foreign Minister Downer's trip there in 2001.

In his final year as Australia's foreign minister before being transferred to the position of minister for defence, Stephen Smith delivered three major Africa-focused speeches: one while visiting South Africa and Botswana, one on relations with the African continent, and a third speech commemorating Africa Day celebrations in Australia. During his visit to South Africa, Smith's speech recognized and reiterated that country's importance for Australia as a major trading partner, and suggested mutual priorities in foreign policy such as pursuit of UNSC reform, commitment to the Millennium Development Goals (MDG), dealing with the global financial crisis, support for nuclear non-proliferation, and a resolution of Zimbabwe's political problems (Smith 2010c). Smith's address to the University of Sydney International Forum on Africa in March 2010 represented a major speech cataloguing how far his government had gone in fostering greater engagement with Africa. Smith began by reiterating the government's dedication to broadening and deepening engagement with Africa, making the point that 'from Perth, there is a somewhat different perspective on our region, seeing Australia both as a country of the Indian Ocean, as well as a Pacific nation. Australia needs to look West to Africa. For too long Australia had not given Africa the priority that it deserved'. He then, in the Labor government's now well-rehearsed Afro-optimist tone, focused on the beneficial changes in Africa: 'Africa is changing for the better and this is under appreciated in Australia as it is internationally. It is a more stable, free and prosperous continent than it was a decade ago... the many positive changes I have mentioned herald enormous opportunity not just for Africa but for Australia'. All of this was invoked to highlight the growing Australian private sector presence in Africa, almost exclusively in the resources and mining sector. Smith also pointed out that 'just as there are sound economic reasons for enhancing our engagement with Africa, there are also good strategic and geopolitical reasons', noting that 'African nations have an important and growing influence in multilateral fora. They comprise more than a quarter of the membership of the World Trade Organization, the United Nations and the Commonwealth'. As Smith added 'for Australia it made strategic sense to engage with Africa bilaterally, regionally and through the African Union' because 'it is difficult to imagine progress on issues such as climate change, the millennium development goals, trade liberalisation, disarmament, and United Nations reform without working closely with Africa, African countries and the African Union'. Australia's foreign minister concluded his speech by stating that 'Australia is committed to Africa for the long term. This commitment is based neither on sentiment nor short term expediency but on the mutual economic, social and political interests Australia and Africa can advance together' (Smith 2010e).

The major feature of Foreign Minister Smith's last substantive Africa-related foreign policy speech, delivered at the May 2010 Africa Day celebrations in Canberra, was the announcement that 'in recognition of the African Union's vital role and growing global influence, Australia will open a new embassy in Addis Ababa' (Smith 2010f). This gave further muscle to his government's proclaimed foreign policy of 'broadening' and 'deepening' engagement with Africa. An embassy and diplomatic representation at the AU would allow Australia to keep abreast of continent-wide issues, and maintain regular contact with diplomats from more than just a handful of African countries (in which it has diplomatic posts), but perhaps more importantly, it represented a commitment to long-term engagement with not only Ethiopia, but also the AU.

During 2010, DFAT facilitated the establishment of further diplomatic relations with African states, this time Sao Tome and Principe, Togo, Equatorial Guinea, Cape Verde, the Central African Republic, and Somalia (DFAT 2010, 62). After Foreign Minister Smith's visit to South Africa and Botswana, Australia again experienced a few high-level diplomatic visits from Africa. In March 2010, Botswana's President, Ian Khama, visited the country, which was two weeks later followed by visits from Erastus Mwencha, the Deputy Chairman of the African Union Commission, South Africa's Deputy Foreign Minister Susan van der Merwe, and Zimbabwe's Finance Minister Tendai Biti (Smith 2010d, e; University of Sydney 2010). In late June 2010, Australia was also visited by Alhaji Muhammad Mumuni, Ghana's minister for foreign affairs, who became the first foreign minister from his country to officially visit Australia (Smith 2010g).

As noted above, Stephen Smith was transferred to the defence portfolio to make room for Foreign Minister Kevin Rudd, and served as Australia's defence minister between 2010 and 2013. He was involved in a rare instance of a possible deployment of Australian Defence Force (ADF) personnel in Africa, so it is worthwhile conducting a brief assessment of Australia's security cooperation with Africa during his government. Much like during the Howard conservative government, there is very little of substance to report with regards to Australia's security cooperation with African states during the Labor years. A detailed review of Department of Defence (DOD) annual reports from between 1996 and 2013 highlights that Australia's strategic goals and interests in Africa were exclusively confined to the realm of non-military or peace-keeping affairs. Within this there were issues such as membership of the UNSC, support for famine relief, or a passing interest in Somali piracy. However, all of those issues were dealt with almost entirely within the confines of Australia's diplomatic, economic, and development cooperation with African states. Indeed, a survey of DOD annual reports highlights that with regards to security cooperation, the Labor government, for all of its rhetoric about 'broadening' and 'deepening' engagement with Africa, did not much surpass the Howard government's levels of engagement.

Following in the footsteps of the Howard government, the Labor government also maintained a very thin focus on UN operations in Africa, providing mostly monetary support. Even after Defence Minister Joel Fitzgibbon's visit to the AU in February 2009, Australia's security cooperation with African states remained largely unchanged. The greatest novelty was the appointment of an Australian Defence Attaché to the AU (DOD 2011, 81). Australia continued supporting AU/UN missions in the Sudan; there was some activity in supporting anti-piracy initiatives off the coast of the Horn of Africa; some funding for the UN trust fund for the African Union Mission in Somalia, and the UN trust fund for Mali; and grants for educational and training activities of African peace keepers.

The most high-profile security issue related to Africa during the Labor government was what Stephen Smith later described as a 'shock horror story about our SAS doing a lot of work in Africa'.[20] In March 2012 Australian journalists broke a story about a squadron of Australian Special Air Services (SAS) soldiers operating in several African countries (such as Zimbabwe, Nigeria, and Kenya) for the purposes of 'gathering intelligence on terrorism and scoping rescue strategies for Australian civilians trapped by kidnapping or civil war'. The major argument was that such clandestine operations by military personnel were conducted 'at the outer reaches of Australian and international law' (Epstein and Welch 2012). At the time, Defence Minister Smith would not confirm whether SAS troops were in fact in Africa, merely stating that 'the suggestion...that somehow we've got Australian Defence Force personnel or SAS personnel operating at large in Africa, rubbing up against the boundaries of the law is just wrong...everything which occurs in that general area is done in accordance with our domestic law', and international legal obligations (Griffiths and Bourke 2012). Although Smith noted in an interview for this research that he 'debunked' the story at the time, in reality, he had not—he merely argued that Australian military personnel operating anywhere in the world did so in accordance with international and domestic laws and legislations. This would fall somewhat short of denying such operations were actually taking place. In any case,

---

[20] Phone interview with Stephen Smith, 25 September 2014.

Smith made it clear that no substantive or prominent Africa-related issue ever came across his desk while he was Australia's defence minister, and the same could be said about the whole term of the Labor government.[21]

JSCFADT's 'Inquiry into Australia's Relationship with the Countries of Africa'

At this time of Australia's growing interest in furthering foreign policy engagement with Africa, and with the support of Prime Minister Kevin Rudd and Foreign Minister Stephen Smith, on 30 October 2009, the Australian Parliament's Joint Standing Committee on Foreign Affairs, Defence and Trade (JSCFADT) officially launched an *Inquiry into Australia's Relationship with the Countries of Africa* (Foreshaw 2013, 53–54). Although there had been several previous inquiries into various Africa-related issues, JSCFADT had never prior to 2009 held an inquiry into Australia's relations with African countries continent-wide.[22] The inquiry provided further parliamentary 'publicity' and interest in Australia's engagement with Africa which was welcomed by the Labor government as it 'was consistent with the government's increased focus on Africa' (Foreshaw 2013, 53). This inquiry and its recommendations provided the government with further strength in justifying its policy of 'broadening' and 'deepening' engagement with Africa, as it could argue that this was not just a Labor Party policy, but one also receiving bipartisan support from the Parliament.

An argument favouring the view that furthering engagement with Africa was a foreign policy that the Labor government would have pursued on its own merits, and not only for the purposes of securing membership of the UNSC in 2012 was expressed by the Chairman of the

---

[21] Phone interview with Stephen Smith, 25 September 2014.

[22] There were only a handful of previous Australian Parliamentary inquiries into African issues, none of which had a pan-African character but were either regional, country-based, or focused on Australian overseas diplomatic representation and aid. These are: the 1980 *Inquiry on Zimbabwe*; the 1982 *Inquiry on Namibia*, the 1983 *The provision of developmental assistance and humanitarian aid to the Horn of Africa*, and *Some observations on Australia's diplomatic representation in Africa and adjacent Indian Ocean island states* inquiries; the 1984 *Regional conflict and superpower rivalry in the Horn of Africa* inquiry; the 1996 *Australia's relations with Southern Africa* inquiry; and the 2006 *Australia's Trade and Investment Relations with North Africa* inquiry.

JSCFADT, Senator Michael Forshaw. Foreshaw was at pains to point out that despite the conservative oppositions 'assertions and attempts at political point scoring', his government's refocus on Africa and the JSCFADT inquiry was not motivated by Labor's campaign 'to be elected to the UN Security Council'. Foreshaw argued that he 'raised the proposal for an inquiry into our relations with Africa' when he became chair of the JSCFADT in February 2008, a month prior to Prime Minister Kevin Rudd's announcement that Australia would run for a seat at the UNSC, and that it was 'clearly in Australia's economic and political interests to increase our engagement with the African continent' (Forshaw 2013, 57).

The Committee presented its report in June 2011 and offered 17 recommendations (JSCFADT 2011). It is not necessary to expand on all of them, but will suffice to say that while the government supported or agreed with all of them in principle, two were never acted upon. Recommendation 10 which advised that the Department of Education, Employment and Workplace Relations help fund a Centre for African Studies was not taken up by the government due to lack of funds in that department, and in the same way, recommendation 16 which advised that DFAT fund an Africa-Australia Council was also rejected for a lack of departmental funds (Australian Government 2012). Since Labor's own 2007 *Constitution and National Platform*—its main pre-election policy document—argued that when in government, it would establish an Africa-Australia Council (ALP 2007, 236), its failure to do so when in government does strengthen the argument that its 'new engagement' with Africa was mostly for the purposes of its UNSC membership bid. The government easily found hundreds of millions of dollars to fund development cooperation with African states, yet it was unwilling to find a paltry two or three million dollars to support two very practical suggestions that would have at the least helped to establish the beginnings of a long-term focus on African engagement within the government as well as Australian academia.

Kevin Rudd's African Safari

Prime Minister and then Foreign Minister Kevin Rudd's role in bringing about an environment conducive of reinvigorating Australia's engagement with Africa was immense. Rudd was Labor's shadow minister for foreign affairs for just over five years between 2001 and 2006, and was the central figure in developing his party's foreign policy outlook and direction. This much was evident from his authorship of the Labor Party's 2004 *Foreign Policy Statement* (discussed in more detail in Chapter 5), and the record of foreign policy direction his party maintained when in government between 2007 and 2013. Furthermore, when asked if personalities made a difference in foreign policy-making towards Africa, one senior DFAT official and Rudd's foreign affairs adviser argued that they certainly did, particularly in Kevin Rudd's case. As the official pointed out, Kevin Rudd had a 'pre-existing interest in diplomacy', and 'firm belief in Australia as a global engager'—Rudd was an Australian diplomat before becoming a politician. But, he stated, it wasn't that Rudd 'loved Africa'; he was 'motivated by his Christian religion' towards giving more aid—increasing Australia's total ODA to 0.5% of GNI—and had a clear sense of 'the role that Australia ought to play internationally'—hence, his government's UNSC membership campaign 'naturally fitted his worldview'.[23] This view was echoed by another senior DFAT official and foreign affairs adviser to Kevin Rudd who made it clear that personalities matter in foreign policy, because it is up to individuals (such as prime ministers and foreign ministers) to recognize opportunities and shape change in foreign policy by amongst other things exploiting wider structural factors.[24] When queried about whether it was the executive government (prime ministers and foreign ministers) or the bureaucracy (DFAT) that 'pushed' or 'drove' Australia's renewed engagement with Africa during the Labor government, a number of senior DFAT officials explicitly stated that it was the agency of the executive government rather than the bureaucracy that served as a key driver of this engagement.[25]

Kevin Rudd's centrality in driving Australia's reinvigorated engagement with Africa stemmed primarily from his personal religious and political disposition (the latter intimately tied to the Labor Party's 'middle power' foreign policy outlook) towards believing in Australia's need

---

[23] Phone interview with senior DFAT official, 13 October 2014.

[24] Interview with senior DFAT official, Canberra, 23 April 2015.

[25] Phone interview with senior DFAT official, 8 April 2014; Interview with retired senior DFAT official, Canberra, 19 May 2014; Interview with senior DFAT official, Canberra, 30 May 2014; Interview with retired senior DFAT official, Canberra, 12 August 2014; Phone interview with senior DFAT official, 13 October 2014; Phone interview with senior DFAT official, 15 October 2914; Interview with senior DFAT official, Canberra, 23 April 2015.

to actively engage with the world, increase its standing internationally, and increase its humanitarian assistance globally.[26] It was because of these factors that Rudd firmly believed in an increase in Australia's ODA—he was 'central' to pushing through Labor's commitment of increasing ODA to 0.5% of GNI by 2015—which given the existing developmental challenges there, coupled with the South Pacific's saturation with Australian aid, was to an extent logically targeted at Africa.[27] Rudd was also a central figure in pushing for Australia's pursuit of UNSC membership, which likely would not have happened had the Labor Party not won the 2007 federal election.[28] However, because he was so closely associated with Australia's UNSC membership bid, some senior DFAT officials, and former Foreign Minister Stephen Smith, have argued that Kevin Rudd was not the main driver of Labor's greater engagement with Africa policy; although he talked it up generically, he was more interested in the UNSC seat, while Stephen Smith, on the other hand, was more about African engagement per se.[29] While it is obvious that Rudd left much of the Africa engagement policy to Smith's running, the view that Rudd was only interested in the 'bigger picture' and not African engagement per se has been contested by one of Kevin Rudd's former foreign affairs advisers. While Kevin Rudd's affinity for African issues should not be overemphasized, his interest in (or at least acquaintance with) them was at least partly consolidated by his status as a Commonwealth election observer during the 2002 Zimbabwe presidential elections, and according to the aforementioned adviser, Rudd exhibited a significant interest in humanitarian issues in

---

[26] Interview with Bob McMullan, Australia's Parliamentary Secretary for International Development Assistance 2007–2010, Canberra, 1 June 2016. McMullan argued that Kevin Rudd was 'central' to Labor's commitment of increasing Australia's ODA to 0.5% of GNI.

[27] Interview with senior Australian Council for International Development official, Canberra, 28 August 2014; Interview with senior DFAT official, Canberra, 30 May 2014; for Rudd's Christian influences, see also Marr (2010, 10, 60–61).

[28] In an interview for this research, Bob McMullan argued that the UNSC campaign would have still most probably happened regardless of Kevin Rudd's role, but that the timing of the campaign was very much determined by Rudd.

[29] Interview with retired senior DFAT official, Canberra 12 August 2014. Phone interview with Stephen Smith, 25 September 2014; Phone interview with senior DFAT official, 13 October 2014.

Africa—especially the Darfur situation (as highlighted by Labor's 2004 *Foreign Policy Statement*)—and 'could recite to you the MDGs'.[30] Kevin Rudd may not have been 'in love with Africa', but he made it clear very early upon becoming prime minister of Australia that his country should have a strategy for enhancing engagement with Africa, and according to the aforementioned advisor, this strategy was flagged even before Rudd made and announced his decision in March 2008 that Australia would run for UNSC membership.[31] In any case, regardless of the degree of Kevin Rudd's personal affinity for African issues, his interest in Australia becoming a greater international player and understanding of his country as an active 'middle power' were key factors allowing him to perceive greater engagement with Africa as a worthwhile foreign policy agenda. This is why, as another one of Rudd's foreign affairs advisers noted, 'I can't remember ever pushing Africa with Kevin, ever. I did not need to. Because, as I said, it fitted with his natural agenda'.[32]

A few months after he was deposed from the country's prime ministership by his deputy Julia Gillard, in September 2010, Kevin Rudd became Australia's minister for foreign affairs. What followed in terms of high-level diplomatic engagement with Africa was unprecedented. In a single year—2011—Foreign Minister Rudd visited the African continent six times; only one trip less than his two predecessors (foreign ministers Stephen Smith and Alexander Downer) had done together in roughly 14 years (1996–2010). In fact, by the end of his tenure as Australia's foreign minister in February 2012, Rudd would mark a unique and largely unnoticed record in Australian political history: he became the foreign minister with by far the most trips to Africa. Rudd had in total visited Africa seven times, while Australia's longest-serving foreign minister, Alexander Downer, in his time in office between 1996 and 2007 visited the continent four times. Moreover, as a testament to its pursuit of closer engagement with Africa as well as UNSC membership, the Labor government Kevin Rudd served as prime minister and foreign minister

---

[30] Interview with senior DFAT official, Canberra, 23 April 2015; see also ALP (2004, 87–89). Rudd's ability to remember and marshal ('know his') facts appear to be at least partially confirmed by Marr (2010, 72).

[31] Interview with senior DFAT official, Canberra, 23 April 2015. This view appears consistent with ALP's (2007) *Constitution and National Platform* which highlighted enhancing foreign policy engagement with Africa as a distinct policy in its own right.

[32] Phone interview with senior DFAT official, 13 October 2014.

had between 2007 and 2013 sent its foreign ministers on 12 official visits to Africa. This constituted more visits to Africa than all of Australia's foreign ministers put together had made in the country's entire history. Now, not all of Foreign Minister Rudd's trips to Africa were primarily of a bilateral nature, and some of the trips should more properly be seen in the context of actively campaigning for the UNSC seat and pursuing multilateral as well as bilateral engagement. However, even if the primary motivation for many of his trips to Africa may have been Australia's UNSC membership campaign, such high-level diplomatic representation still had an effect on enhancing foreign policy engagement with African states, and provided further strength to the Labor government's rhetoric of 're-engagement' with the continent.

Although Kevin Rudd had been Australia's foreign minister for only about three months in 2010, he still managed to deliver one major foreign policy speech with a large Africa focus. In a November 2010 speech to the University of Western Australia, Rudd outlined his vision of *Australia's Foreign Policy Looking West*. The speech exhibited a strong degree of Afro-optimism and Rudd made it clear that although there were many development challenges in Africa, his overall focus was on the opportunities ushered in by changes on the continent: 'and as many nations within the continent of Africa resolve long-standing security problems, proceed down the path of economic development, and open their significant energy and resources markets to the world, Africa's economic significance is growing as well'. Rudd recognized the importance of Western Australian-based resource companies in driving Australia's economic engagement with Africa, recognizing that his government would be 'increasingly called upon to advance these economic interests in Africa', and 'provide diplomatic and consular support to its companies and its citizens'. The foreign minister concluded that he was hearing one message from the Australian mining industry, and that was that they wanted 'Australia to be more engaged with the affairs of the continent, not less. And that too is the resolve of the Australian Government' (Rudd 2010a).

Australia's diplomatic engagement with Africa during Kevin Rudd's tenure as Australia's foreign minister began on a relatively high note when in September 2010, at the UN Summit in New York, Minister Rudd signed a Memorandum of Understanding with the Chairman of the AU, Jean Ping (Rudd 2011a). This was followed by Australian aid support for South Sudan's upcoming January 2011 Independence

Referendum, where the country's aid agency (AusAID) also provided funding for South Sudanese in Australia to vote in the referendum (Rudd 2010b). Then, in December 2010, Kevin Rudd made his first bilateral visit to Africa, where he helped to celebrate the 60th anniversary of Australia–Egypt diplomatic relations in Cairo (Rudd 2010c). In a month's time, Australia's foreign minister was back in Africa, this time in Ethiopia. Rudd used the opportunity to engage with the country bilaterally—marking Australia Day celebrations and meeting the country's Prime Minister Meles Zenawi and Foreign Minister Hailemariam Desalegn—but also fronted the AU's Executive Council to deliver a speech. It was on this occasion that Rudd told the AU that his country was one from the 'south' and not the 'north'—it was not American or European, but 'simply Australian'—a developed country surrounded by developing countries and therefore better placed to understand them than many 'northern' countries whose closest neighbours were other wealthy countries. In pitching his country as one without colonial baggage and more from the global 'south' than the 'north', the Australian foreign minister was no doubt aiming for African support in Australia's upcoming UNSC membership bid, but his government's interest in a closer engagement with Africa was by that stage already clearly expressed. As the Australian foreign minister concluded, Australia had 'confidence in Africa's future' and wished to 'embrace a new engagement' with Africa for the future (Rudd 2011b).

In June 2011, Foreign Minister Rudd visited Equatorial Guinea for the opening session of another AU Executive Council Meeting (Rudd 2011c). Rudd's visit to the AU, his second of the year, would have highlighted to African governments his country's dedication and commitment to fostering greater engagement with the continent, as well as strengthening Australia's UNSC membership candidature. A few weeks later, and in the context of the famine affecting the Horn of Africa, Rudd travelled to Somalia and Kenya, where he was accompanied by the Executive Director of the World Food Programme, Josette Sheeran. Since Rudd was accompanied by such a high-level executive from a key UN agency, this trip would have further highlighted Australia's seriousness in not only caring about development and humanitarian issues in the Horn of Africa, but also its commitment to working through the UN to help mitigate them. In 2011, Australia also formally recognized South Sudan, and by the end of the year had established diplomatic relations with 53 African states (DFAT 2011, 62).

In late October 2011, Australia hosted a Commonwealth Heads of Government Meeting (CHOGM) in Perth. The choice of Perth as the meeting's venue was symbolic of the Australian government's recognition of the need for its foreign policy to 'Look West'. This was important if Australia was to successfully achieve its short-term goal of UNSC membership, but also its long-term goal of enhancing engagement with Africa. Unlike the Zimbabwe issue which dominated the last CHOGM taking place on Australian soil in 2002, this time, there were no substantive African issues to debate, and the Commonwealth was not during these years a highly relevant conduit for Australia's engagement with Africa. In the lead up to the Commonwealth Summit, Foreign Minister Rudd penned an opinion piece in *The Australian* newspaper, highlighting the Australian resources sector's investments in Africa. Rudd argued that Africa was changing for the better and business opportunities were on the rise, before concluding that Australian 'miners have worked this out, and are making a real impact' offering African states something world class and uniquely Australian. This was 'worth the continuing support of the Australian government' (Rudd 2011d).

The most notable Africa-related issue at the 2011 CHOGM was the launch of the Mining for Development Initiative (Gillard 2011). The scheme was aimed at helping 'developing countries use their natural resources to improve their economies in a sustainable manner', and its centrepiece was the International Mining for Development Centre, based at the University of Western Australia in Perth. While the initiative itself was global in focus, a large number of countries it aimed to support were African. To further highlight the importance of this initiative, Foreign Minister Rudd, and Australia's Minister for Resources and Energy Martin Ferguson, made it a point to mention their consultations with specifically Australian companies operating in Africa and the overall support of the resources industry for the scheme (Rudd and Ferguson 2011). At CHOGM, Kevin Rudd also used an opportunity to address the Australia–Africa Foreign Ministers' Mining Breakfast, where he expressed his government's support for African development and Australian mining companies operating on the continent, further promoting the Mining for Development Initiative (Rudd 2011e).

Kevin Rudd's term as Australia's foreign affairs minister came to an end in late February 2012, and as fate would have it, one of the last overseas trips on his agenda was a trip to Ethiopia. Rudd's second trip to Ethiopia came in late January 2012, where he formally opened the Australian Embassy's new chancery building (the Embassy had up to that point operated from a hotel), signed a bilateral development agreement with Ethiopia, and again attended the AU Summit (Rudd 2012a). In his year-and-a-half tenure as Australia's foreign minister, Kevin Rudd followed in his predecessor Stephen Smith's footsteps in further contributing to the enhancement of Australia's engagement with Africa. Although given the context and nature of Rudd's trips to Africa, his engagement with the continent should, to a large extent, be seen in the context of supporting Australia's UNSC campaign, it was still important in terms of Australia's 're-engagement' with Africa that the next Australian foreign minister after Stephen Smith maintained his links with, and interest in African issues.

Finally, it is worth noting that Kevin Rudd's successor as Australia's foreign minister, Bob Carr followed in his predecessors' footsteps in actively promoting Australia's 'new engagement' with Africa. This is evidenced by Carr's several trips to North Africa, as well as his May 2012 announcement that his government planned to open a new Australian embassy in Senegal; Australia's first-ever embassy in a Francophone African country (Carr 2012). In addition to the planned establishment of a new embassy in Senegal, Carr made another announcement that signalled Australia's more durable engagement with Africa: his country would pursue membership of the African Development Bank (AfDB) (Carr and Swan 2012). The Australian government had since at least the mid-1980s and the Jackson Report on Australia's overseas aid been advised to become a member of the AfDB, and membership was also advised by Australia's 2011 *Independent Review of Aid Effectiveness* (Hollway et al. 2011, 11–12, 141). Membership of the AfDB is an indicator of interest in the longer term engagement with and development of African states mostly because the organization is the primary multilateral financial institution participating in the development of African states, and the rather significant size of initial membership contributions indicates a country's more durable interests in African development. Australia was committed to investing around AUD 88 million to join the AfDB, and it was to also make a contribution of around AUD 161 million to join the African Development Fund (Ripoll 2013). This was a serious expenditure, valued at more than half of the country's total ODA to Africa at the time, and as such was unlikely to have been contemplated purely for the short-term expediency of securing UNSC support, especially as Australia's rivals for the UNSC seat—Finland and Luxembourg—were long-standing members of the organization (Pijović 2014).

The Rise of the 'Africa Down Under' as a Key Pillar of Australia's Economic Engagement with Africa

As already noted in the previous chapter, in the last few years of the Howard conservative government and coinciding with the global resources boom, Australia's foreign policy-makers slowly recognized the vast commercial opportunities for particularly the Australian resources industry in Africa. Building on the support provided by DFAT during the dying years of the Howard government, the Labor government moved vigorously to support Australian commercial interests in Africa as widely as possible. As argued elsewhere, the Labor government's policy of expanding diplomatic contacts with African states, which could in turn 'foster or support an environment more conducive to economic activity' was one of the 'newest' aspect of Australia's 'new engagement' with Africa (Pijović 2013, 112). This proactive stance in attempting to help foster greater economic links through a widening diplomatic engagement with African states stood in stark contrast to the Howard government's overall 'reactive' approach in waiting for substantial economic links to justify greater diplomatic contacts (Ford 2003, 31).

During the Labor government's time in office, the Africa Down Under mining conference held annually in Perth would become a key foundation of Australia's enhanced diplomatic and economic engagement with Africa. The ADU has over the years become the second largest Africa-focused mining conference in the world—just after Cape Town's Mining Indaba conference. Although the ADU had been running since 2003, DFAT only began recognizing its strategic importance for enhancing Australia's commercial interests in Africa from 2007. This was evidenced by a newly adopted practice of having all of Australia's African-based ambassadors and high commissioners attend the conference every year.[33] In the years after 2007, the ADU was to become a key focus of Australia's enhanced diplomatic engagement with Africa. As Richard Marles, the then Parliamentary Secretary for Foreign Affairs and Trade noted in 2013, Australia's foreign policy engagement with Africa

---

[33] Phone interview with senior Australian diplomat and DFAT official, who was in 2007 heading an Australian diplomatic mission in an African country, 13 October 2014. Still, it was only in DFAT's 2009–2010 annual report that the department for the first time explicitly mentioned the ADU; see DFAT (2010, 68–70).

4 AUSTRALIA RE-DISCOVERS AFRICA...AND THEN TRIES ... 103

was led by the private sector and particularly Western Australian-based mining companies.[34]

Former Foreign Minister Stephen Smith noted in an interview for this research that he had not been to an ADU conference before becoming foreign minister, but that attending the conference helped him to understand how the various strains of Australia's engagement with Africa could work together:

> ...from my perspective a lot of this stuff did crystallize with conversations that took place in and around the Africa Down Under event. You would have a half a dozen of our ambassadors there...you would have African ministers, and you would have mining companies wanting to engage, and so for a day you could have any number of conversations about what people are doing and thinking about Africa and out of that things would emerge in discussions with high commissioners and ambassadors, such as: yes it would be a really good idea to go to the African Union Ministerial Conference, or yes it would be a really good idea if when you went to the United Nations General Assembly in September you sat down and did a bilateral meeting with all these people [African ministers and ambassadors]...the Africa Down Under thing certainly enabled a bit of good old-fashioned teambuilding where people thought they were all trying to move in the same direction. Mining companies who wanted to enhance engagement for their industry or commercial reasons, ambassadors who wanted to enhance the relationship between a particular country, and then it became a more general thing which is, well it just makes sense to do all these things because we need to enhance our engagement with Africa generally...[35]

In addition to the ADU as an important conduit for supporting Australia's economic interests in Africa, DFAT and the Australian Trade Commission (Austrade) had also since February 2007 co-hosted Australia's representation at the world's largest Africa-focused mining conference, the Mining Indaba conference in Cape Town. This event allowed Australia to further showcase its government's interest in supporting economic cooperation between the two continents, but also support Australian companies operating or wishing to operate in Africa.

---

[34] *Building Sustainable Peace in Africa: Engaging Australians* public workshop at the University of Melbourne, 3 May 2013, author notes.

[35] Phone interview with Stephen Smith, 25 September 2014.

It was in the context of the Mining Indaba conference in February 2010 that Australia's Minister for Trade, Simon Crean, made the only visit to Africa by an Australian Minister for Trade during the Labor government. During his time at the Mining Indaba in South Africa, Crean held bilateral meetings with mining Ministers from South Africa, Tanzania, Mozambique, Ghana, Senegal, Eritrea, and Namibia (Crean 2010). But Crean's presence at Mining Indaba was also important for another reason; it was during his visit that DFAT organized a round table with Australian-based mining industry stakeholders in which the government for the first time formally tried to offer its support to them.[36] One of the organizers of that round table from the industry side explained that it was a 'terrific meeting' in which he was asked to help organize a more formal structure that could work with the government from the industry side, which was how the Australia Africa Mining Industry Group—the Australia Africa Minerals & Energy Group (AAMEG), as it is known today—came about.[37] AAMEG represents the Perth-based small and mid-tier mining and services companies operating across Africa and its activities include advocating for greater engagement with Africa as well as particular support for companies operating in African countries.

Around September 2010, the importance of the ADU conference for Australia's high-profile engagement with Africa was further highlighted when the Secretary of DFAT, Dennis Richardson, formally opened the conference, and DFAT 'established a partnership with the newly created Australia Africa Mining Industry Group' (DFAT 2011, 70). Foreign Minister Bob Carr also followed the pattern set by his predecessor Stephen Smith of ministerial attendance at the ADU, which he attended both in August 2012, and the same time in 2013 (Carr 2014, 149, 451–453). While Kevin Rudd did not attend the ADU conference when he was foreign minister of Australia, he did attend and deliver a speech as a government backbencher in 2012 (Rudd 2012b). This overall high-profile ministerial representation at the ADU would continue with the conservative governments of Tony Abbott and Malcolm Turnbull, with Foreign Minister Julie Bishop attending the event in 2015 and 2017. Hence, in a matter of several years (2007–2011), and in the context of the global

---

[36] Interview with retired DFAT official, Canberra, 7 April 2014.

[37] Phone interview with senior Africa Down Under conference organizer and Paydirt Media official, 31 July 2014.

resources boom and growing Australian commercial interests in Africa, the ADU became a key conduit for the pursuit of Australia's greater commercial engagement with Africa.

THE CONSERVATIVES TRY TO FORGET AFRICA...AGAIN

From September 2013 and up to the time of this writing, Australia was governed by another conservative government, and the country's engagement with Africa experienced another round of disengagement. The Tony Abbott-led conservative Liberal-National Party coalition came to government in September 2013 with a foreign policy outlook and agenda reminiscent of, and actively reinvoking, that of the Howard government. While the Labor years may have given rise to a notion that Australia had enduring national interests in Africa which could not simply disappear with a change in government, the actions undertaken by the conservative government after 2013—and especially during its first two years in power—strongly implied that even if such interests could not be wished away, they could for the most part be ignored. Australia, under the conservative governments of Prime Minister Tony Abbott and his successor, Prime Minister Malcolm Turnbull, made it clear that it was not interested in maintaining the previously observed levels of engagement with Africa.

The End of the Global Resources Boom and Australia's Engagement with Africa

In the 1990s, it was the 'Decline of Africa' that underpinned the Howard conservative government's disengagement from Africa, and in the late 2000s, it was the 'Rise of Africa' that underpinned the Rudd and Gillard Labor government's 'new engagement' with Africa. As stated already, although these structural forces underpinned Australia's changing approach to engagement with Africa, they did not definitively determine it. This section utilizes the example of the ending of the global resources boom and the Australian conservative government's disengagement from Africa to highlight that while structural conditions play a role in underpinning a country's foreign policy, it is the active agency of governments that in the end ultimately defines and determines that foreign policy.

The global resources boom came to an end in the second half of 2014. The prices of fuel and metals decreased significantly, with oil prices declining by 57% between June 2014 and January 2015, and iron ore prices by 37% in the same period (World Bank 2015, 5). Given that so much of Australia's commercial engagement with Africa from the mid-2000s was driven by the booming demand for global resources and Australian resources companies' investments in Africa, one can argue that in the absence of that demand, Australia's engagement with Africa was bound to experience a diminishing intensity. This by itself would help explain why the newly appointed conservative Tony Abbott-led Australian government changed tack on engagement with Africa. However, there are two main problems with this argument. Firstly, while the resources boom did come to an end in the mid-to-late 2014, Africa's economic rise did not; and secondly and more importantly, the Abbott government's disengagement from Africa actually preceded the ending of the global resources boom, and so could not have been driven by it.

The ending of the booming commodities cycle contributed to economic slowdown in Africa, but did not end the continent's economic growth. While there has been plenty of debate about whether Africa really is 'rising' in the absence of greater industrialization on the continent (Rowden 2013; Robertson and Moran 2013), in September 2013, when the conservatives entered government in Australia, Africa's economic picture was largely positive. There was great heterogeneity in the drivers of economic growth on the continent: the economies of Angola, Nigeria, and Mozambique were growing primarily because of natural resources, but the economies of Rwanda and Ethiopia were not (Noman and Stiglitz 2015, 1). Back in 2010, the McKinsey report made clear that Africa's economic growth was based on more than just resources, noting that natural resources directly accounted for around 24% of Africa's GDP growth between 2000 and 2008, and concluding that 'the key reasons behind Africa's growth surge were improved political and macroeconomic stability and microeconomic reforms' (Roxburgh et al. 2010, 2). The World Bank argued in 2015 that SSA's GDP growth, while affected by the end of the global resources boom, was still 4.2% in 2013, 4.5% in 2014, and forecast to rise above that by 2017 (World Bank 2015, 4, 9). Ernst & Young in its 2014 *Africa Attractiveness Survey* highlighted that notwithstanding the global slowdown in the demand for commodities, there was a dramatic improvement in investor perceptions of Africa as a good business and investment destination

(Ernst & Young 2014, 6). In 2011, Africa was ranked eighth in attractiveness as an investment destination, climbing to fifth place in 2012 and 2013, coming second to only North America (and on par with Asia) in 2014, before falling to fourth place in 2015 (Ernst & Young 2015, 29).

However, one could argue that whether Africa's economic rise ended or not mattered less for Australia's engagement with the continent than whether the global resources boom was over, because most of the country's commercial engagement with African states was driven by the global demand for commodities. Here, the evidence for a diminishing Australian investment presence in Africa was in 2014—and remains— far from clear. Certainly many resources companies would have suffered because of the downturn in global demand for resources, but it is unclear how significant the drop in overall numbers of Australian companies operating across Africa had been in 2014 and 2015. As the Chief Executive Officer of Austrade, Bruce Gosper (2014), made clear in his address to the Mining Indaba conference several months after Tony Abbott's conservatives formed government in September 2013, there were still over 200 Australian Stock Exchange-listed resources companies operating over 700 projects in around 40 African countries, with the current and potential investment value estimated at more than AUD 40 billion. And the Australian Foreign Minister Julie Bishop herself made clear in speeches delivered at Africa Day celebrations in May 2015 as well as the 2015 Australia Down Under conference, that Australian companies were still highly active in operating across Africa, again quoting some 200 Australian companies operating over 700 projects in around 40 countries with the value of such investments in the 'order of tens of billions of dollars' (Bishop 2015b, c).

It is reasonable to suggest that many small and medium-sized Australian resources companies operating across Africa would have experienced significant financial troubles due to the decrease in commodity prices from mid-to-late 2014 onwards. But by that time the Abbott government was in office for almost a year, and had already undertaken clear actions which did not correlate with its rhetoric of supporting economic engagement with Africa. Days before the September 2013 federal election, the conservatives released their final election commitments document which cut the planned opening of Australia's first-ever embassy in Senegal (Hockey and Robb 2013). In the context of the conservatives' pre-election narrative of a 'budget emergency' they would inherit due to the Labor government's unfettered spending, this move appeared to make sense, especially if—as the conservatives cynically thought—Labor's 'new engagement' with Africa was all about Australia's pursuit of UNSC membership (*Insiders* 2013). Hence, when the Abbott government, in its 2015 budget, did find funds for opening five new diplomatic posts—the largest expansion of Australia's diplomatic network in the past two decades—none of them were in Africa. Given that by 2015 it was still unclear how much the global slowdown in the demand for resources had actually affected Australian commercial interests in Africa, looking at only the structural factors underpinning Australia's engagement with Africa does not offer clear answers as to why the Abbott government appeared determined to disengage from Africa.

A Government Intent on Disengaging from Africa

As noted above, in September 2013, Australia elected a conservative government, headed by Prime Minister Tony Abbott. Exactly two years later, in September 2015, Abbott was replaced as prime minister of Australia by Malcolm Turnbull, and at the July 2016 federal election, Turnbull kept the conservatives in power. Both Prime Ministers Tony Abbott and Malcolm Turnbull exhibited a clear focus on domestic politics and only engaged with foreign policy issues that sat at the core of the country's foreign policy agenda—resonating more with the Australian public and therefore being more easily exploitable for domestic political gains. This meant that Australia's engagement with Africa was firmly in the hands of the country's foreign minister, Julie Bishop. However, in line with the centrality of prime ministers in influencing Australian foreign policy, Tony Abbott and Malcolm Turnbull's clear lack of interest in engagement with Africa set an overarching 'dampener' on their foreign minister's ability to pursue and foster a greater degree of engagement with Africa. Not that this was necessary, as even if Foreign Minister Bishop herself favoured greater engagement with Africa—and it is by no means clear that she did—she was influenced in her thinking by the conservatives' traditional foreign policy outlook of 'bilateralist regionalism', which did not see a need for engagement with Africa in order to enhance and advance Australia's place in the world.

Just like her Labor predecessor Stephen Smith, Julie Bishop is a Western Australian-based politician, and just like Kevin Rudd, she was a Commonwealth election observer in 2002 in Zimbabwe, so has at least a minimal acquaintance with African politics (Neuhaus 2013,

Part 1, 13). Furthermore, according to a senior Australian Council for International Development (ACFID) official, Julie Bishop had on numerous occasions, both privately and publicly, stated to the Australian non-governmental and development sector that she was a politician from Perth who looked across the Indian Ocean and knew Africa was important, acknowledging that there was a role for Australia's aid programme in Africa.[38] Bishop's interest in engagement with Africa or at least open-mindedness to its continued place in Australian foreign policy was also related to her constituencies in Perth. For example, on her only trip to Africa during the time period under review, visiting South Africa, Madagascar, and Mauritius in 2014, Bishop was accompanied by some of her local electorate constituents, and announced new funding for a non-governmental organization from that electorate, Australian Doctors for Africa (Bishop 2014c). As Australia's former foreign minister, Stephen Smith observed, 'that is a definite "Western Australian" thing. So why would I fall into the company of some "mad" Western Australian miners, it's a "Western Australian" thing. Why would you take some doctors to Mozambique or Mauritius or wherever she went, it's a "Western Australian" thing'.[39]

However, from September 2013 and up until the writing of this book, Julie Bishop had presided over a foreign policy which on the whole unambiguously disengaged from Africa. Regardless of Foreign Minister Bishop's proclaimed support for engagement with African issues, her consistent framing of Australia's place in the world was foremost dictated by an adherence to the conservatives' traditional 'bilateralist regionalism' foreign policy outlook. Bishop also exhibited a cynical view of Australia's engagement with Africa during the Labor years, and this was clear from her statements made in parliamentary debates in 2009, when she labelled the Labor government's pursuit of UNSC membership as Prime Minister Kevin Rudd's 'personal crusade', accusing them of a 'vote buying spree in Africa' (Bishop 2009a, b). Her views on this did not change when she became Australia's foreign minister, as was confirmed by a senior DFAT official working closely with her office on African issues.[40]

---

[38] Interview with senior Australian Council for International Development official, Canberra, 28 August 2014.

[39] Phone interview with Stephen Smith, 25 September 2014.

[40] Interview with senior DFAT official, Canberra, 10 March 2015.

As already mentioned, in September 2014, Foreign Minister Julie Bishop made her only trip to Africa during the time period under review. Bishop visited Madagascar, Mauritius, and South Africa for the purposes of strengthening bilateral cooperation, as well as highlighting the importance her government placed on Indian Ocean Rim cooperation, as Australia was chairing the Indian Ocean Rim Association (IORA) in October of the same year (Bishop 2014a). The Australian foreign minister's first trip to mainland Africa was to South Africa because this was the country with the strongest commercial and historical links with Australia, and the only country's the conservatives traditionally cared to maintain at least commercial links with. A trip to Ethiopia and the headquarters of the AU which might have indicated the conservative government's continued support for pan-African engagement was not contemplated, partly because it was questionable whether Bishop would have received an invitation for such a visit from the AU's Chairperson (AU Summit sessions are closed to non-AU members unless such an invitation is granted).[41] In any case, while Australia in 2014 arguably sat at the pinnacle of global multilateralism, having a seat at the UNSC and chairing both IORA and G20 meetings, this did not translate into the country exhibiting much interest in high-profile African issues. This much was clearly highlighted by the 2014 Ebola epidemic and the Australian government's reluctance to engage with it. As the outbreak of Ebola in West Africa intensified from March 2014, and the US, UK, Cuba, and other countries moved quickly to provide medical personnel and troops to help fight the disease, Australia limited its contributions to funds for the World Health Organization, taking some eight months to finally dispatch a small force of health workers to the disease stricken region (Pijović 2016, 555; Bishop 2014b).

Julie Bishop did maintain support for the ADU conference as Australia's primary and high-profile vehicle for promoting commercial engagement with Africa, especially as her government's emphasis on 'economic diplomacy' as a key pillar of Australia's foreign policy made such an approach logical. She sent a recorded video message to the opening session of the 2014 conference, and attended the 2015 and 2017 conferences. In these appearances, she made speeches reiterating

---

[41] Interview with senior DFAT official, Canberra, 10 March 2015.

the high number of Australian resource companies operating across Africa, and emphasizing her government's belief in the private sector being central to the mission of poverty reduction around the world as well as in Africa. It was also at her 2015 ADU speech that Bishop announced the creation of the Advisory Group on Australia-Africa Relations (AGAAR) (Bishop 2015c). Although AGAAR was a pretty low priority for the government—meeting Minister Bishop only once since its inception—in December 2016, it nevertheless produced an eleven-page *Strategy for Australia's Engagement with Africa* (AGAAR 2016). The document offered some 23 recommendations on what the government should do, and while all were positive for fostering greater engagement with Africa, it is highly questionable whether the conservative government will adopt many of them into policy. In any case, as of the time of writing, there has been no formal response by the Australian government on AGAAR's strategy.

Overall, notwithstanding Foreign Minister Bishop's rhetorical support for maintaining at least commercial engagement with Africa, the conservative government made clear moves that displayed its lack of interest in engagement with Africa past the generic rhetoric of 'economic diplomacy'. For example, when Australia's Foreign Minister Bob Carr announced in May 2012 the Labor government's intention to open a first-ever Australian embassy in Senegal, he argued that such a move would 'provide a significant boost to Australia's growing commercial and political interests in West Africa' (Carr 2012). Many Australian resources companies were active in Francophone West Africa, but could only count on support from Australian diplomatic missions in Ghana or France. As noted already, the conservatives abandoned this plan before even elected to government in 2013, and when they found money for five new Australian diplomatic posts, none of them were in Africa (Bishop 2015a). If the argument for not opening a post in Senegal was a lack of funds—and implicitly it was—then why not open a post there when the funds became available? The conservative government did, in 2017, open a new Australian embassy in Morocco, but within Australian foreign policy thinking, that was more a post in the Middle East, than in Africa. After all, within DFAT's structure and publications, North Africa is always lumped in with the Middle East. In any case, while the opening of the diplomatic post in Morocco was certainly a welcome move for Australian consular and commercial interests in North Africa, it has little flow-on effect for boosting Australia's diplomatic representation in SSA.

Another example of the Australian government's clear lack of interest in engagement with Africa was the savaging of Australia's aid to Africa. Although under the Abbott and Turnbull conservative governments Australia's total ODA in general experienced its largest cuts in the country's history, the bilateral aid budget to SSA was the second most disproportionately cut of all bilateral country/region budgets after Latin America and the Caribbean.[42] The strategy to deal with this 'inconvenient truth' has been to highlight Australia's high contributions to multilateral funding (primarily to the UN) which end up being spent on Africa, while avoiding talking about the country's ridiculously low bilateral aid budget to SSA—in 2017, amounting to roughly AUD 32 million. Foreign Minister Bishop had on occasion defended her government's cuts to the bilateral SSA aid budget by arguing that 'at its peak, in 2012 Australian aid to Africa amounted to 0.7 [%] of the total aid budget'—which was too little to make a significant impact in the region—while, on the other hand, highlighting that her government provided close to AUD 500 million through multilateral institutions to support 'Africa's development and security' (Bishop 2015c). Naturally, the estimates for Australian multilateral aid reaching Africa are 'generous' because such funds are given to multilateral bodies to spend on programmes and regions they see fit, and DFAT does not publish the actual numbers of the proportion of Australian-donated funds spent on Africa. It is therefore impossible to know exactly how much of the Australian supplied funds are actually spent on multilateral programmes in Africa, and prove or disprove Bishop's statement. On the other hand, the foreign minister's other claim, that Australia's peak 2012 budget to Africa made up only 0.7% of the country's total aid budget was patently false. As the discussion of Australian aid to Africa in Chapter 5 makes clear, the figure was closer to 10% of the total aid budget in 2012, which constituted the highest level of Australian bilateral aid to SSA since 1990.

---

[42] Based on the comparison of Australian ODA from the last Labor government budget in 2012/13 and estimates for the Turnbull conservative government's 2017/2018 ODA budget (for references, see Chapter 5). Australian ODA to Latin America was the most severely cut, by some 83%, but from a very low base—from AUD 35.9 million in 2012/2013 to AUD 5.9 million in 2017/2018; ODA to SSA was cut by some 73%—from AUD 401.2 million in 2012/2013 to AUD 108 million in 2017/2018.

In sum, the Australian government in 2018 in many ways brought Australia's contemporary engagement with Africa full circle: from the Howard government's disengagement from Africa in the 1990s, through Labor's 'new engagement' in the late 2000s, to the Abbott and Turnbull government's disengagement from Africa. Notwithstanding the significant changes in Africa's fortunes, and Australia's engagement with African states that took place in the decade between 2003 and 2013, the Abbott and Turnbull governments tried to wind back the clock and downgrade engagement with Africa to what it had been during the Howard years. The irony completely lost on the current crop of Australian conservative politicians is that even the Howard government's engagement with Africa was less ideologically driven than theirs, and did not remain blind to growing Australian interests on the continent, which—no matter how reactively—the Howard government in its last few years in power still attempted to support. The conservative Australian governments between 2013 and 2018 simply decided to forget those interest even existed.

Trading with Africa 2007–2018

As shown in the Appendix which outlines Australia's historical merchandise trade with Africa, Australian exports to the continent between 2007 and 2018 experienced a steady growth and largely followed the geographic patterns already present during the Howard government. Australia's largest export market on the continent was South Africa, followed by Egypt, Mozambique, Sudan, and Ghana. The only notable change in Australia's exports to Africa was the slight drop in exports to South Africa, which from 2013 received 'only' around 40% of total Australian merchandise exports to Africa, which was down from the usual 50% or above. On an average basis, for the whole period between 1996 and 2017, Australian exports to South Africa made up almost 50% of the country's total exports to Africa. In terms of the composition of those exports, Australia mainly exports ores and agricultural produce to African countries. While Australia's exports to Africa, aside from their growing volume, remained largely concentrated in the same African countries throughout the past two decades, the country's imports of merchandise from Africa changed significantly from 2011 onwards. The distinct changes in imports from African countries during the Labor years can be summarized in one phrase: 'thirst for oil'. In 2012, and for the first time in the modern history of Australia's engagement with Africa, a country overtook South Africa as Australia's number one two-way trade partner (imports + exports) from the African continent. This was not the result of a great boom in Australia's exports to that country, but purely a result of Australia's thirst for crude oil from the country in question—Nigeria. The West African country, which was only the eighth largest source of imports from Africa between 1996 and 2009, became the number one import source country from Africa between 2011 and 2014. While South Africa remained an important source of African imports and ranked second, further significant changes in rankings followed. Gabon became Australia's third largest import source country from Africa, the Republic of Congo became fourth (it was ninth up until 2010), and Libya became fifth (it had not even rated as a top import country until 2011). All of this made the ratio of Australia's imports from its traditionally largest trade partner—South Africa—change dramatically. Between the early 1990s and 2010, imports from South Africa made up on average 74% of total Australian merchandise imports from Africa. Since then, those imports have made up only around 30% of total imports—dropping to as low as 13% in 2012. This was partially due to a decrease in imports from South Africa, and mainly because of the growth in imports from these African oil-exporting countries. This made the main trend characterizing Australian imports from Africa between 2010 and 2015 a decrease in imports of processed or finished manufactured goods from Africa (such as motor vehicles made in South Africa), and a rapid increase in imports of crude oil.

Overall, Australian exports to Africa during this time maintained a steady decrease, shrinking from just over AUD 4.3 billion in 2008 to just over AUD 3.4 billion in 2017. However, exports to Africa did not change much in terms of geographic distribution, and Australia's most important export markets remain in Southern (South Africa and Mozambique), and North Africa (Egypt, Algeria, Morocco, and the Sudan). The country's imports from Africa were, however, more volatile. While South Africa remained the only major import source country offering processed merchandise to the Australian economy, in the late 2000s, there was a significant degree of change in other sources of imports as well as their value. From 2008 onwards, Australia's thirst for African oil saw Nigeria, Gabon, the Republic of Congo, and Libya become highly prominent sources of imports from Africa. Imports from these countries peaked between 2012 and 2014, and exhibited the kind of volatility usually associated with booming commodities cycles—no Libyan or Nigerian exports reached Australia in 2015 and 2016. However, notwithstanding such volatility, and Australia's shrinking exports to Africa, the country's two-way trade with Africa actually steadily increased between the early 1990s and late 2000s. Since then, it has experienced some volatility—driven by the volatility of Australia's oil imports from Africa—rising from around AUD 4.9 billion in 2009 to around AUD 10.3 billion in 2012, before falling back down to around AUD 5.2 billion in 2016.

But what of the Australian government's attitude towards trading with Africa during these years? In contrast to the Howard government's reactive approach, the Labor government after 2007 moved quickly in its first term in power to support Australia's economic interest across Africa, and not just primarily South Africa—as was the case with the Howard government. Although the Labor government was certainly interested in maintaining close economic links with South Africa, it recognized that the growth of Australian resource companies operating across the African continent required a wider gaze. Hence, it expanded Australia's nominal diplomatic coverage to all 54 African countries that are members of the UN, announced an opening of a first-ever Australian Embassy in Francophone West Africa, opened two new Austrade posts in Kenya and Ghana, and utilized the Africa Down Under conference to support Australian resource-based interests in Africa. The Abbot and Turnbull conservative governments, on the other hand, appeared happy to exhibit an Afro-optimist attitude supportive of greater economic engagement with Africa—'talk the talk'—but were not willing to honour commitments to actions set in motion by the Labor government which would have indicated an unambiguous practical support for that engagement—'walk the walk'. Therefore, the continuity of a positive attitude towards trading with Africa during the Abbott and Turnbull conservative governments was inconsistent with their lack of support for opening a new Australian Embassy in Senegal, which was, as the Labor government had argued, important for supporting Australian economic interests in Francophone West Africa. Although exhibiting an Afro-optimist attitude and support for the Africa Down Under conference, as well as at least rhetorically recognizing the breadth of Australian economic interest across Africa, the Abbott and Turnbull conservative governments were on the whole disinterested in substantially supporting those commercial interests across the continent.

Conclusion

The purpose of this chapter was to tell the story of how Australia in 2008 re-discovered Africa, and how from 2013 onwards it tried to forget about Africa. The chapter firstly examined the wider structural factor termed the 'Rise of Africa' to highlight how events in Africa, as well as the global resources boom and the growth in Australian resources companies' operations in Africa all helped to underpin an environment more conducive of greater engagement with Africa. The second and third sections of the chapter looked in turn at how Australia's Labor government between 2007 and 2013 embarked on a 'new engagement' with Africa, doing much to reinvigorate the country's relations with African states and issues; and then how Australia's conservative governments after 2013 changed tack and did much to disengage from Africa. What this chapter also tried to highlight was that although wider structural factors—such as the 'Rise of Africa'—helped to underpin Australia's re-discovery of Africa in the late 2000s, as the examination of the Tony Abbott conservative government showed, it was the agency of the Australian government and its prime ministers and foreign ministers that ultimately decided and shaped that foreign policy engagement. Chapters 3 and 4 have provided ample empirical detail to substantiate the argument that Australia's contemporary engagement with Africa suffers from political partisanship. The following chapter will take that argument further by explaining how Labor's and the Liberal-National coalition's foreign policy outlooks shape Australia's politically partisan engagement with Africa, and how this affected Australia's development assistance to Africa in the past two decades.

References

AAP. 2008. Australian Miners' Investment in Africa Climbs to Almost $24 bln. 4 September.

Advisory Group on Australia-Africa Relations (AGAAR). 2016. *A Strategy for Australia's Engagement with Africa*. December. http://dfat.gov.au/about-us/publications/Pages/a-strategy-for-australias-engagement-with-africa.aspx. Accessed on 7 May 2018.

Australian Government. 2012. *Government Response to the Report of the Joint Standing Committee on Foreign Affairs, Defence and Trade Inquiry into Australia's Relationship with the Countries of Africa*. Canberra: Commonwealth of Australia. 22 March.

Australian Labor Party (ALP). 2004. *The Three Pillars: Our Alliance with the US, Our Membership of the UN, and Comprehensive Engagement with Asia. A Foreign Policy Statement by the Australian Labor Party.* http://parlinfo.aph. gov.au/parlInfo/search/display/display.w3p;query=Id%3A%22library%2F-partypol%2FZMZD6%22. Accessed on 7 May 2018.

Australian Labor Party (ALP). 2007. *National Platform and Constitution.* http:// parlinfo.aph.gov.au/parlInfo/search/display/display.w3p;query=Id%3A%22library%2Fpartypol%2F1024541%22. Accessed on 7 May 2018.

Bishop, Julie. 2009a. Questions Without Notice Prime Minister. *House of Representatives.* 14 May.

Bishop, Julie. 2009b. Matters of Public Importance. Australia's Foreign Relations. *House of Representatives.* 19 November.

Bishop, Julie. 2014a. *Visit to South Africa, Madagascar and Mauritius.* Minister for Foreign Affairs. Media Release. 11 September.

Bishop, Julie. 2014b. *New Funding for Australian Doctors for Africa.* Minister for Foreign Affairs. Media Release. 16 September.

Bishop, Julie. 2014c. *Australian Health Workers Depart for Sierra Leone to Fight Ebola.* Minister for Foreign Affairs. Media Release. 24 November.

Bishop, Julie. 2015a. *2015 Foreign Affairs Budget.* Minister for Foreign Affairs. Media Release. 12 May.

Bishop, Julie. 2015b. *Address to Africa Day Celebrations Botswana High Commission.* Minister for Foreign Affairs. Speech. 27 May, Canberra.

Bishop, Julie. 2015c. *Address to Africa Down Under Conference.* Minister for Foreign Affairs. Speech. 4 September.

British Petrol (BP). 2017. *Statistical Review of World Energy 2017.* http:// www.bp.com/en/global/corporate/energy-economics/statistical-review-of-world-energy.html. Accessed on 22 May 2018.

Carr, Bob. 2012. *Opening of New Embassy in Senegal.* Minister for Foreign Affairs. Media Release. 9 May.

Carr, Bob. 2014. *Diary of a Foreign Minister.* Sydney: NewSouth Press.

Carr, Bob and Wayne Swan. 2012. *Australia to Pursue Membership of the African Development Bank to Help Overcome Poverty.* Minister for Foreign Affairs and Deputy Prime Minister and Treasurer. Joint Media Release. 17 July.

Crean, Simon. 2010. *Strengthening the Australia-Africa Partnership.* Ministers for Trade. Media Release. 5 February.

Department of Defence (DOD). 2011. *Annual Report 2010–2011.* Canberra: Commonwealth of Australia.

Department of Foreign Affairs and Trade (DFAT). 2008. *Annual Report 2007–2008.* Canberra: Commonwealth of Australia.

DFAT. 2009a. *Annual Report 2008–2009.* Canberra: Commonwealth of Australia.

DFAT. 2009b. *Africa Task Force Report Memorandum.* 31 March.

118   N. PIJOVIĆ

DFAT. 2010. *Annual Report 2009–2010*. Canberra: Commonwealth of Australia.
DFAT. 2011. *Annual Report 2010–2011*. Canberra: Commonwealth of Australia.
Donnelly, Roger and Benjamin Ford. 2008. *Into Africa: How the Resources Boom Is Making Sub-Saharan Africa More Important to Australia*. Lowy Institute Paper 24.
The Economist. 2011. Africa Rising: The Hopeful Continent. 3 December.
The Economist. 2013. Aspiring Africa: The World's Fastest Growing Continent. 2 March.
Epstein, Rafael and Dylan Welch. 2012. Secret SAS Squadron Sent to Spy in Africa. *Sydney Morning Herald*. 13 March.
Ernst & Young. 2014. *Executing Growth: EY's Attractiveness Survey Africa 2014*.
Ernst & Young. 2015. *Making Choices: EY's Attractiveness Survey Africa 2015*.
Ford, Jolyon. 2003. Australian–African Relations 2002: Another Look. *Australian Journal of International Affairs*. 57:1, 17–33.
Forshaw, Michael. 2013. The JSCFADT Inquiry into Australia's Relations with the Countries of Africa. In David Mickler and Tanya Lyons (eds.), *New Engagement: Contemporary Australian Foreign Policy Towards Africa*. Melbourne: Melbourne University Press, 51–65.
Gillard, Julia. 2011. *Launch of Australian Mining Initiative*. Department of Prime Minister and Cabinet. Media Release. 25 October.
Gosper, Bruce. 2014. *Address to Mining Indaba Conference*. Speech by Brice Gosper, CEO Austrade. 4 February. http://www.austrade.gov.au/news/speeches/address-to-mining-indaba-conference. Accessed on 22 May 2018.
Governor General. 2009. *Governor General's Visit to Africa*. Media Release. 11 March.
Griffiths, Emma and Emily Bourke. 2012. Smith Tight-Lipped on SAS Africa Claims. *ABC News 24*. 13 March.
Hockey, Joe and Andrew Robb. 2013. *Final Update on Federal Coalition Election Policy Commitments*. Costings Table. 5 September. http://www.liberal.org.au/latest-news/2013/09/05/final-update-federal-coalition-election-policy-commitments. Accessed on 17 February 2016.
Hollway, Sandy, Bill Farmer, Margaret Reid, John Denton, and Stephen Howes. 2011. *Independent Review of Aid Effectiveness*. Canberra: Commonwealth of Australia.
International Monetary Fund (IMF). 2018. *World Economic Outlook Database*. May. http://www.imf.org/external/pubs/ft/weo/2015/01/weodata/index.aspx. Accessed on 22 May 2018.
International Monetary Fund (IMF). n.d. *IMF Primary Commodity Prices*. http://www.imf.org/external/np/res/commod/index.aspx. Accessed on 17 February 2016.
Insiders. 2013. Hockey Says Labor 'Wrecking the Joint on the Way Out'. http://www.abc.net.au/insiders/content/2012/s3762329.htm. Accessed on 17 February 2016.

Joint Standing Committee on Foreign Affairs, Defence, and Trade (JSCFADT). 2011. *Inquiry into Australia's Relationship with the Countries of Africa.* Canberra: Commonwealth of Australia.

Le May, Rebecca. 2007. Strengthened Australia–Africa Relations Underpinned by Mining. *AAP.* 14 September.

Marr, David. 2010. Power Trip: The Political Journey of Kevin Rudd. *Quarterly Essay.* 38, 1–91.

Merrillees, Louise. 2014. Australian Mining Companies Look to Africa for New Investment Opportunities. *ABC News.* 3 September.

Neuhaus, Matthew. 2013. Interview with Matthew Neuhaus. *Commonwealth Oral History Project.* Part 1, 2. http://www.commonwealthoralhistories. org/2014/interview-with-matthew-neuhaus/. Accessed on 17 February 2016.

Noman, Akbar and Joseph E. Stiglitz. 2015. *Industrial Policy and Economic Transformation in Africa.* New York. Columbia University Press.

Pijović, Nikola. 2013. The Opportunities and Challenges of a One-Dimensional Relationship. In David Mickler and Tanya Lyons (eds.), *New Engagement: Contemporary Australian Foreign Policy Towards Africa.* Melbourne: Melbourne University Press, 97–114.

Pijović, Nikola. 2014. Did Aid 'Buy' African Votes for Australia's Security Council Seat? *The Conversation.* 17 November. https://theconversation. com/did-aid-buy-african-votes-for-australias-security-council-seat-34189. Accessed on 7 May 2018.

Pijović, Nikola. 2016. The Liberal National Coalition, Australian Labor Party and Africa: Two Decades of Partisanship in Australia's Foreign Policy. *Australian Institute of International Affairs.* 70:5, 541–562.

Radelet, Steven. 2010. *Emerging Africa: How 17 Countries Are Leading the Way.* Washington, DC: Centre for Global Development.

Ripoll, Bernie. 2013. *African Development Bank Bill 2013, Second Reading.* House of Representatives. 30 May.

Robertson, Charles and Michael Moran. 2013. Sorry But Africa's Growth Is Real. *Foreign Policy.* 11 January.

Robertson, Charles, Yvonne Mhango, and Michael Moran. 2012. *The Fastest Billion: The Story Behind Africa's Economic Revolution.* Renaissance Capital.

Rowden, Rick. 2013. The Myth of Africa's Rise. *Foreign Policy.* 4 January.

Roxburgh, Charles, Norbert Dorr, Acha Leke, Amine Tazi-Riffi, Arend van Wamelen, Susan Lund, Mutsa Chironga, Tarik Alatovik, Charles Atkins, Nadia Terfous, and Till Zeino-Mahmalat. 2010. *Lions on the Move: The Progress and Potential of African Economies.* McKinsey Global Institute. June.

Rudd, Kevin. 2007. *Future Challenges in Foreign Policy.* Speech to the Lowy Institute. 5 July, Sydney.

Rudd, Kevin. 2008. *Press Conference, United Nations, New York.* Department of Prime Minister and Cabinet. Interview. 30 March.

120   N. PIJOVIĆ

Rudd, Kevin. 2010a. *Speech at University of Western Australia: Australia's Foreign Policy Looking West*. Minister for Foreign Affairs. Speech. 12 November, Perth.

Rudd, Kevin. 2010b. *Australia Provides Assistance to Sudan Referendum*. Minister for Foreign Affairs. Media Release. 16 November.

Rudd, Kevin. 2010c. *Joint Statement on the Occasion of the 60th Anniversary of Australia–Egypt Relations*. Minister for Foreign Affairs. Media Release. 11 December.

Rudd, Kevin. 2011a. *Speech to Mark the Opening of Australia's Embassy in Addis Ababa*. Minister for Foreign Affairs. Speech. 26 January, Addis Ababa.

Rudd, Kevin. 2011b. *Executive Council Speech, African Union*. Minister for Foreign Affairs. Speech. 27 January, Addis Ababa.

Rudd, Kevin. 2011c. *Foreign Minister to Visit Burma*. Minister for Foreign Affairs. Media Release. 24 June.

Rudd, Kevin. 2011d. Africa Provides a Rich Seam for Resources Sector. *The Australian*. 24 October.

Rudd, Kevin. 2011e. *Australia—Africa Foreign Ministers' Mining Breakfast*. Minister for Foreign Affairs. Speech. 27 October, Perth.

Rudd, Kevin. 2012a. *Australia Supporting a Healthy Ethiopia*. Minister for Foreign Affairs. Media Release. 26 January.

Rudd, Kevin. 2012b. *Chinese Economic Growth and Implications for the Australian Economy*. Speech to the Africa Down Under Conference. Member for Griffith. 30 August, Perth.

Rudd, Kevin and Martin Ferguson. 2011. *Transcript of Joint Press Conference*. Minister for Foreign Affairs and Minister for Resources and Energy. 27 October, Perth.

Severino, Jean-Michel and Olivier Ray. 2011. *Africa's Moment*. Cambridge: Polity Press.

Smith, Stephen. 2008a. *Africa Day*. Minister for Foreign Affairs. Speech. 26 May, Canberra.

Smith, Stephen. 2008b. *A New Era of Engagement with the World*. Minister for Foreign Affairs. Speech. 19 August, Sydney.

Smith, Stephen. 2009a. *Visit to Ethiopia and the African Union*. Minister for Foreign Affairs. Media Release. 27 January.

Smith, Stephen. 2009b. *Presentation to the Executive Council of the African Union*. Minister for Foreign Affairs. Speech. 29 January, Addis Ababa.

Smith, Stephen. 2009c. *Africa Day*. Minister for Foreign Affairs. Speech. 25 May.

Smith, Stephen. 2009d. *Visit to Australia by Tanzanian Minister for Foreign Affairs and International Cooperation*. Minister for Foreign Affairs. Media Release. 25 May.

Smith, Stephen. 2009e. *Visit to Australia by Kenyan Minister for Foreign Affairs*. Minister for Foreign Affairs. Media Release. 12 June.

Smith, Stephen. 2009f. *Visit to Australia by Rwandan Minister for Foreign Affairs and Cooperation*. Minister for Foreign Affairs. Media Release. 15 June.

Smith, Stephen. 2009g. *Visit by Botswana Minister of Foreign Affairs and International Cooperation*. Minister for Foreign Affairs. Media Release. 17 June.

Smith, Stephen. 2009h. *Participation in the Non-aligned Movement Summit in Egypt and Travel to Malta*. Minister for Foreign Affairs. Media Release. 12 July.

Smith, Stephen. 2009i. *Visit to Perth by Mozambican Minister of Foreign Affairs and Cooperation*. Minister for Foreign Affairs. 11 September.

Smith, Stephen. 2010a. *Visit to Botswana*. Minister for Foreign Affairs. Media Release. 25 January.

Smith, Stephen. 2010b. *Visit to South Africa*. Minister for Foreign Affairs. Media Release. 26 January.

Smith, Stephen. 2010c. *Multilateral Engagement: Priorities for Australia and South Africa*. Minister for Foreign Affairs. Speech. 26 January, Pretoria.

Smith, Stephen. 2010d. *Visit to Australia by the President of Botswana*. Minister for Foreign Affairs. Media Release. 1 March.

Smith, Stephen. 2010e. *Australia and Africa: Looking to the Future*. Address to the University of Sydney International Forum on Africa. Minister for Foreign Affairs. Speech. 19 March, Sydney.

Smith, Stephen. 2010f. *Africa Day 2010*. Minister for Foreign Affairs. Speech. 25 May, Canberra.

Smith, Stephen. 2010g. *Visit to Australia by the Foreign Minister of Ghana*. Minister for Foreign Affairs. 30 June.

Sy, Amadou and Fenohasina Maret Rakotondrazaka. 2015. *Private Capital Flows, Official Development Assistance, and Remittances to Africa: Who Gets What?* Policy Paper. Washington, DC: The Brookings Institution, May.

United Nations Conference on Tarde and Development (UNCTAD). 2017. *UNCTADStat* Based on the Statistical Annexes of the UNCTAD *World Investment Report 2017.* http://unctadstat.unctad.org/wds/TableViewer/tableView.aspx?ReportId=96740. Accessed on 22 May 2018.

University of Sydney. 2010. *Leaders Come Together to Re-engage with Africa.* 19 March. http://sydney.edu.au/news/84.html?newsstoryid=4637. Accessed on 17 February 2016.

World Bank. 2015. *Africa's Pulse*. Office of the Chief Economist for the Africa Region. 11 April.

CHAPTER 5

Political Partisanship and Australia's Volatile Aid to Africa

Although the previous two chapters provided much empirical material to highlight the political partisanship affecting Australia's contemporary engagement with Africa, this chapter seeks to offer a detailed analytical discussion of why this is so. The chapter begins by outlining in greater detail the foreign policy outlooks of Australia's two main political forces, the conservative Liberal-National Party coalition, and the centre-left Labor Party. It does this so that readers have a clear understanding of how these foreign policy outlooks are distinct and why they matter for Australia's foreign policy in general. Then, the chapter proceeds to briefly explain why within a foreign policy agenda which is generally politically bipartisan—that is, when in government, both the conservatives and Labor do similar things when it comes to the fundamental pillars of the country's foreign policy—engagement with Africa can be so partisan. After that, the chapter analyses Africa's place in the conservative and Labor foreign policy outlooks by focusing on their foreign policy documents and speeches. This analysis highlights very clearly how Australian politicians from both sides of the ideological divide have since the mid-1990s conceptualized Africa's place in Australian foreign policy. Finally, the second section of the chapter utilizes the case study of Australia's development assistance to Africa to highlight the great volatility this political partisanship has caused. Through this examination of significant cuts and expansions of Australia's aid to Africa, this section

© The Author(s) 2019
N. Pijović, *Australia and Africa*, Africa's Global
Engagement: Perspectives from Emerging Countries,
https://doi.org/10.1007/978-981-13-3423-8_5

123

124 N. PIJOVIĆ

will make clear how the political partisanship affecting engagement with Africa saps the ability of Australian decision-makers to develop any form of strategic and long-term engagement with Africa.

POLITICAL PARTY FOREIGN POLICY OUTLOOKS AND AUSTRALIA'S PLACE IN THE WORLD[1]

The importance of political parties in driving a country's foreign policy depends on many factors, most obviously, the nature of the country's political system and the level of the institutionalization of political parties. In multiparty democratic political systems where several ideologically distinct parties band together to form coalition governments, foreign policy formulation could depend on negotiating (at times difficult) compromises. On the other hand, in Westminster style (two-party) political systems—such as in the United Kingdom or Australia—such compromises on foreign policy rarely happen, and the party that wins office is for the most part free to implement its own foreign policy outlook and agenda. In Australia's political system, the conservative Liberal-National Party coalition, and the centre-left Labor Party are the two main political forces, and both are fond of promoting their distinct foreign policy outlooks. Although foreign policy achievements are built on the work of successive governments regardless of their ideological affinity, differing foreign policy outlooks can, and do, affect foreign policy decisions and direction. How states imagine themselves, and how others perceive that imagining influences the making of foreign policy, and the purpose of a foreign policy outlook is to offer a vision for the country's place and role in the world, and how it should go about achieving that status (Patience 2014, 211).

Both the conservatives and Labor claim to embody differing understandings of Australia's place in the world, and differing approaches to advancing the country's standing (Baldino et al. 2014, 19–38). These foreign policy outlooks can be considered traditions (or myths) based on the foreign policy behaviour of previous party officials in government.

---

[1] This section of the chapter draws on work previously published in Pijović, Nikola. 2016. The Liberal National Coalition, Australian Labor Party and Africa: two decades of partisanship in Australia's foreign policy. *Australian Institute of International Affairs*, 70:5, 541–562, parts of which are reprinted here by permission of Taylor & Francis Ltd, on behalf of the Australian Institute of International Affairs.

However mythical they may be—given that the conservatives and Labor employ similar means in the pursuit of mostly bipartisan foreign policy objectives—they can be highly salient determinants of foreign policy behaviour. The foreign policy outlooks of particular Australian governments, as based on the traditions or 'myths' about their political party's distinct understanding of Australia's place in the world, have been salient in affecting a volatile and changing engagement Africa. Simply put, these foreign policy outlooks *as interpreted* by key decision-makers have provided a frame of reference for how and why such changes would take place. Foreign policy outlooks in Australia have been profoundly shaped by key decision-makers, such as prime ministers and foreign ministers, with the former holding primary significance for the 'big picture' direction of the country's foreign policy. While there may be disagreements between foreign and prime ministers on issues of specific policy decisions, usually the overall direction of policy is determined by the prime minister.[2] As former Australian Foreign Minister Gareth Evans argued, 'when in doubt in making judgements about why political things get done, you don't usually have to look much farther than who is in charge and explanations at the top'.[3] There is a clear hierarchy in which prime ministers set the tone their foreign ministers are expected to follow.

Bilateralist Regionalism vs. the Middle Power

The conservative approach to Australia's place in the world can be called 'bilateralist regionalism'. This 'bilateralist regionalism' is underpinned by a realist and liberal understanding of international relations, and conservatives place an emphasis on maximizing the country's power through

---

[2] One high-profile example of differences on specific policy positions in the time period under review is the difference between Labor's Prime Minister Julia Gillard and Foreign Minister Bob Carr over a November 2012 vote to accord Palestine 'observer status' at the United Nations. As Gillard makes clear in her autobiography, she was in favour of a 'no' vote, while Carr strongly disagreed, favouring an abstention. In an unusual move, the disagreement was brought before the full Cabinet of government—all the ministers—which agreed with Carr and Australia abstained from voting. However, this was an exception which proved the rule that prime ministers have the final say in foreign policy decisions. As Gillard made clear, 'on significant and sensitive issues', foreign policy decisions are made by the prime minister. See Gillard (2014, 209), Carr, Bob (2014b, 231–241), and Coorey (2012).

[3] Interview with Gareth Evans, Canberra, 17 September 2015.

maintaining close ties with culturally, linguistically, and politically similar countries that Australia's longest-serving prime minister, Robert Menzies, described as 'great and powerful friends' (Wesley and Warren 2000, 13; Menzies 1970, 44). Notwithstanding slight changes over the past half century, the conservatives' foreign policy outlook remains predominantly focused on regional issues displaying three key features: Australia as a significant regional power; Australia that prefers bilateral management of foreign affairs; and Australia that should primarily aim to enhance its traditional partnerships with key allies. Modern foundations of the conservative foreign policy outlook were set during the long reign of Prime Minister Robert Menzies (1949–1966). Robert Menzies viewed international politics through the prism of the conflict between global communism and the West, and argued that in order to meet this existential threat, Australia should rely on its traditional alliances—its 'great and powerful friends'. 'Menzies was not an advocate of a particularly activist or independent role for Australia in world affairs', and this view has remained a key strain of the conservative foreign policy outlook (Ungerer 2007, 543). The criticisms raised by the Menzies-led opposition at the post-World War II Australian Labor government highlight examples of the conservative approach to foreign policy. Menzies' party often criticized the Labor government for '"meddling" in international relations, instead of obeying the dictates of "real power"', and made disparaging remarks about Labor's devotion to internationalism and the 'experimental' United Nations (UN) system (Lowe 1997, 63–66; Menzies 1946b). The underlying theme of conservative critiques of Australian foreign policy during those years was one of 'theory' versus 'reality', highlighting the Labor government's meddling in international affairs by toying with 'theory and procedure', and 'ignoring the realities of the distribution of power' (Lowe 1997, 68; McEwen 1946; Menzies 1946a). By framing its own foreign policy agenda as more endowed with realism and pragmatism than that of Labor, Menzies' party set the foundations for the conservative view of Australia's role in the world: a self-interested, pragmatic, and realist regional power, preferring a bilateral management of foreign affairs.

On the other hand, ever since the mid-1940s, and Labor's Minister for External Affairs Herbert Evatt's proactive and prominent role in developing the UN at the San Francisco Conference in 1945, the Labor party has imagined Australia as an active 'middle power'. This translates into a foreign policy emphasizing the good use of multilateral architectures, and looking beyond Australia's immediate region for foreign policy engagement and relationships (Evans 1997, 18; Cotton and Ravenhill 2011, 1–2; Whitlam 1961; Hasluck 1980, 207–217).[4] Labor governments label themselves as 'good international citizens' who are driven by values as well as self-interest in foreign policy, and rather than reactively following the dictates of great powers or global trends, seek to proactively and creatively lead globally where possible (Evans 1997, 18; Wesley and Warren 2000, 19; Ravenhill 1998, 321; Evans and Grant 1995, 34–35; Parke and Langmore 2014).

Without getting side-tracked into (never-ending) discussions about defining 'middle powers', it will suffice to say that a 'middle power' is probably best understood as 'a role in search of an actor' (Cox 1989, 827). This much is complemented by the significant literature which has over the years critically interrogated the concept in the hope of developing an analytically robust understanding (Cooper et al. 1994; Ravenhill 1998; Chapnick 1999; Jordaan 2003; Ungerer 2007; Beeson 2011; Sussex 2011; Carr 2014a; Patience 2014). In any case, although Australian decision-makers from both sides of the ideological spectrum between the 1970s and 1990s periodically invoked Australia's status as a 'middle power', such conceptualizations of Australia's place in the world were rare during the conservative governments of Robert Menzies (1949–1972), John Howard (1996–2007), and Tony Abbott and Malcolm Turnbull (2013–2018).

Why Is Engagement with Africa Such a Politically Partisan Issue?

Regardless of their differing foreign policy outlooks and the speeches conservative and Labor politicians give to differentiate themselves around election time, it is difficult to fight the notion that Australia's foreign policy generally receives bipartisan political support. After all, the women and men charged with implementing that foreign policy at

---

[4]Some have suggested that the first description of Australia as a 'middle power' was by the conservative External Affairs Minister Garfield Barwick in 1964 (Wesley 2009, 335). However, a search of Australian Parliament Hansard archives places the first reference to 'middle power' in 1950, and made by Labor's Member of Parliament Kim Beazley in criticizing the Menzies government for rejecting to label Australia as a 'middle power' when in opposition. Hence, the description of Australia as a 'middle power' was well known by at least 1950; see Beazley (1950). Herbert Evatt (1947) made implicit references to Australia's 'middle power' status in parliamentary speeches in 1947.

least seem to think so: 75% of 242 respondents to a survey of Australian Department of Foreign Affairs and Trade (DFAT) staff perceptions' towards the country's foreign policy agreed with the statement that Australia's foreign policy was 'essentially bipartisan' (Gyngell and Wesley 2007, 315). While both conservative and Labor politicians espouse different ideas about Australia's place in the world, and have utilized them in constructing distinct foreign policy outlooks, those foreign policy outlooks do not necessarily exclude similar means of satisfying often similar foreign policy goals. Moreover, international political and trade structures, and security/economic interdependencies all necessitate a certain degree of continuity and bipartisanship in foreign policy, and given the structure of Australia's two-party political system, the country's foreign policy has in its fundamental aspects enjoyed a high degree of bipartisanship. Regardless of their political rhetoric and adherence to distinct foreign policy outlooks, both the conservatives and Labor accept the same basic pillars of the country's engagement with the world. They are both interested in greater engagement with the Indo-Pacific region; maintaining close ties with major economic and security partners such as the United States, European Union, China, Japan, or Indonesia; and focusing development cooperation primarily on Australia's immediate neighbourhood (particularly Papua New Guinea and the Pacific islands). Hence, in its fundamentals—the relationships and issues that are perceived to be of primal and immediate economic and security importance for the country—Australian foreign policy exhibits a strong degree of political bipartisanship (Pijović 2016, 542).[5]

But if Australia's foreign policy is generally bipartisan—that is, regardless of what they say in opposition, when in power both the conservatives and Labor do the same things—how is it that Australia's contemporary engagement with Africa is marked by such a significant degree of political partisanship? Well, classical literature on political parties and particularly two-party political systems makes clear that major parties will 'agree on any issues that a majority of citizens strongly favour' for the purposes of winning elections. This is why they become 'catch-all parties', pursuing 'votes at the expense of ideology', in an effort to raise their appeal to a growing and widening audience (Downs 1957, 297; Kirchheimer 1966; Williams 2009, 539). This is also how clearly distinguishable

---

[5] This bipartisanship was only really tested with regard to Australia's involvement in the Vietnam War, and the invasion of Iraq in 2003; see McDonald (2013).

policy differences between the parties decrease, disappear, or are relegated to the margins of their political agendas. And it is at the margins of Australia's foreign policy agenda, dealing with issues and regions traditionally perceived to be of limited or minimal importance to the country's economic and security well-being—like engagement with Africa—that politically partisan differences become most visible. Add to this that the conservatives prefer a bilateral management of foreign affairs while Labor's 'good international citizenship' and 'middle power' approach mandate an emphasis on multilateralism, and it is even clearer why Australia's engagement with Africa—traditionally conducted mainly through multilateral fora—is so politically partisan.

As the previous two chapters have demonstrated, Australia's contemporary engagement with Africa has been driven by political partisanship—ideologically different governments have made substantial changes to the country's engagement with Africa going beyond mere rhetoric. And the second section of this chapter will demonstrate how this political partisanship has resulted is a significant degree of volatility in Australia's development assistance towards Africa. However, before tackling that discussion, the following pages will outline Africa's place in Australian political party foreign policy outlooks. This will be done through an examination of key foreign policy documents and speeches written and delivered by conservative and Labor politicians which highlight Africa's place—or lack thereof—in their foreign policy thinking, and the justifications they provide for why it is, or is not, in Australia's interest to engage with the continent.

Africa in the Conservative and Labor Foreign Policy Outlooks: Policy Documents

Conservative Australian governments have since 1996 published three foreign policy white papers—two by the Howard government, and one by the Turnbull government—which also constitute the only three foreign policy white papers the country has ever published. All three of these highlight the conservatives' general lack of interest in engaging with Africa. The first foreign policy white paper, *In the National Interest*, published in 1997 contained a total of six references to 'Africa', one of which was to do with population pressures on the continent, and the rest with Southern Africa, or more specifically South Africa. In the context of the Indian Ocean region, the paper noted that 'the Gulf states,

130   N. PIJOVIĆ

South Africa and countries of South Asia will be important and growing markets for Australia over the next fifteen years', while in the context of Africa, it stated that Australia's interests would 'remain focused on the South African market, which will also provide a base for trading into all the countries of the Southern African Development Community' (DFAT 1997, 67–68). Therefore, for the Howard government in its early days, engagement with Africa was almost exclusively about commercial ties with South Africa, and more broadly, the Southern African region. The second foreign policy white paper published in 2003, *Advancing the National Interest*, offered the African continent somewhat more attention, with engagement with Africa receiving one whole page. In discussing Australia's 'wider global interests', the document outlined the country's interests in Africa as primarily revolving around aid to the continent, or Zimbabwe's poor governance. The document best summarized Australia's interests in Africa during the Howard years by stating that 'Australia's interests in Africa are engaged most directly through our relationship with South Africa and our membership of the Commonwealth' (DFAT 2003, 110). Overall, the Howard conservative government did not entertain any other possible interests or opportunities for engagement with African states. Due to the emphasis on commercial and economic considerations in Australia's engagement with Africa at the time, it is little wonder then that (commercial) engagement with South Africa was the main (and only) thing on the government's mind. However, even this relationship experienced significant turbulences stemming from the 2002/2003 CHOGM suspension of Zimbabwe. Australia's third foreign policy white paper was published by the conservative Turnbull government in 2017—this time without a flashy title—and contained exactly 10 in-text references to Africa (DFAT 2017b). The document displayed the conservatives' traditional disinterest in the African continent as all of those mentions were generic passing references—this time Africa did not even warrant a separate section within the discussion of Australia's 'global partnerships'. So, while two decades had elapsed between Australia's first and third foreign policy white papers, in the minds of Australia's conservative politicians, nothing had essentially changed—Africa was still a place of potential but very distant threats and opportunities which hardly merited any serious consideration.

The Australian Labor Party never published a foreign policy white paper while in power between 2007 and 2013, but did publish two policy documents while in opposition. The first of these was a 2004 *Foreign Policy Statement* issued by Labor's then Shadow Minister for Foreign Affairs and International Security Kevin Rudd, who would be Australia's prime minister and then foreign minister between 2007 and 2013. The document's focus on Africa was small, but recognized that the Howard conservative government had 'largely ignored Africa' in recent years, which should be changed in the future if Australia wanted to be a fully effective participant in the UN and the Commonwealth. It then went on to offer specific policy options for Australia's re-invigorated engagement with Africa: support the Millennium Development Goals through a joint Australia–European Union developmental initiative; downgrade the country's diplomatic representation in Zimbabwe, while at the same time upholding existing sanctions against the government there; grow Australia's humanitarian assistance to Darfur; and work with the Commonwealth on improving its contributions to mitigating development challenges in Africa (ALP 2004, 124–125). Labor's second policy document with relevance to its foreign policy agenda was its *Constitution and National Platform* adopted in April 2007 as the set of policies for the upcoming federal election it ended up winning. Again, the focus on Africa was small, but more specific than anything the conservatives ever put out. After introducing engagement with Africa with a generic line stating that Labor would 'build our relationships with the Indian Ocean Rim and the emerging economies of Southern Africa', the recognition of the need to engage with Africa was made more explicit:

> Labor will rectify the emerging pattern of Australian disengagement from the African continent. Africa lies front and centre in the international community's global development challenge. Australia must re-engage with Africa and, to this end, Labor will establish an Africa-Australia Council as a vehicle for deepening this country's commitment to some of the poorest countries on the planet. Africa also presents significant opportunities for Australian business—as well as enhancing Australia's multilateral leverage through the UN system. (ALP 2007, 235, 236)

In contrast to the conservatives' passing references and generic formulations of Africa's place in Australia's foreign policy agenda, the Australian Labor Party at least presented a coherent and reasonably specific set of reason why it was in Australia's interest to engage with Africa. Even if the Labor-led government never actually established an Africa–Australia

132 N. PIJOVIĆ

Council, it still made clear that as a 'good international citizen' and 'middle power' it should be interested in supporting development internationally, and not just regionally, and that the success of its future multilateral ambitions depended on African support.

Africa in the Conservative and Labor Foreign Policy Outlooks: Foreign Policy Speeches

Key decision-makers on both sides of Australia's political divide have since the mid-1990s made numerus foreign policy speeches outlining their party and government's conceptualization of Australia's place in the world, and Africa's place in the country's foreign policy agenda. While there is no space here to examine every such speech, for the purpose of highlighting the politically partisan understanding of Africa's place in Australian foreign policy, this section will review the speeches that are representative of the conservatives' and Labor's attitude towards engagement with Africa—either by references to that engagement or a lack thereof.

The Howard Conservative Government (1996–2017)
During his tenure as Australia's prime minister, John Howard made only a handful of major foreign policy speeches outlining his ideas about Australia's role and place in the world. What all of those speeches had in common was a heavy focus on Australia's region and almost no interest in engagement with Africa—Howard never delivered a substantive foreign policy speech focusing on Africa. In his August 2001 speech, titled *Australia's International Relations-Ready for the Future*, Howard adhered to the conservatives' 'realist', 'pragmatic', and 'clear sighted' foreign policy outlook, contrasting this with Labor's 'idealism' and 'meddling' in foreign affairs, and pronouncing that 'the maintenance of strong bilateral relationships' was a cornerstone of his government's approach to foreign policy. The key bilateral relationships for Australia were with Japan, China, the United States (US), and Indonesia, and it was only in the context of the upcoming Commonwealth Heads of Government Meeting (CHOGM), that Prime Minister Howard made his only reference to an African issue; the deteriorating political and security situation in Zimbabwe (Howard 2001).

A few years later, in his June 2004 address to the Australian Strategic Policy Institute, Prime Minister Howard reminded his audience that 'there can be no retreat into splendid isolation or paradigms of the past', claiming that 'we cannot put a fence around our country or our region'. However, this line of more 'internationalist' thinking was employed solely to justify Australia's controversial military involvement in the Middle East and Iraq—a significant electoral issue back in 2004—rather than call for a general widening of Australia's strategic and foreign policy focus (Howard 2004). Engagement with Africa this time featured no mention. Finally, in his March 2005 address titled *Australia in the World*, Howard again reiterated his government's focus on 'the region' and Australia's traditional engagement with relationships that were fundamental for the country's security and prosperity (the US, China, Japan, Indonesia, and Papua New Guinea). In that speech, the Australian prime minister made a reference to his country's 'global interests' which were exclusively economic in nature, focusing on the US, European Union, Asia, and 'growingly' the Middle East (Howard 2005). Again, no mention of Africa. In sum, on the few occasions when John Howard gave Australian foreign policy a wider conceptualization that surpassed Australia's region and key bilateral relationships, such 'width' was only imagined within the realm of existing trade relationships. His only reference to Africa in major foreign policy speeches was in the context of the Commonwealth, and given that John Howard's only trips to Africa were for Commonwealth summits and meetings (1999 South Africa, 2002 and 2003 Nigeria), this further confirms that his government's engagement with Africa was largely confined to the Commonwealth.

John Howard's foreign minister, Alexander Downer, during his 11 years in the foreign affairs portfolio, delivered many major foreign policy speeches outlining Australia's place and role in the world, but engagement with Africa was never substantially addressed. Just seven months after being elected into government, in November 1996, Foreign Minister Downer delivered a speech titled *Australia's Place in the World*. Downer specified that the Asia-Pacific region was Australia's 'highest foreign policy priority', and spoke of the importance of Australia's bilateral relations with neighbouring countries (Indonesia, Malaysia), the US, and China. When outlining 'Australia's broader global links'—the area of the speech with the most potential relevance to engagement with Africa—the foreign minister made no reference to Africa (Downer 1996). Hence, in setting the priorities for the country's foreign policy in his government's first term in power, Foreign Minister Downer unambiguously followed the conservatives' foreign policy outlook by focusing heavily on regional issues and the maintenance and enhancement of key bilateral relationships. With such narrow frames of reference for understanding Australia's place in the world, it is little wonder that engagement with Africa hardly featured a mention for many years to come.

In the early 2000s, Alexander Downer delivered several major foreign policy speeches with minimal references to Africa. In January 2000, Foreign Minister Downer delivered a speech on *Australia's Global Agenda*, where he again outlined his government's primary focus on the region, stating that Australia did have broader, more global interests:

> Let me start by saying that the facts of geography tend to determine naturally enough where any country concentrates its foreign policy efforts. In Australia's case the primary focus is the Asia-Pacific Region. But that's not to say we don't have broader interests ... We have broad interests in the European Union. We have interests in Africa. We have interests in Latin America... Nevertheless, like any country, the primary focus of our foreign policy is by necessity on our own region, in our case, the Asia-Pacific region. (Downer 2000)

However, this was the only reference to Africa in the whole speech, and since the rest of his speech focused again on Australia's region, it is clear that such passing references to Africa were largely tokenistic. Furthermore, in four major foreign policy speeches Alexander Downer delivered between 2001 and 2003, Africa did not feature one reference. In his March 2001 speech titled *Australia—Meeting our International Challenges*, Downer spoke at length of globalization, trade, regional issues, Indonesia, and East Timor, making no reference to Africa (Downer 2001). Then, in May 2002, in a speech titled *Advancing the National Interest: Australia's Foreign Policy Challenge*, Downer spoke about his government's foreign policy initiatives and future challenges to Australia, again making no reference to engagement with Africa (Downer 2002a). In August 2002, Downer presented a speech titled *Australia's Foreign Policy and International Relations*, in which he again outlined the government's foreign policy achievements and spoke at greater length about future challenges to global and regional security, trade and investment, and trans-national issues, again not mentioning Africa (Downer 2002b). In November 2003, Downer delivered his *The Myth of Little Australia* speech (Downer 2003). Although his purpose was not to give an overview of the government's foreign policy focus and achievements, he touched upon many issues and regions of significance to Australia's foreign policy, but again engagement with Africa did not feature a single reference.

In the last term of the Howard conservative government, Alexander Downer delivered several major foreign policy announcements, with again no or scant references to engagement with Africa. For example, in July 2006, Downer delivered two major foreign policy speeches. The first, *Should Australia think big or small in Foreign Policy?*, outlined the foreign minister's conceptualization of Australia as a 'considerable power and a significant country' which should think and act big in foreign policy. He then highlighted four key global challenges where Australia's foreign policy had an expansive agenda to pursue: climate change, democracy and freedom, trade, and focus on 'the region'. The whole speech contained no references to engagement with Africa (Downer 2006a). A day later, Alexander Downer delivered a speech titled *40 Years of Australian Foreign Policy—Democracy, Liberalism, and Australia's National Interests* where he gave an account of how Australia's pursuit of liberal values in foreign policy benefited many regions of the world. As Downer (2006b) noted, democracy was the 'core value' of Australia's foreign policy, and helping it spread around the world was 'in Australia's national interest'. He then went on to highlight the advances in good governance achieved in Indonesia, contrasting that with other parts of the world, specifically Africa. Overall, Prime Minister John Howard and Foreign Minister Alexander Downer exhibited very little interest in engagement with Africa, and on the few occasions they did make references to African states and African issues, these were overwhelmingly negative. Their conceptualization of Africa was hardly ever as that of a place of opportunity, but rather that of a problematic and troubled foreign policy space, which the government was mostly comfortable ignoring.

The Labor Government (2007–2013)

The Australian Labor government between 2007 and 2013 had two prime ministers: Kevin Rudd (December 2007–June 2010, and again from June to September 2013), and Julia Gillard (June 2010–June 2013). As discussed in the previous chapter, Labor's foreign ministers Stephen Smith and Kevin Rudd made numerous speeches on engagement with Africa, so there is no need to review them again. Rather, this section will examine major foreign policy speeches which outlined the Labor government's conceptualization of Australia's place in the world, and highlight Africa's place in that thinking. This will showcase how compatible it was for these two issues to overlap, and why Labor politicians generally find it more palatable and easier to justify and promote foreign policy engagement with Africa than their conservative counterparts.

Just like his conservative predecessor John Howard, Prime Minister Kevin Rudd delivered only a handful of major foreign policy speeches outlining his conceptualization of Australia's place in the world, and no major speech on engagement with Africa. However, as the main architect and author of the Labor Party's foreign policy agenda between 2001 and 2006, Kevin Rudd's views on Australia's place in the world and its 'middle power' diplomacy were already well known by the time he became prime minister of the country (Rudd 2007). Rudd often asserted his party's foreign policy outlook of 'middle power' activism, and in a speech delivered a day after his March 2008 announcement that Australia would run for United Nations Security Council (UNSC) membership in 2012, he reiterated that Australia would deploy 'creative middle power diplomacy' both regionally and globally, while prosecuting 'a more activist foreign policy agenda' (Rudd 2008).

Julia Gillard, who replaced Kevin Rudd as prime minister of Australia in June 2010, did not, during her time in office, deliver many major foreign policy speeches. However, contrary to Kevin Rudd—who had a background as an Australian diplomat and whose expertise on foreign policy was well known—Gillard herself noted that foreign policy was not her passion, and that given a choice, she would 'probably be more (comfortable) in a school watching kids learn to read in Australia' than attending 'international meetings' (*ABC News* 2010). In any case, although Gillard (2014, 164) stated that once in the position of prime minister she did 'master foreign policy engagements', by the time she had become prime minister of Australia, the government's foreign policy direction was already well established, and she merely perpetuated and reiterated her adherence to Labor's 'middle power' foreign policy outlook. As Gillard (2014, 195) made clear in her autobiography, great Labor governments understood and achieved 'the difficult balance that needs to be struck to have impact as a middle power', and she was determined to do that again during her tenure in office.

Labor's first foreign minister, Stephen Smith—the man instrumental in translating his government's 'middle power' diplomacy into a greater

5 POLITICAL PARTISANSHIP ...   137

focus on renewed engagement with Africa—did not make extensive references to engagement with Africa in his major foreign policy speeches, but did highlight the government's emphasis on that engagement. In an April 2008 speech titled *A Modern Australia for a New Era*, Smith re-invoked Labor's 'middle power' foreign policy outlook and an emphasis on multilateralism by reminding his audience that Australia needed to take 'much greater advantage of international institutions to make a positive contribution to international security'. As 'a good international citizen', Australia could and should do more in the world, and his government exhibited a 'renewed interest in Africa' (Smith 2008a). A few months later, in a speech titled *A New Era for Engagement with the World*, the Australian foreign minister reiterated his government's reinvigoration of 'engagement with the United Nations and other multilateral organizations', repeating that bilateral and multilateral management of foreign affairs were not mutually exclusive. As a 'good international citizen', Australia would strengthen ties with regional groupings, and Smith justified the government's greater engagement with Africa policy by arguing that

> The Government is determined to bring a wider perspective to Australia's relations with Africa. Australian minerals and petroleum resources companies discovered Africa last century and it is time that the Australian Government caught up. We want to broaden and deepen our engagement with Africa to reflect our growing trade, commercial and investment links. (Smith 2008b)

As already noted, Stephen Smith's successor as Australia's foreign minister was Kevin Rudd, and one of his first major foreign policy speeches—titled *Australia's Foreign Policy Looking West*—offered an extensive justification and detailed examination of his government's greater engagement with Africa (Rudd 2010). The speech itself was not just about Africa but the Indian Ocean region more broadly, and Rudd made it clear that Australia was a 'middle power with global interests', such as the stability of the global strategic and economic order, climate change, nuclear non-proliferation, etc. He argued that such global interests required Australia to 'be active in all the regions and capitals of the world' through 'creative middle power diplomacy'. In this context of not only being a 'middle power' with global but also 'profound regional interests', Rudd elaborated on Australia's commercial interests in Africa, noting that Australia's 'interests in the region therefore require an increasingly activist Australian foreign policy'. This speech clearly articulated that it was not only because of the growth in Australian commercial interests in Africa that the government should engage with the continent more closely, but also because that engagement was completely consistent with the Labor government's traditional adherence to viewing Australia as a 'middle power'.

In his next major foreign policy address, a June 2011 speech titled *Australia's foreign policy priorities and our candidature for the UN Security Council*, Foreign Minister Rudd offered a lengthy and detailed justification for his government's pursuit of UNSC membership, as well as reinforcing the need to re-engage with areas of the world like Africa, overwhelmingly neglected by the previous conservative government (Rudd 2011a). As Rudd stated, 'In the Labor tradition of foreign policy, we always seek to be actors rather than informed bystanders in the unfolding events of our region and the world at large', further arguing that Australia sought to mitigate threats to national security and protect its national sovereignty by doing these things 'as a middle power with both regional and global interests', through 'creative, middle power diplomacy'. Australia's foreign minister outlined his government's foreign policy priorities which included (amongst other things) Australia's 'fresh engagement both with Africa and Latin America', before justifying the government's pursuit of UNSC membership. In this vein, Rudd reminded his audience of the foundation of the UN in 1945, when 'Australia, recognised as an influential, capable and responsible middle power, took its place as a member of the first United Nations Security Council'.

Kevin Rudd's last major foreign policy speech as Australia's foreign minister was his November 2011 Charteris Lecture titled *The Australia We Can All Be Proud of* (Rudd 2011b). It was delivered at the fourth anniversary of the election of the Labor government, and used to catalogue the government's objectives and achievements in foreign policy. Rudd began the speech with a reminder that for Australia, no matter how isolated it may appear, there was 'no alternative but to be comprehensively globally engaged'. He then offered his government's foreign policy vision for Australia's place in the world which clearly encapsulated all of Labor's traditional foreign policy outlook themes discussed so far: entrenching the country's 'standing as a middle power with global interests and regional interests—committed to the principles of creative middle-power diplomacy'; building new cooperative institutions to support the peace and stability of the Indian Ocean region; expanding formal engagement with 'Europe, Africa, Latin America and the Middle East...as part of a broader strategy of global engagement'; and acting as and being seen as a 'good international citizen', by 'working in particular through the agency of the United Nations'. The foreign minister added that while relations with Australia's neighbourhood were 'necessarily the core' of the country's foreign policy, his government had also actively sought to strengthen 'relations with regions where our engagement in the past has been thin and where our contemporary interests require greater engagement in the future', mentioning specifically the Middle East, Africa, Latin America, and the Caribbean.

The Tony Abbott and Malcolm Turnbull Conservative Government (2013–2018)

Up to the time of this book's writing in mid-2018, the current Australian conservative government had two prime ministers. Tony Abbot was Australia's prime minister between September 2013 and September 2015, when he was replaced by Malcolm Turnbull, Australia's current prime minister. Regardless of the Labor government's six years of trying to foster closer engagement with Africa, the Abbott and Turnbull governments espoused the conservatives' traditionally narrow frames of reference for understanding Australia's place in the world, displaying a general lack of interest in engagement with Africa. Both Prime Ministers Abbott and Turnbull delivered only a few major foreign policy speeches outlining their assessment of Australia's place in the world, and none of those contained any substantial references to engagement with Africa. Tony Abbott's 2014 *Sir John Downer Oration* made a few references to Australia being the dominant power in the South Pacific, and a 'country with global interests and some global reach', but then focused overwhelmingly on the threat posed by Islamic terrorism. The speech contained one reference to African issues—the 'worrying rise' of Islamic insurgencies and terrorism as displayed by Al-Shabaab and Boko Haram (Abbott 2014). Similarly, aside from a few passing remarks in his 2017 *Address to the Indian Ocean Rim Association Leaders' Summit*, Malcolm Turnbull's major foreign policy speeches also contained no references to Australia's engagement with Africa (Turnbull 2017). There really is no need to further catalogue their other major foreign policy speeches with no references to engagement with Africa.

Tony Abbott and Malcolm Turnbull's foreign minister, Julie Bishop, was more open-minded towards Australia's engagement with Africa. This was to a large extent motivated by her own personal experiences: she was a politician based in Perth—Australia's gateway to the Indian Ocean and Africa; and thanks to the Labor government's successful election to the UNSC in 2012, upon becoming Australia's foreign minister in 2013, she experienced first-hand how important engagement with Africa was for Australia's term at the UNSC. However, Foreign Minister Bishop's understanding of Australia's place in the world was still primarily informed by the conservatives' traditional 'bilateralist regionalism' foreign policy outlook, and her only 'innovation' was an emphasis on 'economic diplomacy'—the commercial underpinnings of foreign policy engagements. As Bishop made clear in her first major foreign policy speech as foreign minister, titled *Friends and Neighbours: Australia and the World*, the country's foreign policy under her government would focus on Australia's neighbourhood and regional issues, placing the emphasis back on bilateral relationships. Economic diplomacy 'was at the heart' of that foreign policy agenda because 'Australia has always taken a clear-eyed, commercial approach to our links with foreign governments', which 'invariably start with trade'. While the speech did spell out specific countries and regions Australia would engage with (Japan, China, US, Indonesia, and Pacific Islands), Australia's engagement with Africa did not feature a mention (Bishop 2014b). Julie Bishop's focus on economic diplomacy as a key pillar of her government's foreign policy was to an extent a novelty in the conservatives' foreign policy outlook, in that while Australian governments of both ideological persuasions were certainly interested in pursuing greater economic and trade connections through multilateral and bilateral means, Julie Bishop's government took this enthusiasm to a more explicitly pronounced level. The irony lost on Bishop was that while her emphasis on economic diplomacy was highly suited for engagement with African states—which had since the mid-2000s experienced a significant growth of Australian businesses operating there—that did not translate into her government's greater support for engagement with Africa. As Bishop made clear, it was in Australia's 'immediate neighbourhood' that the country's economic diplomacy had the power to 'really transform lives' (Bishop 2014c).

Political Partisanship Drives Australia's Volatile Development Assistance to Africa

Out of all of the aspects of a country's foreign policy, the provision of development assistance is often the clearest and most easily measurable factor indicating that country's interest and willingness in engaging with certain foreign policy issues, regions, and countries. This is so because national governments have full control over how and where they chose to spend their development assistance budgets, and at least within the Organization for Economic Cooperation and Development countries, such spending is regularly reported in publicly available publications. Although development assistance statistics are not without their problems, and governments can to an extent 'massage' them to appear to be donating more than is really the case, they are still indispensable in helping highlight a country's foreign policy priorities. This last section of the chapter will use the example of Australia's provision of Official Development Assistance (ODA) to Sub Saharan Africa (SSA) since the 1990s to demonstrate how political partisanship has resulted in a great deal of volatility in Australia's development cooperation with Africa.

The Howard Government Takes Africa Off the Menu

As Table 5.1 indicates, Australia's total ODA during the first half of the 1990s grew steadily until the election of John Howard's conservative government in March 1996. In the first two terms of the Howard government, the country's total ODA budget declined, and took some four years to be brought back to the same nominal levels experienced during the last year of the Paul Keating Labor government. Australia's ODA towards SSA in the first half of the 1990s, with the exception of 1990/1991, hovered around AUD 100 million, making up between 7.6 and 5.5% of Australia's total ODA budget (see also Figs. 5.1 and 5.2). This also changed significantly after the election of the Howard government, and development assistance to Africa declined significantly. Overall, Australia's total ODA to SSA hovered around AUD 50 million until 2003, when it started growing in nominal terms. However, as the ratio data indicate, for the majority of the Howard government's 11 years in power, Australian aid to SSA was shrinking from 4.4% of the total ODA budget in 1997/1998 to just round 3% in 2007/2008.

142 N. PIJOVIĆ

Table 5.1 Total Australian ODA to SSA, and as a percentage of total ODA, 1989/1990–2015/2016

Year	Total Australian ODA	Australian ODA to SSA	SSA to total ODA ratio
Unit	Current prices	Current prices	%
Data type	AUD '000	AUD '000	Ratio
1989–1990	1,173,802	103,968	8.86
1990–1991	1,261,040	78,231	6.20
1991–1992	1,330,263	102,061	7.67
1992–1993	1,386,145	106,371	7.67
1993–1994	1,410,815	90,250	6.40
1994–1995	1,484,980	98,133	6.61
1995–1996	1,567,170	101,503	6.48
1996–1997	1,432,351	79,105	5.52
1997–1998	1,443,300	63,630	4.41
1998–1999	1,531,300	55,100	3.60
1999–2000	1,752,343	58,037	3.31
2000–2001	1,638,895	56,038	3.42
2001–2002	1,765,815	50,540	2.86
2002–2003	1,840,697	58,127	3.16
2003–2004	1,986,447	72,607	3.66
2004–2005	2,211,078	82,921	3.75
2005–2006	2,619,036	77,762	2.97
2006–2007	2,879,571	69,445	2.41
2007–2008	3,047,114	91,730	3.01
2008–2009	3,709,186	179,479	4.84
2009–2010	3,813,224	147,114	3.86
2010–2011	4,259,638	271,108	6.36
2011–2012	4,765,000	442,998	9.30
2012–2013	4,856,457	401,201	8.26
2013–2014	5,051,533	263,876	5.22
2014–2015	5,054,032	268,137	5.30
2015–2016	4,032,558	163,331	4.05

Note Aid to SSA as a percentage of total Australian ODA is based on author's calculations
Source DFAT (n.d.b, Table 4), April 2018

Guided by its traditional 'bilateralist regionalism' foreign policy outlook, the Howard government made it clear from the beginning of its tenure that Australia's aid programme would focus mainly on the Asia Pacific, with Papua New Guinea, Pacific island countries, and the poorest regions of East Asia being the areas of 'highest priority' (DFAT,

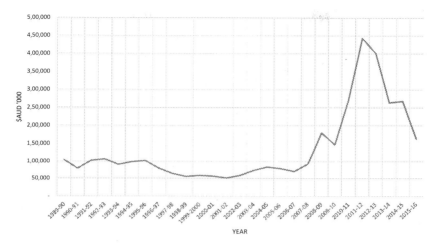

Fig. 5.1 Total Australian ODA to SSA, current prices, 1989/1990–2015/2016, AUD '000

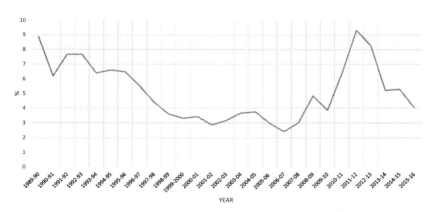

Fig. 5.2 Total Australian ODA to SSA as a percentage of total Australian ODA, 1989/1990–2015/2016

n.d.a). In 1999, the conservative government published *A new framework for aid to Africa*, which even further narrowed the geographic and sectoral focus of development assistance towards SSA. Although the

144   N. PIJOVIĆ

Keating Labor government had already focused Australian aid on predominantly Eastern and Southern Africa, Australia would from now on focus its aid on only a handful of African countries, primarily South Africa, Mozambique, and Zimbabwe (AusAID 2005, 6). This focus was clearly visible in the Australian Development Agency's (AusAID) annual reports and budget statements which year after year specified funding for only two countries; South Africa and Mozambique. These two would between themselves receive roughly two thirds of Australia's total annual Africa-designated bilateral funding (AusAID 2000, 52; 2001, 42–43). Australia's 'retreat from Africa' to its southern tip was mainly due to South Africa's status as the continent's largest economy, and one with the most economic potential and interest for Australia. However, in cutting aid to Africa, the Howard government was actually out of step with public support for development engagement with the continent. While in the decade between 1987 and 1997 on average over 40% of public donations went to Australian non-governmental organizations' (NGOs) funded programmes in Africa, the Howard government was in its first three years in power directing less than 5% of its total ODA to Africa (ACFOA 1999, 5–6).

In any case, by the time the Howard government published its second strategy for development cooperation with Africa in 2005, its preference for focusing development assistance to Australia's neighbourhood was well entrenched. Nothing summarized the conservatives' perception of Africa in Australia's overall development assistance program better than the statement that Australia's aid was focused 'on the Asia-Pacific region, where Australia has a leading role and special responsibilities recognized by the international community, while Africa is increasingly the major focus of other international donors' (AusAID 2005, 4). Simply put, Australia had enough to worry about in its own region, and Africa was anyway someone else's development concern. This approach was philosophically consistent with the Coalition's 'bilateralist regionalism', and was re-invoked again by the Abbot conservative government to justify its own development disengagement from Africa after 2013 (see below).

Labor Puts Africa Back on the Menu and in Bigger Serves

With the election of the Labor government in November 2007, Australia's development cooperation with Africa changed significantly. Firstly, as Table 5.1 and Figs. 5.1 and 5.2 indicate, Australia's total ODA budget grew considerably and consistently, with the Labor government increasing the aid budget much more rapidly than its conservative predecessors. It took the Howard conservative government 11 years to raise Australia's total ODA by roughly AUD 1.4 billion (from AUD 1.4 billion in 1996–1997 to AUD to 2.8 billion in 2006–2007), while it took the Labor government less than half that time to raise the country's total ODA budget by roughly AUD 1.1 billion (from AUD 3.7 billion in 2007–2008 to AUD 4.8 billion in 2012–2013). In line with the growing ODA budget, Australia's development assistance to SSA also increased during the Labor government, which, as compared to its highest level during the Howard government, grew four-fold in nominal terms, and almost three-fold as a ratio of total ODA. Hence, in 2008/2009, Australia's total ODA to SSA was AUD 91.7 million, or 3% of the total ODA budget, which grew to a high of AUD 442 million and 9.3% of the total ODA budget in 2011/2012, before dropping to AUD 401 million and 8.2% of total ODA in 2012/2013. Yes, Australia's total ODA budget was overall growing during the Labor government, but the levels of aid to Africa were still greater as a percentage of total Australian ODA as compared to the previous conservative government.

When Kevin Rudd's Labor government entered office in late 2007, it brought with itself a stated dedication to increasing Australia's total ODA to 0.5% of Gross National Income (GNI) by 2015, which at their time of entering office was just below 0.3%. In addition to this, a year into his first term as prime minister, Kevin Rudd also announced Australia would bid for a non-permanent UNSC seat in 2012. These two factors combined to drive a 'supercharged' development engagement with Africa which saw the above-described increase in Australia's aid to the continent. As one senior DFAT official noted, part of the reason for such an increase in Australia's total ODA towards Africa was that much of Australia's immediate region was already saturated with Australian aid, and Africa was the natural choice for any expansion, especially given the pursuit of Millennium Development Goals.[6] A survey of Australia's annual development budget statements between 2007–2008 and 2012–2013 highlights how Australia's aid to Africa exploded; while the Howard government had problems even spending its estimated budget

[6] Interview with senior DFAT official, Canberra 30 May 2014.

146   N. PIJOVIĆ

Table 5.2   Budget estimates for total Australian ODA to Africa between 2007 and 2013, AUD Million

Budget year	Budget estimate	Estimated outcome	Difference
2007/2008	94.4	101.2	+6.8
2008/2009	116.4	132	+15.6
2009/2010	163.9	157.3	−6.6
2010/2011	200.9	290.7	+89.8
2011/2012	286.3	389.0	+102.7
2012/2013	354.8	385.6	+30.8

Note The column 'Budget Estimate' shows estimates provided in the May budget of the first budget year; the column 'Estimated Outcome' shows actual funds spent as estimated in May of the second year
Source Author calculations based on AusAID development budget statements, 2007/2008–2012/2013. Table 2. *Total Australian ODA from all agencies and programmes to partner countries and regions*

for aid towards Africa, the Labor government mostly overspent them. As Table 5.2 indicates, with the exception of the 2009/2010 budget, Australia's estimated aid budget to Africa was consistently overspent, from a low of AUD 6.8 million in 2008, to a high of AUD 102.7 million in 2012.

The Labor government's provision of development assistance to Africa was consistent with its 'middle power' foreign policy outlook and status as a 'good international citizen'. Aid to Africa was given in support of the continent's 'progress towards the MDGs' (AusAID 2009, 55), and the government further justified its expanding development engagement with Africa as being 'informed by Australia's interests as a middle power' which included 'the stability, security and prosperity' of the Indian Ocean region (AusAID 2010, 3). As far as Australia's focus was concerned, it would concentrate provision of aid mainly to Eastern and to a lesser extent Southern Africa, and would focus largely on areas of comparative advantage for Australian expertise, such as maternal and child health, water supply and sanitation, agriculture and food security, and Australia Award scholarships (AusAID 2010, 8–15).

Development assistance during this time also exhibited a noticeable pan-African aspect which was largely driven by Australia's UNSC campaign. As one of Kevin Rudd's foreign affairs advisors argued, Australia's need to secure UNSC membership votes meant that the country's 'traditional' emphasis on Eastern and Southern Africa no longer mattered:

One of the key dynamics of what has changed over the last 20 years has been a shift away from a focus on East and Southern Africa and the Commonwealth states, to a focus on basically everywhere in the region. One of the things that made it difficult to define Australia's interest in Africa, in the Rudd period, was that they were not defined geographically. Because a vote by Burkina Faso was as valuable as a vote by Mozambique...[7]

This approach in turn led to some tension between 'identity and/or visibility and aid effectiveness': between Australia's 'continent-wide approach' that sought to build relationships, visibility and Australia's 'middle power' status, and the government's 'aid effectiveness agenda', which sought to 'sharpen focus and promote depth and delivery of aid with a light footprint' (Negin and Denning 2011, 13). While that tension was never fully resolved during the Labor government, it did help indicate Australia's preparedness to be a more active development partner in Africa. This sentiment was further strengthened by the Labor government's commitment to joining the African Development Bank (AfDB), a move also recommended by the country's 2011 *Independent Review of Aid Effectiveness* (Hollway et al. 2011, 11–12).

The government's growth of aid to Africa, and its commitment to joining the AfDB were complemented by two other initiatives which helped to highlight its interest in a more long-term development engagement with Africa. The first was the 2010/2011 launch of the Australia Africa Community Engagement Scheme (AACES) which entailed a cooperative funding model between the government and 10 Australian NGOs, worth around AUD 90 million over five years (AusAID 2011, 61).[8] AACES indicated the government's support for working with Australian NGOs and by extension the broader Australian community which favoured greater development engagement with Africa, and its willingness to remain engaged with African development issues past the UNSC campaign. The second was the considerable growth and expansion of the Australian Centre for International Agricultural Research's (ACIAR) focus on operations in Africa. ACIAR's projects and programmes 'link Australian scientists with their counterparts in developing

---

[7] Phone interview with senior DFAT official, 13 October 2014.

[8] AACES was built on a similar scheme—the Australian Partnership with African Communities—in place from 2004.

148   N. PIJOVIĆ

countries of the Asia-Pacific and parts of Sub-Saharan Africa, to increase agricultural productivity and sustainability', and as such were an important component of AusAID's key focus on agriculture and food security in Africa (AusAID 2011, 117). In 2008/2009, ACIAR's expenditure in Africa constituted only 1% of the organization's overall expenditure; by 2012/2013, it was up to 24% (AusAID 2008, 60; 2012, 131; ACIAR 2009, 5; 2013, 5).

While the Howard years stood out as indicating a time period of Australia's low interest in development cooperation with the African continent, the Labor years stood out as indicating the opposite. However, this does not mean that development cooperation with Africa was swiftly becoming a key component of Australia's overall development programme or that the Labor government was overwhelmingly focused on increasing development cooperation with Africa only. In line with its 'middle power' foreign policy outlook—which informed the Labor government's pursuit of a non-permanent UNSC seat and commitment to grow the country's aid budget to 0.5% of GNI by 2015—Australia was, during the Labor years, overall giving more aid to several regions of the world. In fact, although starting from a very low base, regions such as 'Latin America and the Caribbean', and 'Other Asia' benefitted much more in relative terms from the Labor government's growing ODA budget than Africa. Nevertheless, between 1996 and 2018, Australia's development cooperation with Africa was never higher in terms of overall aid levels, or a as percentage of total ODA than during the Labor government.

Abbott and Turnbull Destroy Aid to Africa

The period of the Tony Abbott and Malcolm Turnbull conservative governments between 2013 and 2018 again clearly demonstrated how changes in government drove the already noted volatility in Australia's development cooperation with Africa. The conservatives overall cut Australia's aid budget to its lowest levels in history, and aid to Africa was disproportionately affected (Devpolicy 2018). After winning the election in September 2013, the Abbott government in January 2014 announced a reduction of the 2013–2014 ODA budget from Labor's announced AUD 5.7 billion to just above AUD 5 billion (Bishop 2014a). This level was maintained in the 2014–2015 budget with total ODA hovering above AUD 5 billion, but the 2015/2016 budget cut that by almost

AUD 1 billion, with the total ODA budget left at just above AUD 4 billion (DFAT, n.d.c, Table 1). The Abbott government implemented the largest cumulative cuts to Australia's total ODA budget ever enacted, as well as the largest cut in a single year, which sliced the ODA budget by 20% (Howes and Pryke 2014). This was, however, not the end to Australia's ODA budget cuts, with the Turnbull government's 2017–2018 total ODA budget estimated at AUD 3.9 billion (DFAT 2017a). Such cuts hit the Africa budget particularly hard. As Table 5.3 illustrates, although the Labor government in its last aid budget cut Australia's total ODA to SSA by some AUD 41 million or almost 10%, the cuts under the Abbott and Turnbull conservative governments were much more significant. By the 2017–2018 aid budget, as compared to the last full-term Labor government budget in 2012–2013, Australia's total ODA to Africa had overall been cut by some 73%: from a nominal AUD 401 million to AUD 108 million.[9]

The Abbott and Turnbull conservative governments were much less interested than their Labor predecessors in providing aid to Africa, and that attitude could be gauged by their unwillingness to join the AfDB, an important indication of a country's long-term interest in foreign policy and development engagement with Africa. As noted already, the Labor government had made a commitment to join the AfDB—an issue long supported by governmental and independent reviews of Australia's overseas aid programme—and moved to introduce Parliamentary legislation to enable the country's membership. The Bill to join the AfDB lapsed at the dissolution of Australia's 43rd Parliament before the September 2013 federal election, and was never reintroduced. In its 2014 report on *Australia's overseas aid and development assistance*, the Australian Senate's Foreign Affairs, Defence and Trade References Committee recommended that 'the Australian Government reintroduce and support legislation to enable Australia to become a member of the African Development Bank Group' (SFADTRC 2014, 95). The conservative government did not agree with this recommendation, responding that it had already 'advised the President of the African Development

---

[9] These are nominal figures or current prices and as such are not the best tool for comparison as they are not adjusted for inflation. However, they are the best figures currently available. The 75% figure represents the total value of cuts comparing the 2012–2013 and 2017–2018 budgets; Table 5.3 indicates year-on-year successive cuts to Australian ODA to Africa.

Table 5.3 Year-on-year cuts to Australia's total ODA to SSA 2011/2012–2017/2018, current prices, AUD Million

Budget year	Labor government		Conservative government				
	2011/2012	2012/2013	2013/2014	2014/2015	2015/2016	2016/2017	2017/2018
Total ODA to SSA	442,998	401,201	263,876	268,137	163,331	89,500	108,200
% change	−9.4	−34.2	+1.6	−39.1	−45.2	+20.9	
∓AUD Mil change	−41,797	−137,325	+4261	−104,806	−73,831	+18,700	

Note The figures for 2017–2018 are estimates

Source Author calculations based on DFAT (n.d.c, 11); DFAT 2016–2017 and 2017–2018 budgets

Bank Group that it would not pursue Australian membership of the African Development Bank and the African Development Fund' (Australian Government 2014, 3).

The Abbott and Turnbull governments' overall cuts to Australia's ODA budget proved to be consistent with their 'tendency to view foreign policy through the lens of domestic politics, even undermining core foreign policy commitments in the process', something not entirely new in Australian foreign policy, but particularly acute during Tony Abbott's prime ministership (McDonald 2015, 664). As highlighted by Foreign Minister Julie Bishop's speeches outlined above and in the previous chapter, development cooperation disengagement from Africa was consistent with the primacy the conservative government accorded to focusing development cooperation on Australia's own region. This regional focus was in itself consistent with the Coalition's traditional 'bilateralist regionalism' foreign policy outlook, and the perception within the conservative government and particularly by Foreign Minister Julie Bishop that Labor's 'new engagement' with Africa was really all about winning the UNSC seat in 2012.[10] Overall, foreign policy engagement with Africa under the Abbott and Turnbull conservative governments was experiencing a return to the John Howard era principles of episodic engagement. Australia's contemporary engagement with Africa had indeed come full circle.

CONCLUSION

The purpose of this chapter was to utilize the case study of Australia's development assistance to Africa in highlighting how the political partisanship plaguing Australia's contemporary engagement with Africa resulted in a highly volatile aid engagement with the continent between 1996 and 2018. The chapter outlined why the foreign policy outlooks of Australia's two main political forces—the 'bilateralist regionalism' of the conservatives vs. Labor's 'middle power' approach—influence a politically partisan foreign policy engagement with Africa, and how such partisanship is even possible in what is generally a politically bipartisan approach to Australian foreign policy. The chapter's review of policy documents and speeches delivered by conservative and Labor politicians

[10] Interview with senior DFAT official, Canberra, 10 March 2015.

demonstrated how these differing foreign policy outlooks were utilized by individual prime ministers and foreign ministers to inform their thinking on Australia's place in the world, and justify the direction and focus of their foreign policy. Whether these politicians personally believed in their Party's foreign policy outlooks or were simply 'toeing the party line' is irrelevant; what is relevant is their publicly pronounced adherence and belief in such foreign policy outlooks. Once on the public record and part of public memory, such pronouncements contribute to a narrative, tradition, and myth of a distinctive contribution which conservative and Labor politicians help define through their own agency in prioritizing and managing Australia's foreign policy. In the end, the great volatility in Australia's development assistance to Africa, and the broader fickleness of Australia's engagement with Africa, should make it clear why the country is unable to assess its strategic and long-term interests in Africa, and implement policies that would enable it to advance those interests.

REFERENCES

Abbott, Tony. 2014. *Sir John Downer Oration.* Delivered to the University of Adelaide. Department of Prime Minister and Cabinet. Speech. 21 August, Adelaide.

ABC News. 2010. Foreign Policy Not My Thing, Says Gillard. 6 October.

ACIAR. 2013. *Annual Report 2012–2013.* Canberra: Commonwealth of Australia.

Australian Centre for International Agricultural Research (ACIAR). 2009. *Annual Report 2008–2009.* Canberra: Commonwealth of Australia.

Australian Council for Overseas Aid (ACFOA). 1999. *'Ubuntu' an Agenda for Australia's Involvement in Africa.* NGO Position Paper on Africa. Canberra: ACFOA Africa Working Group.

Australian Government. 2014. *Australian Government Response to the Senate Foreign Affairs, Defence and Trade Reference Committee Report on Australia's Overseas Aid and Development Assistance Program.* Canberra: Commonwealth of Australia. August.

Australian Labor Party (ALP). 2004. *The Three Pillars: Our Alliance with the US, Our Membership of the UN, and Comprehensive Engagement with Asia.* A Foreign Policy Statement by the Australian Labor Party. http://parlinfo. aph.gov.au/parlInfo/search/display/display.w3p;query=Id%3A%22library%2Fpartypol%2FZMZD6%22. Accessed on 7 May 2018.

Australian Labor Party (ALP). 2007. *National Platform and Constitution.* http://parlinfo.aph.gov.au/parlInfo/search/display/display.w3p; query=Id%3A%22library%2Fpartypol%2F1024541%22. Accessed on 7 May 2018.

AusAID. 2000. *Annual Report 1999–2000.* Canberra: Commonwealth of Australia.

AusAID. 2001. *Australia's Overseas Aid 2001–02.* Statement by the Honourable Alexander Downer MP, Minister for Foreign Affairs. 22 May. Canberra: Commonwealth of Australia.

AusAID. 2005. *Australia and Africa: Facing the Challenges as Partners 2003–2007.* March. Canberra: Australian Agency for International Development.

AusAID. 2008. *Australia's International Development Assistance Program 2008–2009.* Statement by the Honourable Stephen Smith MP, Minister for Foreign Affairs and the Honourable Bob McMullan MP, Parliamentary Secretary for International Development Assistance. 13 May. Canberra: Commonwealth of Australia.

AusAID. 2009. *Australia's International Development Assistance Program. A Good International Citizen.* Statement by the Honourable Stephen Smith MP, Minister for Foreign Affairs and the Honourable Bob McMullan MP, Parliamentary Secretary for International Development Assistance. 12 May. Canberra: Commonwealth of Australia.

AusAID. 2010. *Looking West: Australia's Strategic Approach to Aid in Africa 2011–2015.* December. Canberra: Australian Agency for International Development.

AusAID. 2011. *Australia's International Development Assistance Program 2011–2012.* Statement by the Honourable Kevin Rudd MP, Minister for Foreign Affairs. 10 May. Canberra: Commonwealth of Australia.

AusAID. 2012. *Australia's International Development Assistance Program 2012–2013.* Statement by Senator the Honourable Bob Carr, Minister for Foreign Affairs. 8 May. Canberra: Commonwealth of Australia.

Baldino, Daniel, Andrew Carr, and Anthony J. Langlois. 2014. *Australian Foreign Policy: Controversies and Debates.* Melbourne: Oxford University Press.

Beazley, Kim. 1950. Question International Affairs. *House of Representatives.* 21 March.

Beeson, Mark. 2011. Can Australia Save the World? The Limits and Possibilities of Middle Power Diplomacy. *Australian Journal of International Affairs.* 65:5, 563–577.

Bishop, Julie. 2014a. *Five Billion Dollar Aid Budget to Focus on the Region.* Minister for Foreign Affairs. Media Release. 18 January.

154   N. PIJOVIĆ

Bishop, Julie. 2014b. *Friends and Neighbours: Australia and the World*. Address to the Sydney Institute. Minister for Foreign Affairs. Speech. 6 March, Sydney.

Bishop, Julie. 2014c. *Address to Economic Diplomacy Policy Launch*. Minister for Foreign Affairs. Speech. 18 August, Sydney.

Carr, Andrew. 2014a. Is Australia a Middle Power? A Systemic Impact Approach. *Australian Journal of International Affairs*. 68:1, 70–84.

Carr, Bob. 2014b. *Diary of a Foreign Minister*. Sydney: NewSouth Press.

Chapnick, Adam. 1999. The Middle Power. *Canadian Foreign Policy Journal*. 7:2, 73–82.

Cooper, Andrew F., Richard A. Higgott, and Kim Nossal. 1994. *Relocating Middle Powers: Australia and Canada in a Changing World Order*. Vancouver: UBC Press.

Coorey, Phillip. 2012. Gillard Reassures Israel of Backing Despite UN Vote. *Sydney Morning Herald*. 29 November.

Cotton, James and John Ravenhill (eds.). 2011. *Middle Power Dreaming: Australia in World Affairs 2006–2010*. Melbourne: Oxford University Press.

Cox, Robert W. 1989. Middlepowermanship, Japan, and Future World Order. *International Journal*. 44:4, 823–862.

Devpolicy. 2018. *Australian Aid Tracker. Trends*. http://devpolicy.org/aidtracker/trends/. Accessed on 7 May 2018.

Department of Foreign Affairs and Trade (DFAT). n.d.a. *Annual Report 1997–1998*. Section 1.4 Interests in the South Pacific, Africa and the Middle East. http://dfat.gov.au/about-us/publications/corporate/annual-reports/annual-report-1997-1998/subprog14.html. Accessed on 18 February 2016.

DFAT. n.d.b. *Statistical Summary and Time Series Data*. 'Australia's Official Development Assistance (ODA) Standard Time Series'. Table 4. http://dfat.gov.au/about-us/publications/aid/statistical-summary-time-series-data/Pages/australias-official-development-assistance-standard-time-series.aspx. Accessed on 7 May 2018.

DFAT. n.d.c. *Budget Highlights 2015–16*. http://dfat.gov.au/about-us/corporate/portfolio-budget-statements/Pages/budget-highlights-2015-16.aspx. Accessed on 18 February 2016.

DFAT. 1997. *In the National Interest: Australia's Foreign and Trade Policy White Paper*. Canberra: Commonwealth of Australia.

DFAT. 2003. *Advancing the National Interest: Australia's Foreign and Trade Policy White Paper*. Canberra: Commonwealth of Australia.

DFAT. 2017a. *2017–18 Australian Aid Budget Summary*. 11 May. http://dfat.gov.au/news/news/Pages/2017-18-australian-aid-budget-summary.aspx. Accessed on 7 May 2018.

DFAT. 2017b. *The 2017 Foreign Policy White Paper*. November. Canberra: Commonwealth of Australia. https://www.fpwhitepaper.gov.au/. Accessed on 7 May 2018.

5   POLITICAL PARTISANSHIP ...   **155**

Downer, Alexander. 1996. *Australia's Place in the World.* Minister for Foreign Affairs. Speech. 26 November, Sydney.

Downer, Alexander. 2000. *Australia's Global Agenda.* Minister for Foreign Affairs. Speech. 31 January.

Downer, Alexander. 2001. *Australia—Meeting Our International Challenges.* Minister for Foreign Affairs. Speech. 1 March, Canberra.

Downer, Alexander. 2002a. *Advancing the National Interest: Australia's Foreign Policy Challenge.* Minister for Foreign Affairs. Speech. 7 May, Canberra.

Downer, Alexander. 2002b. *Australia's Foreign Policy & International Relations.* Minister for Foreign Affairs. Speech. 21 August, Canberra.

Downer, Alexander. 2003. *The Myth of 'Little' Australia.* Minister for Foreign Affairs. Speech. 26 November, Canberra.

Downer, Alexander. 2006a. *Should Australia Think Big or Small in Foreign Policy?* Minister for Foreign Affairs. Speech. 10 July, Sydney.

Downer, Alexander 2006b. *40 Years of Australian Foreign Policy—Democracy, Liberalism and Australia's National Interests.* Minister for Foreign Affairs. Speech. 11 July, Adelaide.

Downs, Anthony. 1957. *An Economic Theory of Democracy.* New York: Harper & Row.

Evans, Gareth and Brice Grant. 1995. *Australia's Foreign Relations in the World of the 1990s.* 2nd Edition. Melbourne: Melbourne University Press.

Evans, Gareth. 1997. The Labor Tradition: A View from the 1990s. In David Lee and Christopher Waters (eds.), *Evatt to Evans: The Labor Tradition in Australian Foreign Policy.* St. Leonards: Allen & Unwin, 11–22.

Evatt, Herbert Vere. 1947. Question International Affairs. *House of Representatives.* 5 June.

Gillard, Julia. 2014. *My Story.* Sydney: Knopf.

Gyngell, Allan and Michael Wesley. 2007. *Making Australian Foreign Policy.* 2nd Edition. Melbourne: Cambridge University Press.

Hasluck, Paul. 1980. *Diplomatic Witness: Australian Foreign Affairs 1941–1947.* Carlton: Melbourne University Press.

Hollway, Sandy, Bill Farmer, Margaret Reid, John Denton, and Stephen Howes. 2011. *Independent Review of Aid Effectiveness.* Canberra: Commonwealth of Australia.

Howard, John. 2001. *Australia's International Relations—Ready for the Future.* Address to the Menzies Research Centre. Department of Prime Minister and Cabinet. Speech. 22 August, Canberra.

Howard, John. 2004. *Address to the Australian Strategic Policy Institute.* Department of Prime Minister and Cabinet. Speech. 18 June, Sydney.

Howard, John. 2005. *Address at the Opening of the Lowy Institute of International Policy.* Department of the Prime Minister and Cabinet. Speech. 31 March, Sydney.

156   N. PIJOVIĆ

Howes, Stephen and Jonathan Pryke. 2014. Biggest Aid Cuts Ever Produce Our Least Generous Aid Budget Ever. *DevpolicyBlog*. 15 December. http://devpolicy.org/biggest-aid-cuts-ever-produce-our-least-generous-aid-budget-ever-20141215-2/. Accessed on 17 February 2016.

Jordaan, Eduard. 2003. The Concept of a Middle Power in International Relations: Distinguishing Between Emerging and Traditional Middle Powers. *Politikon South African Journal of Political Studies*. 30:1, 165–181.

Kirchheimer, Otto. 1966. The Transformation of the Western European Party. In Joseph LaPalombara and Myron Weiner (eds.), *Political Parties and Political Development*. Princeton: Princeton University Press, 177–200.

Lowe, David. 1997. Dividing a Labor Line: Conservative Constructions of Labor's Foreign Policy, 1944–49. In David Lee and Christopher Waters (eds.), *Evatt to Evans: The Labor Tradition in Australian Foreign Policy*. St. Leonards: Allen & Unwin, 62–76.

McDonald, Matt. 2013. Foreign and Defence Policy on Australia's Political Agenda, 1962–2012. *Australian Journal of Public Administration*. 72:2, June, 171–184.

McDonald, Matt. 2015. Australian Foreign Policy Under the Abbott Government: Foreign Policy as Domestic Politics? *Australian Journal of International Affairs*. 69:6, December, 651–669.

McEwen, John. 1946. Foreign Affairs—Missions Overseas—Ministerial Statement. *House of Representatives*. 20 March.

Menzies, Robert Gordon. 1946a. Foreign Affairs—Missions Overseas—Ministerial Statement. *House of Representatives*. 20 March.

Menzies, Robert Gordon. 1946b. Question: International Affairs Speech. *House of Representatives*. 13 November.

Menzies, Robert Gordon. 1970. *The Measure of the Years*. Melbourne: Cassell.

Negin, Joel and Glen Denning. 2011. *Study of Australia's Approach to Aid in Africa. Commissioned as Part of the Independent Review of Aid Effectiveness*. Final Report, 21 February.

Parke, Melissa and John Langmore. 2014. The Labor Tradition in Australian Foreign Policy. In Daniel Baldino, Andrew Carr, and Anthony J. Langlois (eds.), *Australian Foreign Policy: Controversies and Debates*. Melbourne: Oxford University Press, 29–37.

Patience, Allan. 2014. Imagining Middle Powers. *Australian Journal of International Affairs*. 68:2, 210–224.

Pijović, Nikola. 2016. The Liberal National Coalition, Australian Labor Party and Africa: Two Decades of Partisanship in Australia's Foreign Policy. *Australian Institute of International Affairs*. 70:5, 541–562.

Ravenhill, John. 1998. Cycles of Middle Power Activism: Constraint and Choice in Australian and Canadian Foreign Policies. *Australian Journal of International Affairs*. 52:3, 309–327.

Rudd, Kevin. 2007. *Leading, Not Following: The Renewal of Australian Middle Power Diplomacy*. Future Directions in Australian Foreign Policy (Speech Delivered to The Sydney Institute on 19 September 2006). The Sydney Papers. Summer.

Rudd, Kevin. 2008. *The Australia-US Alliance and Emerging Challenges in the Asia-Pacific Region*. Address to The Brookings Institution. Department of Prime Minister and Cabinet. Speech. 31 March, Washington.

Rudd, Kevin. 2010. *Speech at University of Western Australia: Australia's Foreign Policy Looking West*. Minister for Foreign Affairs. Speech. 12 November, Perth.

Rudd, Kevin. 2011a. *Australia's Foreign Policy Priorities and Our Candidature for the UN Security Council*. Minister for Foreign Affairs. Speech. 1 June, Canberra.

Rudd, Kevin. 2011b. *The Australia We Can All Be Proud of*. Charteris Lecture at the Australian Institute of International Affairs. Minister for Foreign Affairs. Speech. 24 November, Sydney.

Senate's Foreign Affairs, Defence and Trade References Committee (SFADTRC). 2014. *Report on Australia's Overseas Aid and Development Assistance Program*. Canberra: Commonwealth of Australia. 27 March.

Smith, Stephen. 2008a. *A Modern Australia for a New Era*. Minister for Foreign Affairs. Speech. 9 April, Sydney.

Smith, Stephen. 2008b. *A New Era of Engagement with the World*. Minister for Foreign Affairs. Speech. 19 August, Sydney.

Sussex, Matthew. 2011. The Impotence of Being Earnest? Avoiding the Pitfalls of 'Creative Middle Power Diplomacy'. *Australian Journal of International Affairs*. 65:5, 545–562.

Turnbull, Malcolm. 2017. *Address to the Indian Ocean Rim Association Leaders Summit*. Speech. 7 March, Jakarta. https://www.pm.gov.au/media/address-indian-ocean-rim-association-leaders-summit. Accessed on 7 May 2018.

Ungerer, Carl. 2007. The 'Middle Power' Concept in Australian Foreign Policy. *Australian Journal of Politics and History*. 53:4, 538–551.

Wesley, Michael. 2009. Foreign Policy in Asia. In Keith Windschuttle, David Martin Jones, and Ray Evans (eds.), *The Howard Era*. Sydney: Quadrant Books, 335–350.

Wesley, Michael and Tony Warren. 2000. Wild Colonial Ploys? Currents of Thought in Australian Foreign Policy. *Australian Journal of Political Science*. 35:1, 9–26.

Whitlam, Gough. 1961. Question: International Affairs Speech. *House of Representatives*. 11 April.

Williams, Michelle Hale. 2009. Catch-All in the Twenty-First Century? Revisiting Kirchheimer's Thesis 40 Years Later: An Introduction. *Party Politics*. 15:5, 539–541.

CHAPTER 6

Conclusion

The purpose of this book was twofold: to tell the story of Australia's engagement with Africa and analyse its main characteristics, and through that analysis highlight the country's uniqueness as an emerging country engaging with Africa. The book therefore makes two contributions: one to the study of Australia's engagement with Africa and the other to the study of emerging countries and 'new' actors engaging with the continent. This conclusion will firstly reiterate the major arguments made in each chapter, and then assess Australia's status as an emerging country engaging with Africa, and how its example challenges some of the key commonalities ascribed to emerging and 'new' actors' engagement with Africa. The last section of the conclusion will offer some final observations on the future of Australia's engagement with Africa.

Chapter 2 of this book examined Australia's historical engagement with Africa, from its earliest contacts to the end of the Cold War and apartheid in South Africa. The purpose of this chapter was to highlight several important themes which contribute to an understanding of Australia's contemporary engagement with Africa, but also Africa's place in Australia's foreign policy. The chapter argued that it was during the conservative governments of Prime Minister Robert Menzies and his successors (1949–1972) that Australia's engagement with Africa acquired its recognizable contours. Engagement with Africa was overwhelmingly multilateral (through the Commonwealth and United Nations [UN]), and since at least the 1960s, almost entirely focused

© The Author(s) 2019
N. Pijović, *Australia and Africa*, Africa's Global
Engagement: Perspectives from Emerging Countries,
https://doi.org/10.1007/978-981-13-3423-8_6

159

on racially discriminatory governance and apartheid in Southern Africa. What this chapter tried to highlight—and what is conveniently forgotten in Australia today—is the country's 'flawed' history of supporting British colonialism in Africa, and sympathizing with apartheid and 'outnumbered whites' in Southern Africa. The underpinning (neo)colonialist and racist mindsets that helped generate that support and sympathy have since the 1970s been mostly exhibited by the conservative side of Australian politics. It is in this context that we can understand the strong opposition Australia's conservative Prime Minister Malcolm Fraser faced in the 1970s and early 1980s by many within his own government and party over his vocal opposition to apartheid and racism in Africa. It is also within this context that we can understand the conservative leader John Howard's opposition to Australian sporting and financial sanctions against apartheid South Africa in the 1980s, and his criticisms of the Labor government' immigration policy 'discriminating' against white South Africans. And, it is within this context that we can understand Australia's conservative Home Affairs Minister Peter Dutton's March 2018 comments about his preference for 'persecuted' white South African (farmer) immigrants who would work hard and integrate into Australian society—implying that immigrants from other races do the opposite (McCulloch 2018). Such statements were never the wishful thinking of irrelevant, fringe Australian politicians, but the embodiments of the colonialist and racist sentiment still present in Australian society as articulated by powerful leaders of one of the country's most popular political parties.

Chapter 2 also highlighted how Australia's foreign policy between the early 1970s and 1990s experienced a rare occurrence of political bipartisanship which was driven by Australian political leaders' commitment to the fight against apartheid. This was also the only time before the late 2000s that Australia's engagement with Africa exhibited anything resembling a strategic and long-term understanding of Australian interests in Africa, and how it was best to go about advancing them. However, that bipartisanship came to an end with the end of apartheid in the early 1990s, and given that the apartheid issue was overwhelmingly the main focus of Australia's engagement with Africa since at least the early 1960s, the mid-1990s saw a recalibration in the intensity of Australia's engagement with Africa.

Chapters 3 and 4 examined Australia's contemporary engagement with Africa—that is, engagement since the end of the Cold War,

6 CONCLUSION **161**

and more specifically, the end of apartheid in South Africa. Both chapters began with an examination of the wider structural factors that have helped underpin Australia's changing engagement with Africa during this time. One of the key overall arguments of this book—and reason for highlighting issues of structure and agency—is that structural factors *underpin* but do not by themselves *affect* the course of a country's foreign policy because they do not directly determine outcomes, merely helping shape the potential range of options and strategies decision-makers can choose. This range of options is uneven and biased, and it is up to decision-makers to exercise their agency in deciding which course of action to pursue. Hence, it is the active, purposeful, and deliberate decision-making or agency of governments and their key decision-makers—such as prime ministers and foreign ministers—that fundamentally affects a country's foreign policy by determining it.

Chapter 3 argued that Australia—under Prime Minister John Howard's conservative government—between 1996 and 2007 largely tried to forget Africa. This was made easier by the highly salient structural factor underpinning Australia's engagement with Africa in the 1990s termed the 'Decline of Africa'. The end of the Cold War in Africa in the late 1980s allowed for greater international pressure to be exerted on the South African government which in the early 1990s—in addition to the internal liberation struggle—helped bring about the end of apartheid. Since the anti-apartheid struggle was so central to Australia's engagement with Africa for over two decades, apartheid's ultimate demise influenced a diminished intensity in that engagement. At the same time, changes in Australia's political leadership in the early 1990s also signalled a lessening interest in the Commonwealth as well as an increasing focus on Australia's engagement with Asia, which also took some of the intensity out of engagement with Africa. More broadly, the end of the Cold War took away much of Africa's overall international strategic value, further exposing some of the long-standing development issues prevalent in many African countries. This coupled with a string of highly publicized conflicts in Somalia, Rwanda, Sierra Leone, Liberia, the Democratic Republic of Congo, Angola, and the Sudan contributed to a global narrative of a 'hopeless Africa' running through much of the 1990s.

However, this broader context only set the background scene for the Howard government's engagement with Africa—it was the agency of that government that ultimately determined the nature and extent of

Australia's disengagement from Africa. As stated by Australia's foreign minister at the time, engagement with Africa was 'episodic' rather than strategic, and it can be added, on the whole reactive. The Howard government did not conceptualize Africa as a policy space with much relevance past the Commonwealth connection. It was not interested in fostering proactive engagement initiatives, and up until the mid-2000s maintained only a steady interest in economic engagement with South Africa. Australia's main episode of engagement with Africa came with the 2002/2003 suspension of Zimbabwe from the Commonwealth, and the country's overall contacts with Africa during this time were mostly confined to the Commonwealth. There was a widening of this gaze in 2004 and 2005 with the opening of Australia's High Commission in Ghana and Consulate General in Libya, but these were largely 'reactive' policies, responding to the growth of Australian consular and economic interests on the ground.

Chapter 4 told two stories: one of the Australian Labor government's re-discovery of Africa between 2007 and 2013, and the other of the conservative government's attempts to forget Africa again after 2013. The Labor government's re-discovery of Africa, and its efforts to develop a 'new engagement' with the continent were made easier by the highly salient structural factor underpinning Australia's engagement with Africa from the late-2000s onwards, termed the 'Rise of Africa'. From the early 2000s, the continental trend of Africa's greater political stability and macroeconomic growth, coinciding with the global resources boom, all contributed to a growing recognition that things in Africa were changing for the better. This recognition in turn fed the 'Rise of Africa' narrative which also influenced the Afro-optimist outlook of Australia's Labor government. Overall, the Labor government's engagement with Africa between 2007 and 2013 displayed a more proactive and strategic approach when compared to both the John Howard conservative government preceding it, and Tony Abbott and Malcolm Turnbull conservative governments succeeding it. During Labor's time in office, the Commonwealth was no longer Australia's main 'window' into African issues. There were no major or high-profile Africa-related issues on the Commonwealth's agenda during the Labor years, and the Australian government itself moved to expand Australia's contacts with African states both bilaterally as well as through other multilateral fora, particularly the African Union (AU). Hence, the government opened an Australian embassy in Ethiopia (also accredited to the AU), two new Australian Trade Commission offices in Ghana and Kenya, and committed itself to joining the African Development Bank (AfDB) as well as opening a first-ever Australian Embassy in Senegal (covering French-speaking West Africa). Australia's engagement with Africa during this time was driven by a strategic and long-term assessment of Australian interests in Africa for several reasons. Labor's traditional 'middle power' foreign policy outlook provided support and justification for Australia's engagement with Africa. This should not be taken to suggest that engagement with Africa was suddenly becoming a key pillar of Australia's foreign policy agenda, because it was not—Labor's 'middle power' approach mandated that Australia engage more with all regions of the world through bilateral and multilateral means in general, and engagement with Africa formed only one small part in the grand scheme of things. However, the 'middle power' approach to understanding Australia's place and role in the world allowed the government to profess a long-term aspirational goal of enhancing and broadening engagement with Africa, which was 'supercharged' by two specific policy objectives: securing membership of the United Nations Security Council (UNSC) in 2012, and increasing the country's total Official Development Assistance (ODA) budget to 0.5% of Gross National Income by 2015.

As Chapter 4 also argued, the Abbott conservative government's approach to disengaging from Africa was not influenced by changes in wider structural factors. While the 'Rise of Africa' was still a factor helping promote or at least sustain Australia's enhanced engagement with Africa, the Abbott government made it clear in 2013 and 2014 that it had little interest in maintaining such engagement. This is further proof in support of the argument that while broader structural factors help underpin foreign policy direction, it is the agency of governments and decision-makers that ultimately determines it. And so it is that Australia's conservative governments since 2013 overall exhibited no interest in maintaining their predecessors' enhanced engagement with Africa. While there was rhetorical support for that engagement at least on the economic front, the government's actions quickly exposed the limits of such rhetoric. The Tony Abbott and Malcolm Turnbull-led conservative Australian governments have generically talked up economic engagement with Africa as an important aspect of the development of African states, but subscribed to a cynical view that Labor's 'new engagement' with Africa was wholly driven by Australia's UNSC membership bid, and once that was over, there was no need to proactively pursue engagement with Africa anymore. Hence, the conservatives abandoned the proposed opening of a new Australian embassy in Senegal, and decided not to join the AfDB. While the Turnbull government did open a new Australian embassy in Morocco in 2017, driven by their own traditional 'bilateralist regionalism' foreign policy outlook, the conservatives saw little need to engage with Africa, and were wholly comfortable returning to the Howard era's episodic and reactive engagement with Africa. Suffice it to say that the Australian government in 2018 in many ways brought Australia's contemporary engagement with Africa full circle: from the Howard government's disengagement from Africa between the mid-1990s and mid-2000s, through Labor's 'new engagement' between 2007 and 2013, to the Abbott and Turnbull government's current disengagement from Africa. Notwithstanding the significant changes in Africa's fortunes, and Australia's engagement with African states that took place in the decade between 2003 and 2013, the Abbott and Turnbull Australian governments tried to wind back the clock and simply forget about Africa.

The purpose of this book's Chapter 5 was to firstly explain what drives the political partisanship in Australia's contemporary engagement with Africa, and then use the case study of Australia's development assistance to Africa to highlight how that partisanship has resulted in a great deal for volatility. All of this added further evidence to the book's central argument that Australia does not know what it wants in African because it is unable to assess its strategic and long-terms interests on the continent. Given such volatile and comprehensive changes in Australia's engagement with Africa—as described throughout Chapters 3–5—it is no wonder that Australian decision-makers do not have the time and space to not only assess why Australia should engage with Africa and what interests the country has there, but also implement policies aimed at supporting and advancing those interests.

Chapter 5 argued that Australian political party foreign policy outlooks frame politicians' thinking about Australia's place in the world, and that such thinking, as espoused in relevant foreign policy documents and speeches, in turn supports and perpetuates those foreign policy outlooks. This represents a mutually reinforcing cycle: Australian politicians use their party's foreign policy outlooks to frame and justify their foreign policy direction and priorities, thereby creating traditions of foreign policy outlooks for future generations to invoke in justifying their own foreign policy direction. The main reason why such foreign policy outlooks are so influential in framing politicians' thinking about Australia's

6 CONCLUSION 165

place in the world is because the vast majority of those politicians come to office with very little or no knowledge of, or interest in, foreign policy.

The conservative Liberal-National Party coalition subscribes to a foreign policy outlook which conceptualizes Australia as a significant regional power, driven by pragmatism and realism in the pursuit of foreign policy, overwhelmingly interested in regional engagement and maintaining links with key strategic and economic partners, and preferring bilateral management of foreign affairs. The conservatives are comfortable following the dictates of great powers and strive to maintain the established status quo. This has been termed the 'bilateralist regionalism' understanding of Australia's place and role in the world, and such a foreign policy outlook allowed the conservative governments of John Howard, Tony Abbott, and Malcolm Turnbull to feel less compelled to proactively seek out engagement with African states—past traditionally established links with South Africa and the Commonwealth. On the other hand, the Australian Labor Party subscribes to a foreign policy outlook which conceptualizes Australia as an active 'middle power' which is equally as interested in regional engagement, but more open-minded to actively seeking engagement with issues and countries outside of Australia's immediate region, favouring multilateral management of foreign affairs, and labelling the country as a 'good international citizen' which sees a place for values as well as interests in foreign policy. Labor governments seek to transcend the dictates of great powers by actively fostering coalitions of like-minded states to try and influence global affairs and build a stable and rules-based international order. This has been termed the 'middle power' understanding of Australia's role and place in the world and it made the Kevin Rudd and Julia Gillard Labor governments more compelled or at least willing to seek greater engagement with African states (moving beyond traditionally established links), and justify that engagement both in its own right, as well as in the context of Australia's pursuit of UNSC membership and an expanding Australian aid budget.

Overall, as Chapter 5 argued, there are two main reason why these differing foreign policy outlooks—as adhered to and interpreted by Australian politicians—have been such highly salient drivers of change and volatility in Australia's engagement with Africa. As was made clear with reference to Otto Kirchheimer's (1966) classical writing on 'catch-all' political parties in two-party Westminster political systems, as parties drive towards the centre of the political spectrum attempting to capture as many votes as possible, real and substantive policy differences are often relegated to the margins of their political agendas. At the same time, engagement with Africa has traditionally been perceived as relatively peripheral and marginal to Australia's overall foreign policy agenda. Combined, these two reasons highlight why Australia's contemporary engagement with Africa receives such politically partisan approaches. The reason why this partisanship was not evident between the early 1970s and 1990s was largely because of a bipartisan dedication to the anti-apartheid struggle by Prime Ministers Gogh Whitlam, Malcolm Fraser, Bob Hawke, and Paul Keating, and to an extent their pronounced bipartisan conceptualization of Australia as a 'middle power'.

It is also worth noting that Chapters 3 and 4 offered at times lengthy discussions of the idiosyncratic and highly personal factors that have played a part in affecting the agency of Australian prime ministers and foreign ministers as they were relevant to engagement with Africa. While such factors are random and individual, and therefore difficult to theorize, they are important in informing an empirically rich analysis of Australia's engagement with Africa. In this light, an overall argument was made that Australian prime ministers are more likely to engage on foreign policy issues deemed to be of fundamental importance for the country's overall economic and security well-being, as well as ones that resonate more with domestic opinion and are therefore more easily exploitable for domestic political gains. This generally allows their foreign ministers more leeway and space to formulate polices towards issues and areas considered relatively marginal and peripheral on Australia's overall foreign policy agenda. However, this also means that foreign ministers are less likely to risk or waste time and resources—and political capital—on vigorously pursuing policies towards such marginal issues if the prime minister strongly favours a different course of action, or actively exhibits little interest in them. The prime minister is the central figure in setting the overall direction of Australian foreign policy, and their foreign ministers—like all other ministers—take their cue from her/him.

However, it is important to stress that no Australian prime minister since the end of the Cold War—and probably ever—has had a particular interest in, or affinity for Africa. None of them were 'in love' with Africa. What has allowed them to be more or less open-minded to the need for Australia to engage with Africa was primarily their political party's foreign policy outlook—the prism through which the vast majority of Australian politicians understand their country's foreign policy. It is in this context that we can understand why conservative Prime Ministers Howard, Abbott, and Turnbull found little reason to exhibit any interest in engagement with Africa—and how this influenced their foreign ministers' perceptions of Africa's place in Australian foreign policy, as well as how much attention they should/could attach to engagement with African. This context also helps us understand why Labor's Prime Minister Kevin Rudd wanted his country to be more active in engaging countries beyond Australia's immediate region, and how this allowed his foreign minister to devote a significant amount of time and resources to pursuing a 'new engagement' with Africa.

To sum up, Prime Minister John Howard's contacts with African issues came exclusively through the Commonwealth, and there is evidence to suggest that his bruising experience with South Africa's president Thabo Mbeki at the 2002/2003 Commonwealth Heads of Government Meetings may have further influenced or re-trenched his lack of interest in engagement with Africa. After 2003, Prime Minister Howard did not deal with any substantive African issue during his remaining four years in office. Howard's foreign minister, Alexander Downer, may have been more open-minded to engaging Africa—particularly with the growth of Australian interests on the continent in the mid-2000s—but he too did not entertain a more strategic conceptualization of that engagement. Labor's Prime Minister Kevin Rudd displayed a significantly Afro-optimist and proactive attitude towards engagement with Africa, whether on its own merits, or in support of broader agendas such as the pursuit of UNSC membership and increases in Australia's aid budget. These two specific policies were influenced by Rudd's perception of Australia's place in the world and the role it should play globally, as well as his Christian values and the belief in a responsibility to help the world's poor. Closer engagement with Africa was wholly compatible with these goals. Such attitudes allowed Rudd's foreign minister, Stephen Smith, to more vigorously pursue greater engagement with Africa—something Smith was interested in doing due to his own understanding of Australia's geostrategic and economic interests in Africa. Given his Western Australian base and constituents, Smith was perhaps more than the average Australian foreign minister attuned to the growth of Australian commercial interests across Africa, and his more 'west coast'-minded thinking on foreign policy helped inform his engagement with Africa. Finally, Prime Ministers Tony Abbott and Malcolm Turnbull displayed no interest in engagement with Africa which would have set a general dampener on their foreign minister's abilities to maintain Labor's levels of engagement with the continent. Foreign Minister Julie Bishop, with her own Western Australian base and constituents was, much like Stephen Smith, aware of Australian interest across Africa, and somewhat interested in looking west for greater foreign policy engagements. However, Bishop subscribed to a cynical view that Labor's engagement with Africa was driven exclusively by the expediencies of Australia's UNSC campaign, and did not see a need for maintaining that engagement once UNSC membership was secured.

Australia the Sui Generis Emerging Engager with Africa

So far, the book has only implicitly engaged with the question of what kind of an emerging engager with Africa Australia is. However, as noted in the introduction, answering this question is only possible after discussing what Australia wants in Africa. While the bulk of this book was primarily aimed at answering that question, it still provided ample evidence from which to build an argument that Australia is a rather unique—*sui generis*—emerging country engaging with Africa. The overarching reason why this is so is because, unlike most of the countries covered in the literature on emerging countries and 'new' actors in Africa, Australia does not know what it wants on the continent—it has so far been unable to assess its strategic and long-term interests in Africa. As a result, Australia's engagement with Africa is not driven by the same motives and enacted in the same way as that of many other emerging countries and 'new' actors in Africa.

The countries usually identified as 'new' actors and emerging countries engaging with Africa are a heterogenous lot, ranging from ex-superpowers like Russia or current global powers like China, to regional powers like Saudi Arabia, India, the Republic of Korea, and Brazil. Aside from China—about whose engagement with Africa much has been written in the past 15 years—the academic literature on these other emerging countries' engagement with Africa is still very much under development. That is to say, while journalistic, descriptive, and largely superficial accounts of their engagement with Africa can easily be found, systematic and analytical scholarly studies are only beginning to be published more regularly. With this in mind, and noting the great heterogeneity of emerging countries' engagement with Africa, it is to be expected that every new

6 CONCLUSION   169

contribution to the literature could revise the conclusions of the last one. Hence, some have, for example, criticized previous attempts at explaining the drivers of Brazil's engagement with Africa—interest in African resources and desire to secure support for UNSC reform—as 'unconvincing', before arguing that Brazil's engagement with Africa is primarily driven by the country's desire to enhance its own international status and gain recognition as a 'great power' (Stolte 2015, 6, 7). Notwithstanding such contestability between older and newer research in this relatively young field of study, it is possible to identify several factors currently common to most 'new' actors and emerging countries engaging with Africa.

As some scholars have suggested, emerging countries' engagement with Africa shares three main common features. Firstly, these countries engage with Africa with the aim of securing important resources they lack in their own countries and/or are required to fuel economic growth back home. Secondly, these countries also engage with Africa to offset or counter the influence of strategic rivals or at least 'catch-up' to them—hence, they engage for geopolitical and strategic reasons. Lastly, these engagements with Africa are generally undertaken through 'collusion and support between the spheres of government and business'—often state-owned companies—which is particularly important for accomplishing the objective of securing valuable African resources (Van der Merwe et al. 2016, 8).[1] To these three could be added a fourth commonality which is less often highlighted in the literature, and that is an emerging engager's general desire to enhance their international standing, reputation, and influence. Taken together, such commonalities highlight the very strategic and reasonably well thought out—if at times still incoherent—nature of emerging countries' engagement with Africa.

The main reason why Australia appears unique when compared to other emerging countries' engagement with Africa is because it shares none of these commonalities, save for perhaps the last one—and even that was only exhibited for a short period of time. As the previous chapters have demonstrated, Australia's contemporary engagement with Africa is not nearly strategic enough to be guided by such rational considerations. For one, its engagement with Africa is certainly not about securing valuable resources for the Australian economy. In Australia's

---

[1] For case studies that highlight these commonalities in emerging countries' engagement with Africa, see in general Cheru and Obi (2010), Carmody (2013, 2016), Allan et al. (2013), and Van der Merwe et al. (2016).

capitalist and liberal economy, the Australian government does not govern the country's acquisition of resources. In fact, the government is so hands-off in its management of resources that every now and then it is reminded that it doesn't even have the 90 days' worth of reserves of fuel mandated by its membership of the International Energy Agency (*SBS News* 2018). Australia is also one of the world's leading exporters of resources and minerals, and the resources that it lacks—such as oil—it mainly imports from its own region or the Middle East. This is not to say that Australia does not import oil from Africa—because it does, and quite significantly since 2011—but rather that those imports are not actively strategically governed or guided. For example, when Australia's imports of Nigerian oil exploded in 2012, even the Australian High Commissioner in Abuja at the time didn't know who was responsible for the import of over AUD 2.5 billion worth of oil. As he stated, 'despite oil being seen as this very strategic commodity where you plan your sources of energy, Australia does not seem to work like that'.[2] As far as he, or any other Australian diplomat interviewed for this research knew, there has been no involvement by the Australian government in the country's growing petroleum imports from Africa.

Certainly, Australian governments since 1996—and particularly the Labor government between 2007 and 2013—have invoked the importance of Australian commercial interests for the country's engagement with Africa, and most of those commercial interest have been in the resources sector. But aside from looking to support those interests by opening new diplomatic posts and Australian Trade Commission offices in African countries, the government's main form of assistance to Australian commercial interests in Africa has been one of business contact facilitation and consular assistance. Even its cooperation with the Australia-Africa Minerals & Energy Group (AAMEG)—the industry body representing the interests of the Western Australian-based small and medium-sized mining and resources companies operating in Africa—has been fairly superficial and tokenistic. Yes, Australian Department of Foreign Affairs and Trade officials meet with AAMEG regularly once or twice a year, but those meetings often revolve around discussions of advocacy initiatives for greater engagement with Africa—they are not meetings in which a strategy for the exploitation of African resource is

---

[2] Phone interview with senior DFAT official, 15 October 2014.

thrashed out. Therefore, Australia's commercial interests in Africa are not coordinated between the national government and Australian business companies—the latter operate completely independently of the government. They will certainly seek diplomatic support with host governments in the hope of positively influencing the ease of doing business, but are not directed by the Australian government on where and how to do business. Simply put, in Australia's liberal economy in which partially or wholly state-owned companies are mainly the national broadcaster, the post, ports, and a handful of domestic electricity and gas providers, the government plays no role in directing the foreign investments of privately owned Australian companies. Hence, although Australian businesses operating in Africa are predominantly in the resources sector, their activities are not guided by the desires of the government of the day, or geostrategic and geopolitical considerations.

Furthermore, Australia's contemporary engagement with Africa is not motivated by geopolitical strategies or the desire to offset and counter the influence of a strategic rival. Australia does not have a traditional strategic rival in the way that other Asia-Pacific powers do—India vs. China, Japan vs. China, China vs. the United States—and the only region in which it would contemplate strategic rivalry with anyone is the South Pacific. Australia has traditionally seen itself as the main power in the South Pacific and would have serious concerns over China's growing engagement with, and influence over Pacific Island States. But the South Pacific is a long way from Africa, and there was nothing encountered in the research for this book that would suggest any desire on behalf of the Australian government to engage with Africa because it wanted to 'catch-up' to, or offset and counter another power's influence there.

The closest Australia gets to sharing the same commonalities with other emerging countries' engagement with Africa is with regard to its desire to enhance its international standing, reputation, and influence. And here there is a similarity with Brazil. Brazil's engagement with Africa is argued to be motivated by a desire to gain recognition as a 'great power' by exhibiting its willingness and capability to contribute to global problem-solving and the maintenance of a rules-based international order—what in Australia is usually called 'good international citizenship' (Stolte 2015, 7). Australia's engagement with Africa under the Labor government between 2007 and 2013 was also partially motivated by its desire to enhance the country's international reputation and influence, and to that effect, it also ran for UNSC membership in 2012.

172   N. PIJOVIĆ

However, that was only because of the Labor government's 'middle power' foreign policy outlook, and conservative Australian governments, while also interested in enhancing Australia's international standing and influence, try to do so through their close association with 'great and powerful friends' such as the United States. They do not see engagement with Africa as a means to enhance Australia's reputation, and the conservatives' record on engagement with Africa while in government between 1996 and 2018 clearly attests to that. To conclude, aside from some—and short lived—similarities to Brazil in its motivation for closer engagement with Africa, Australia on the whole is rather *sui generis* when compared to other emerging countries engaging with Africa, and its example highlights that not all emerging countries engage with Africa with the same motivations and in the same ways.

The Future of Australia's Engagement with Africa

Australia's history of engaging with Africa is a troubled one. Its direct military support for British imperialism and participation in the colonization of Africa has largely remained unacknowledged and swept away by modern interpretations of the courageous, loyal, and liberating role Australian forces played whenever called upon to serve alongside the British. Australia's long-standing sympathy for 'outnumbered whites' and their white-minority and apartheid governance in Southern Africa is also an inconveniently remembered past, usually explained away by reference to the *zeitgeist* of the era in which it was expressed. In many ways, these sympathies are enjoying the same fate as the country's racially discriminatory 'White Australia' immigration policy which sought to keep non-whites outside of Australia—both were a regrettable, but understandable, product of 'their time', and should be forgotten because Australia is today a successful multicultural society. The problem with this view is that the racism that underpinned both Australian sympathies for whites and apartheid in Southern Africa, and the 'White Australia' immigration policy regularly rears its ugly head not only in the Australian public, but within the highest echelons of Australian politics. And it is that largely unacknowledged and papered-over racism, coupled with a sense of cultural superiority and colonialist and ethnocentric mindset, that still informs some of the thinking on engagement with Africa in Australian politics.

6 CONCLUSION   **173**

Australia's contemporary engagement with Africa—although appearing bereft of its colonial and racist history—is also troubled. The political partisanship that has plagued that engagement since the mid-1990s has resulted in volatility and fickleness. Driven by their own distinct foreign policy outlooks— the conservative's 'bilateralist regionalism' and Labor's 'middle power' approach—ideologically different Australian governments have in the past two decades adopted markedly different approaches to engagement with Africa. While Labor governments have been more comfortable with, and open-minded to enhancing engagement with Africa, the conservatives have for the most part tried to forget about the black continent, not seeing much value in that engagement. Although political partisanship in itself is not necessarily a completely negative thing for a country's foreign policy—it can promote the contestability of ideas and approaches that seek to revise poorly thought out policies—this has not been the case with Australia's engagement with Africa.

These two factors, (a) a never fully acknowledged and condemned historical 'baggage' in the country's engagement with Africa, whose underlying mindsets of colonialism, racism, and sympathy for apartheid still to an extent influence conservative thinking on engagement with Africa, and (b) a politically partisan approach to that engagement, have resulted in Australia's inability to understand what it wants in Africa. While one side of Australian politics exhibits at least some understanding of why Australia should engage with Africa and what interests it has on the continent, the other largely sees no value or reward in that engagement, choosing to forget those interests exist. Therefore, since it appears impossible for Australian decision-makers to offer a non-partisan justification for why it makes sense to engage with Africa, it remains equally impossible for them to assess the country's strategic and long-terms interests on the continent, and start putting in place the types of policies and initiatives that can help Australia advance those interests. The closest both sides of Australian politics have ever come to sharing an appreciation for the need for engagement with Africa is with regard to the country's pursuit of multilateral goals—more specifically, pursuit of UNSC membership. This, however, has only resulted in an appreciation of the need to lobby African votes 'when the time comes', and given that UNSC membership campaigns usually take place at least decades apart, engagement with Africa will remain cyclical, episodic, and superficial.

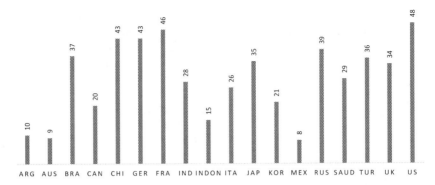

Fig. 6.1 A snapshot of G20 member states' Embassies and High Commissions in Africa in 2018. *Note* South Africa is excluded

To end this book on a more positive note, it would be easy to say that regardless of who is in power in Australia, the country's interest in Africa will at some stage force the Australian government to take engagement with Africa more seriously. Such a structuralist argument would, however, run contrary to one of the central arguments of this book, and that is that agency matters. Regardless of wider structural factors—such as the potential future growth of Australia's commercial, political, developmental, and geostrategic interests in Africa—the country's foreign policy will be made by governments and ministers, and it is their agency that will ultimately determine the shape and course of Australia's engagement with Africa. Unfortunately, that agency has so far been failing Australia's interests on the African continent. As Fig. 6.1 makes clear, for a country that is the second or third (depending on which statistics you read) wealthiest G20 member in per capita terms, Australia was until 2017 tied with Mexico as having the least—eight—diplomatic posts in Africa. It currently has nine diplomatic posts in Africa, but one wonders how such a wealthy country could allow itself to rival the much poorer Mexico and Argentina in the size of its diplomatic footprint in Africa. While it is unreasonable to expect Australia to rival the United States, China, or European nations in their diplomatic coverage of Africa, a comparison with other 'regional' or 'middle powers' from Asia is more apt. While Japan, Korea, and Indonesia are all as geographically distant from Africa as Australia, their diplomatic coverage of the continent makes Australia's record look amateurish.

6 CONCLUSION 175

Finally, one could say that Australia's almost 400,000 strong African-born diaspora will successfully 'push' Australian governments of both ideological persuasions to take engagement with Africa more seriously. This is indeed a seductive argument. While that may happen in the long-term, its short-term prospects are rather low. Yes, over 160,000 African-born Australians are South Africans who can represent a strong, united, and wealthy diaspora voice which could translate into the political wherewithal to successfully lobby the Australian government for greater engagement with Africa. But, the vast majority of these South Africans are whites, and many left the country after democratization and the end of apartheid in 1994.[3] It is therefore questionable how many of them really want Australia to engage more with a South Africa they 'fled', and the continent more generally. On the other hand, while there are tens of thousands of Zimbabweans, Somalis, South Sudanese, Sudanese, Ethiopians, Nigerians, Ghanaian, Congolese, and other Africans in Australia, most of them arrived in the past three decades as refugees and lack the wealth, unity, and connections to become politically influential advocates of greater engagement with Africa.

Australian politicians are happy to regularly tell their audiences that their country constantly 'punches above it weight' in world affairs. Unfortunately, in its engagement with Africa, Australia punches way below its weight. How long it takes for that to change will depend primarily on the Australian political class' recognition of Africa's importance for their country's overall interests and well-being.

REFERENCES

Allan, Tony, Martin Keulertz, Suvi Sojamo, and Jeroen Warner (eds.). 2013. *Handbook of Land and Water Grabs in Africa: Foreign Direct Investment and Food and Water Security*. New York: Routledge.

Carmody, Padraig. 2013. *The Rise of the BRICS in Africa: The Geopolitics of South-South Relations*. London: Zed Books.

Carmody, Padraig. 2016. *The New Scramble for Africa*. 2nd Edition. Cambridge: Polity Press.

Cheru, Fantu and Cyril Obi (eds.). 2010. *The Rise of China and India in Africa: Challenges, Opportunities and Critical Interventions*. London: Zed Books.

---

[3] These figures are taken from the Australian Bureau of Statistics' 2016 Census.

Kirchheimer, Otto. 1966. The Transformation of the Western European Party. In Joseph LaPalombara and Myron Weiner (eds.), *Political Parties and Political Development*. Princeton: Princeton University Press, 177–200.

McCulloch, Daniel. 2018. Peter Dutton Looks to Help 'Persecuted' White South African Farmers. *The Sydney Morning Herald*. 14 March. https://www.smh.com.au/politics/federal/peter-dutton-looks-to-help-persecuted-white-south-african-farmers-20180314-p4z4el.html. Accessed on 8 May 2018.

SBS News. 2018. Fuel Review Ordered Amid Claim of 'Declining Reserves'. 8 May. https://www.sbs.com.au/news/fuel-review-ordered-amid-claim-of-declining-reserves. Accessed on 8 May 2018.

Stolte, Christina. 2015. *Brazil's Africa Strategy: Role Conception and the Drive for International Status*. New York: Palgrave Macmillan.

Van der Merwe, Justin, Ian Taylor, and Alexandra Arkhangelskaya (eds.). 2016. *Emerging Powers in Africa: A New Wave in the Relationship?* London: Palgrave Macmillan.

APPENDIX: AUSTRALIA'S MERCHANDISE TRADE WITH AFRICA

© The Editor(s) (if applicable) and The Author(s),
under exclusive license to Springer Nature Singapore Pte Ltd.,
part of Springer Nature 2019
N. Pijović, *Australia and Africa*, Africa's Global
Engagement: Perspectives from Emerging Countries,
https://doi.org/10.1007/978-981-13-3423-8

178   APPENDIX: AUSTRALIA'S MERCHANDISE TRADE WITH AFRICA

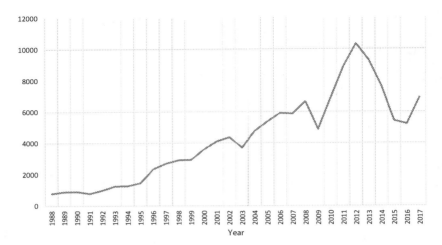

Fig. A.1 Australia's total two-way merchandise trade with Africa, 1988–2017, AUD million (*Source* Author calculations based on Australian Bureau of Statistics 5368.0 Tables 14a and b, May 2018)

Table A.1   Australia's top merchandise export markets in Africa, 1996–2017, AUD million

Year	South Africa	Egypt	Mozambique	Sudan	Mauritius	Ghana	Nigeria	Tanzania	Kenya	Algeria	Morocco	Libya	Total exports to Africa	Ratio exports to South Africa (%)
1996	947	435	8	10	101	34	9	12	44	19	24	19	1727	55
1997	1020	453	14	36	91	73	20	38	43	28	32	91	2013	51
1998	1064	534	21	38	102	54	10	48	41	55	53	90	2191	49
1999	912	471	23	61	106	57	22	82	76	55	12	47	2031	45
2000	1263	554	93	87	120	57	17	93	94	44	29	34	2567	49
2001	1298	740	191	128	137	67	40	130	94	70	48	40	3061	42
2002	1295	667	181	146	139	59	41	111	81	78	78	88	3076	42
2003	1328	236	226	148	99	67	30	54	28	52	7	9	2355	56
2004	1593	646	354	193	123	93	28	76	39	70	31	13	3327	48
2005	1868	355	423	218	101	98	30	40	41	90	54	14	3423	55
2006	2292	417	419	294	118	94	46	30	56	113	34	12	4035	57
2007	2535	353	418	140	86	104	32	31	50	67	15	15	4051	63
2008	2450	359	445	253	110	174	42	67	65	88	24	51	4378	56
2009	1497	433	319	312	97	125	57	102	32	40	40	15	3273	46
2010	1803	497	375	183	97	147	56	100	39	22	36	31	3590	50
2011	1645	561	405	203	99	173	45	98	57	21	15	9	3614	46
2012	1523	511	329	253	106	204	75	80	52	4	24	29	3460	44
2013	1321	480	421	291	94	122	166	126	94	2	33	11	3502	38
2014	1191	483	405	186	110	53	221	58	88	48	46	23	3122	38
2015	1228	540	459	72	100	60	245	116	75	13	15	4	3150	39
2016	975	417	369	8	88	119	191	52	67	6	23	1	2511	39
2017	1393	532	561	10	105	100	217	43	121	32	41	1	3432	41
Total	34,790	13182	6520	3291	2758	2331	1676	1625	1462	1285	739	707	74232	47

Source Author's calculations based on Australian Bureau of Statistics 5368.0 Table 14a, May 2018

Table A.2 Australia's top merchandise import source countries in Africa, 1996–2017, AUD million

Year	South Africa	Nigeria	Gabon	Congo	Libya	Algeria	Morocco	Egypt	Kenya	Total imports from Africa	Ratio imports from South Africa (%)
1996	454	58	18	0	0	0	13	10	13	617	74
1997	473	58	0	58	0	0	14	13	14	682	69
1998	562	0	20	11	0	1	23	14	19	715	79
1999	640	39	18	24	0	0	22	15	18	897	71
2000	851	34	0	0	0	5	34	15	18	1025	83
2001	860	1	0	0	0	2	38	13	21	1033	83
2002	966	0	55	0	0	56	28	28	23	1290	75
2003	1136	0	0	0	0	0	31	16	20	1344	85
2004	1250	0	0	0	0	0	21	35	15	1439	87
2005	1533	0	130	4	43	0	61	14	15	1935	79
2006	1578	0	0	0	0	48	52	15	16	1864	85
2007	1347	0	0	73	0	151	47	17	17	1808	75
2008	1591	0	0	0	0	242	221	22	12	2269	70
2009	912	245	0	0	50	151	28	34	12	1585	58
2010	1103	787	396	202	354	147	52	25	19	3296	33
2011	841	2046	909	683	199	281	91	49	13	5262	16
2012	872	2630	1120	895	1120	0	44	54	14	6876	13
2013	906	1871	976	942	761	82	28	26	30	5788	16
2014	913	1615	712	866	0	2	87	39	34	4506	20
2015	1186	0	592	129	0	0	41	34	41	2258	53
2016	1059	0	604	268	0	370	66	34	30	2695	39
2017	1111	568	571	314	54	467	58	50	34	3473	32
Total	23,591	9960	6134	4469	2581	2027	1223	587	527	54665	43

Source Author calculations based on Australian Bureau of Statistics 5368.0 Table 14b, May 2018

APPENDIX: AUSTRALIA'S MERCHANDISE TRADE WITH AFRICA **181**

Table A.3   Composition of major Australian exports to African states

Country	Type(s) of major export merchandise
South Africa	Alumina,[a] coal, and wheat
Egypt	Wheat and vegetables
Mozambique	Alumina and wheat
Sudan	Wheat
Ghana	Civil engineering equipment and specialized machinery and parts
Mauritius	Wheat, cheese, and meat
Tanzania	Wheat
Nigeria	Wheat
Kenya	Wheat
Algeria	Meat and dairy produce

Source Based on Department of Foreign Affairs and Trade, *Countries, economies and regions*, country fact sheets, May 2018. http://dfat.gov.au/geo/pages/countries-and-regions.aspx
[a]Australia's exports of aluminium ores and concentrates (including alumina) to Africa and the Middle East are not published in Australian Bureau of Statistics international trade data as they are classified as a 'confidential export'. The major confidential component in this code is Alumina (aluminium oxide). The reason why these items are considered confidential is because usually there is only a single producing company involved, and reporting the value of trade could reveal much about that company's sales

Table A.4   Composition of major Australian imports from African states

Country	Type(s) of major merchandise imports
Nigeria	Crude petroleum
South Africa	Passenger motor vehicles
Gabon	Crude petroleum
Republic of Congo	Crude petroleum
Libya	Crude petroleum
Algeria	Crude petroleum
Morocco	Crude fertilisers
Swaziland	Fruit
Egypt	Floor coverings
Tunisia	Clothing

Source Based on Department of Foreign Affairs and Trade, *Countries, economies and regions*, country fact sheets, May 2018. http://dfat.gov.au/geo/pages/countries-and-regions.aspx

INDEX

A

Abbott, Tony, 14–16, 20, 74,
  104–108, 112, 113, 115, 116,
  127, 139, 140, 148, 149, 151,
  162–165, 167
Advisory Group on Australia-Africa
  Relations (AGAAR), 111
Africa Day, 89, 90, 107
Africa Down Under (ADU), 85, 86,
  102–104, 110, 111, 115
African Development Bank (AfDB),
  15, 101, 147, 149, 163, 164
African National Congress (ANC), 36,
  53, 63, 64
African Union (AU), 1, 15, 86–88,
  90–92, 98, 99, 101, 103, 110,
  162
agency, 8, 13, 15, 16, 23, 51, 74, 95,
  99, 105, 116, 139, 144, 152,
  161, 163, 166, 170, 174

Algeria, 44, 67, 68, 79, 114
apartheid, 2–4, 6–9, 12, 13, 19, 23,
  25–28, 30–35, 37–44, 46, 51–57,
  60, 63, 68, 159–161, 172, 173,
  175
Asia-Pacific Economic Cooperation
  (APEC), 54, 55
Australia Africa Community
  Engagement Scheme (AACES),
  147
Australia-Africa Minerals & Energy
  Group (AAMEG), 104, 170
Australian Agency for International
  Development (AusAID), 11, 99,
  144, 146–148
Australian Council for International
  Development (ACFID), 96, 109
Australian Trade Commission
  (Austrade), 15, 66, 69, 103, 107,
  115

© The Editor(s) (if applicable) and The Author(s),
under exclusive license to Springer Nature Singapore Pte Ltd.,
part of Springer Nature 2019
N. Pijović, *Australia and Africa*, Africa's Global
Engagement: Perspectives from Emerging Countries,
https://doi.org/10.1007/978-981-13-3423-8

183

B

'bilateralist regionalism', 16, 74, 108, 109, 125, 140, 142, 144, 151, 164, 165, 173
Bishop, Julie, 1, 15, 104, 107–112, 140, 148, 151, 168
Boer War, 5, 19–21
Botswana, 88, 89, 91
Brazil, 4, 168, 169, 171, 172
Britain, 2, 6, 10, 22, 24, 26–31, 88
Butler, Richard, 60

C

Carr, Bob, 10, 101, 104, 111, 124, 125, 127
China, 4, 8, 9, 27, 128, 132, 133, 140, 168, 171, 174
Cold War, 3, 7, 12, 13, 51–53, 56, 159–161, 166
Commonwealth, 5, 8, 10, 12–15, 19, 20, 22, 24–29, 32–34, 36, 38, 39, 41, 43–45, 53–55, 59, 61–65, 68, 90, 96, 100, 108, 130, 131, 133, 147, 159, 161, 162, 165, 167
Commonwealth Heads of Government Meeting (CHOGM), 7, 38, 39, 41–43, 54, 55, 61–65, 100, 130, 132, 167
Congo, 52, 56, 68, 77, 88, 114, 161

D

Decline of Africa, 13, 52, 56, 74, 105, 161
Department of Defence (DOD), 91
Department of Foreign Affairs and Trade (DFAT), 11, 44, 45, 57, 58, 60, 61, 64, 67, 75, 76, 79, 80, 82, 85–88, 91, 94–97, 99, 102–104, 109, 111, 112, 128, 130, 142, 145, 147, 149, 151, 170
Downer, Alexander, 1, 13, 51, 55, 57–61, 64, 66, 68, 81, 87, 89, 97, 133–135, 167
Dulles, John Foster, 27
Dutton, Peter, 31, 160

E

Ebola, 110
economic diplomacy, 110, 111, 140
Egypt, 5, 21, 22, 24, 27, 44, 66–68, 89, 99, 113, 114
emerging countries, 2–5, 17, 159, 168, 169, 171, 172
emerging engager, 2, 4, 168, 169
Ethiopia, 1, 15, 22, 44, 52, 87, 88, 91, 99–101, 106, 110, 162, 175
Evans, Gareth, 9, 41, 42, 53–55, 86, 87, 125, 127

F

foreign policy outlook, 16, 17, 73, 74, 85, 86, 95, 105, 108, 109, 116, 123–129, 132, 133, 136–138, 140, 142, 146, 148, 151, 152, 163–166, 172, 173
Fraser, Malcolm, 6, 7, 35–40, 59, 63, 160, 166

G

G20, 110, 174
Gabon, 68, 114
Ghana, 14, 15, 25, 26, 44, 58, 67–69, 81, 91, 104, 111, 113, 115, 162, 163
Gillard, Julia, 17, 83, 97, 100, 105, 125, 135, 136, 165
Governor General, 20, 88, 89

INDEX 185

H

Harris Report, 43, 44
Hawke, Bob, 40–43, 54, 166
Howard, John, 7, 13, 14, 16, 31, 46,
   51, 55, 57, 59–69, 74, 79, 84,
   89, 91, 102, 105, 113, 115, 127,
   129–133, 135, 136, 141, 142,
   144, 145, 148, 151, 160–162,
   164, 165, 167
Howson, Peter, 29, 30

I

India, 4, 25, 31, 84, 168, 171
Indian Ocean Rim Association
   (IORA), 110, 139

J

Jackson Report, 43, 101
Japan, 4, 8, 54, 128, 132, 133, 140,
   171, 174
Joint Standing Committee on Foreign
   Affairs, Defence, and Trade
   (JSCFADT), 55, 56, 66, 93, 94

K

Keating, Paul, 40, 54, 55, 141, 143,
   166
Kenya, 15, 44, 67, 68, 88, 89, 92, 99,
   115, 163
Korea, 4, 168, 174

L

Labor Party, 3, 6, 16, 40, 73, 83, 86,
   87, 95, 96, 123, 124, 126, 130,
   131, 136, 165
Liberal-National Party, 3, 14, 16, 35,
   57, 105, 123, 124, 165
Libya, 14, 21, 66–69, 79, 114, 162

M

Mandela, Nelson, 42
Mauritius, 44, 67, 68, 88, 109, 110
Mbeki, Thabo, 62–65, 167
Menzies, Robert, 6, 22–35, 63, 126,
   127, 159
middle power, 14, 16, 73, 86, 95, 97,
   126, 127, 129, 132, 136–138,
   146–148, 151, 163, 165, 166,
   172, 173
Mining for Development, 100
Morocco, 68, 111, 114, 164
Mozambique, 68, 88, 89, 104, 106,
   109, 113, 114, 144, 147
Mugabe, Robert, 39, 62–64

N

Nasser, Gamal Abdel, 22, 24, 27
Nehru, Jawaharlal, 26
'new' actors, 2, 17, 159, 168, 169
new engagement, 10, 14, 73, 74, 94,
   99, 101, 102, 105, 108, 113,
   116, 151, 162–164, 167
Nigeria, 25, 44, 61, 62, 67, 68, 78,
   79, 92, 106, 114, 133
Nkrumah, Kwame, 26

O

Obasanjo, Olusegun, 62
Official Development Assistance
   (ODA), 8, 15, 17, 78, 84, 85,
   95, 96, 101, 112, 141–146,
   148–151, 163
Organization for Economic
   Cooperation and Development
   (OECD), 2, 56, 141
Organization of African Unity, 59, 87

186 INDEX

P

Pacific, 8, 60, 90, 96, 128, 133, 134, 139, 140, 142, 171
Partisanship, 8, 16, 17, 83, 116, 123, 124, 128, 129, 141, 151, 164, 166, 173
Perth, 85, 90, 100, 102, 104, 109, 140
Portugal, 30, 60

R

Rhodesia, 6, 7, 12, 28–30, 33–40, 46, 84
Rhodesian Information Centre, 7, 34, 37
Rise of Africa, 13–15, 74–76, 78–80, 82, 105, 116, 162, 163
Rudd, Kevin, 1, 17, 82–84, 91, 93–101, 104, 108, 109, 131, 135–138, 145, 146, 165, 167

S

Senegal, 5, 15, 101, 104, 107, 111, 115, 163, 164
Sheil, Glenister, 7, 37
Smith, Stephen, 28–30, 83–93, 96, 97, 101, 103, 104, 108, 109, 135–137, 167, 168
Somalia, 40, 54–56, 91, 92, 99, 161
South Africa, 5–8, 12, 15, 20, 21, 25–28, 30, 31, 33–35, 37, 38, 40–44, 46, 51, 53–55, 59, 63, 64, 66–68, 78, 89, 91, 104, 109, 110, 113–115, 129, 130, 133, 144, 159–162, 165, 174, 175
South Sudan, 98, 99, 175
structure, 13, 52, 66, 104, 111, 128, 161
Sudan, 5, 20, 56, 68, 92, 113, 114, 161

Suez Canal, 22, 24, 27, 31
sui generis, 5, 168, 172
Swaziland, 68

T

Tanzania, 44, 45, 68, 88, 89, 104
The Economist, 56, 75–77, 79
trade, 7–9, 12, 31, 34, 35, 42, 44, 66, 67, 90, 93, 102–104, 113–115, 128, 133–135, 137, 140, 149, 163
Turkey, 4
Turnbull, Malcolm, 14–16, 74, 104, 105, 108, 112, 113, 115, 127, 130, 139, 140, 148, 149, 151, 162–165, 167

U

United Kingdom (UK), 8, 24, 25, 27, 29, 30, 39, 45, 57, 63, 110, 124
United Nations (UN), 6, 8, 10, 19, 23, 27–30, 32–35, 37, 40, 45, 54, 60, 83, 90, 92, 94, 98, 99, 103, 112, 115, 126, 131, 137, 138, 159
United Nations Security Council (UNSC), 4, 6, 7, 11, 15, 17, 34, 37, 59–61, 68, 73, 74, 82, 84–87, 89, 91, 93–101, 108–110, 136, 138, 140, 145–148, 151, 163, 165, 167–169, 171, 173
United States (US), 8, 9, 24, 27, 30, 41, 42, 45, 52, 53, 55–57, 60, 66, 77, 78, 86, 110, 128, 132, 133, 140, 171, 172, 174

V

Verwoerd, Hendrik, 26

W

Western Australia, 37, 85, 98, 100, 109, 167
'White Australia', 6, 27, 31, 32, 172
white paper, 129, 130
Whitlam, Gough, 6, 7, 32–34, 127, 166
Wolfensohn, James, 41–43
World War II, 5, 22, 23, 32, 40, 52, 126

Z

Zambia, 7, 39, 44, 54, 88
Zimbabwe, 6, 7, 14, 28, 37–40, 44, 46, 55, 59, 61–66, 68, 84, 89, 91–93, 96, 100, 108, 130–132, 144, 162